IMAGES
of America

CINCINNATI THEATERS

On the Cover: No matter how hard life is outside, the neighborhood theater has always been a place to escape the worries and pressures of everyday life. Often, the elegance and unique architecture of these cinemas presented a stark contrast to the neighborhoods around them. (Cincinnati Museum Center, Cincinnati Historical Society Library.)

IMAGES
of America

CINCINNATI THEATERS

Steven J. Rolfes, Douglas R. Weise, Phil Lind

ARCADIA PUBLISHING

ISBN 978-1-4671-1524-7

Published by Arcadia Publishing
Charleston, South Carolina

Printed in the United States of America

Library of Congress Control Number: 2015944862

For all general information, please contact Arcadia Publishing:
Telephone 843-853-2070
Fax 843-853-0044
E-mail sales@arcadiapublishing.com
For customer service and orders:
Toll-Free 1-888-313-2665

Visit us on the Internet at www.arcadiapublishing.com

To Judy and Isabelle Weise; Terri, Jordan, and Selena Rolfes; and the Lind family

Contents

ACKNOWLEDGMENTS

This book would not have been possible without the help of many very supportive people.

To everyone who had a part in helping us with the research and obtaining images for this project, we say thank you! Special thanks to Diane Mallstrom and everyone associated with the Public Library of Cincinnati and Hamilton County Greater Cincinnati Memory Project and the Southwest Ohio and Neighboring Libraries. We would also like to thank Cierra Earl and the Kenton County Public Library for all the assistance. Thanks also to the Cincinnati History Library and Archives. Thanks to Penny Huber and David Huser of the Mount Healthy Historical Society. Other historical societies who assisted us include College Hill, Catherine Huebner with the Westwood Historical Society, North College Hill, Reading, and Delhi. Thanks to Alicia Krall at the Carnegie, Curtis Trefz, Cincinnati Arts Association, Connie Yeager, the McNamara Collection, the Ray Grothaus Collection, Joe Raphael, Vern Oliver, Pat Kelly, Jim Repogle, Phil Adams, Sharon McCullough, Tom Wernke, Dru Steigert and Ed Miller at the Parkland Theater, Cincinnati Playhouse in the Park, Michel Sheer at the Hilton Netherland Plaza, Mary Casey-Sturk and Sean Mette at Madcap Productions, and Sarah Bradley. Thanks also to Scott Santangelo at Music Hall. Thanks to Jesse Darland, our editor at Arcadia Publishing. We appreciate all your help and encouragement.

We thank our families for all their help and support, especially Jordan Rolfes, of Beagle Rampant Productions, for the beautiful photographs and hours of technical support. Thanks to Isabelle G. Weise for her wonderful photographic contributions. As always, we thank our Lord for his many blessings.

INTRODUCTION

It is impossible to say exactly what the first theater in Cincinnati was. It could have been just a tree stump or a fallen log, an unsteady chair, or possibly the roof of a nearby flatboat that had not yet been taken apart to be repurposed as a cabin. Any structure that would support a fiddler would have sufficed as the Queen City's very first stage, and the recently cleared open ground could have served as its first ballroom.

Despite the gay music, not everyone would have been drinking and dancing. A few men with loaded muskets would have been standing guard, staring out into the blackness of the surrounding wildwood. They were vigilant for the unexpected appearance of the Shawnees, who would be in no mood for dancing.

It would not always be that way. By 1789, Fort Washington was built to secure the settlements in the Northwest Territory. With the presence of soldiers, the tiny encampment known as Losantiville was destined to become a major city. The next year, the rapidly growing river village changed its name to Cincinnati.

A year later, in 1791, Northwest Territory governor Arthur St. Clair suffered a disastrous military defeat in his campaign against the Indians. As soon as word of this debacle spread, many settlers in remote locations abandoned their cabins and fields, fleeing to the safety of Cincinnati.

Overnight, this sudden influx of new people turned the village into a city. Among the amenities of this remote outpost of civilization were no less than three taverns. The fiddler on the tree stump now had a more traditional setting, and the Cincinnati Theater was off and running.

In 1819, the city directory proudly announced the construction of a real theater on Second Street, "to be opened under the management of Messrs. Collins and Jones with a full and respectable corps of comedians." There was no stopping the Cincinnati Theater now!

Cincinnati was still young in 1834 but was quickly becoming the meeting place of the North and the South. That year, Dan Emmett arrived in the burgeoning Queen City. A musician, he carefully listened to the songs of the African American men working on the steamboats and docks and decided to become a soldier. After enlisting in the Army, he was stationed directly across from Cincinnati in Newport, Kentucky. There, he continued his life in music and became part of the marching band. After being stationed in Missouri, where he also listened to African American music, this time from actual slaves, he returned to Cincinnati and left the Army. Around this same time, a New Yorker named Thomas Dartmouth Rice, often known as "Daddy," created a character named Jim Crow. A third songwriter, Stephen Foster, was sitting in his room in a boardinghouse at what is now the Guilford Building, where he penned some of the most well-known songs of all time, including "Oh! Susanna." The uniquely American form of musical theater practiced by these men became known as the minstrel show.

Emmett's days as a soldier were over, but he still loved music. He joined a circus and began to imitate the music he had heard, performing the foot-tapping melodies under a thick coat of black makeup. His troupe, which donned blackface, called themselves the Virginia Minstrels. Among the songs he penned was one that would later become the anthem for the Confederacy—"Dixie."

The minstrel show was extremely popular not only in the years before the Civil War but also throughout the Gilded Age and into the early part of the 20th century. In the decades following the Second World War, however, this form of entertainment was regarded as derogatory, an attempt to humiliate African Americans. Today, it is extinct.

While this uniquely American theatrical experience certainly has no place in today's society, one must always be careful of judging the past by modern standards. To understand the appeal of this curious form of entertainment, one must look at the audience. Presented as a diversion to average, hardworking white men and women, the minstrel show was a three-act romp depicting the Southern plantations as a kind of Elysian Fields with stirring music and sometimes risqué comedy. Men would howl at the dandy character who effectively satirized their foremen and factory owners. A life of singing lively songs, dancing, and loafing was presented to the audience.

Of course, it was all a myth. The reality outside the theater door painted a very different picture. The streets of Cincinnati—and all Northern cities—were filled by African Americans who had escaped the bonds of slavery and, later, the brutal discrimination during Reconstruction. They could tell anyone who would listen that life on the plantation was not a song and dance.

Of course, no one was listening. They were seeking escape in a fantasy realm far from the stress and boredom of the everyday world. But, then, that is what theater is all about.

The fantasy of the Cincinnati Theater was so great that, at Madame Tournaire's French Circus, it nearly changed the course of American history. In 1856, the spot on the corner of Fifth and Vine Streets (where the Hilton Netherland Plaza stands today) was a temptation to delegates in town for the Democratic Convention. Although their constituents had entrusted them with the significant task of selecting the party's candidate to be the next president of the United States, the esteemed representatives kept sneaking away from wearisome meetings and speeches to partake of the joys of Tournaire's circus. Among their favorite activities were thrilling balloon ascensions with "Professor" Pusey. When they finally got down to business, the convention nominated James Buchanan, who later won the election to become president.

Buchanan's administration was a dismal failure, however. Rather than face the challenges of the day, the new president completely ignored the sectional strife and threatening division of the country over the volatile issue of slavery. He even came razor-close to bringing the nation into a war with Paraguay, of all places. Perhaps if there had been a few more balloon rides with Professor Pusey, American history might have been changed for the better.

From the minstrel show, with its mythical South, right up to the modern blockbuster, theater is supposed to be a fantasy world. The theater stage is a barrier between the boredom and stress of everyday realities and a kingdom of beautiful people in romantic encounters amid dramatic, tumultuous events. On the two-dimensional portal to the imagination, Atlanta burns and Rhett carries Scarlett up the stairs, and in the audience, popcorn falls to the floor as mouths remain agape. Rick Blaine, Humphrey Bogart's character in *Casablanca*, was right—the world outside the theater does not give the proverbial "hill of beans" about the average person. But inside the theater, things are very different.

It is only proper and fitting that such a venue would have a luxurious setting to enter this captivating realm of dreams and wild imagination.

Throughout much of the 20th century, every neighborhood had its own theater, creating a sense of territory, a sense of belonging. With few exceptions, these neighborhood theaters showed merely one major film and a B-movie. Downtown was different. It was not regional territory but, rather, belonged to everyone. Downtown was special. It was the realm of great movie palaces such as the Albee, the Shubert, and the National. Beyond the glitter and excitement of downtown, smaller theaters presented the same fare and still struggled to present an exciting and vibrant facade to patrons.

It was a matter of community pride, as well as good business, that neighborhood theaters were so often stunning in their appearance. Art Deco architecture was favored, as it was a genre that was ambitious, defiant, and progressive. Thus attired in a bold modern look, the neighborhood movie house provided mental and physical escape from the comparatively dull world outside.

Born amid this era was a subgenre of theatrical experience. After the Second World War, the automobile replaced trains, buses, and streetcars as the favored mode of transportation. In the increasingly mobile postwar society, one could enjoy an experience almost completely lost to this day's generation—the beloved drive-in move theater. Sure, moviegoers had to sit in their vehicles for the length of the film, but back then, cars were much larger and often more comfortable. Yes, they had to suffer the inconvenience of having a rearview mirror protruding into the middle of the screen, but there was something for everyone in the family. Children were delighted to play in the little playground reserved exclusively for patrons. Young people on dates certainly enjoyed the film, along with a bit of darkness and romantic privacy. And who could deny that there was nothing in the world to rival the taste of a cellophane-wrapped hot dog from the concession stand?

However, changes would soon send these two cherished institutions to the realm of nostalgia.

With the gas shortages of the early 1970s, automobiles became smaller, more fuel efficient, and certainly less comfortable to sit in for two hours to watch a movie. Neighborhood theaters lost ground to multiplex cinemas, where a number of screens would show different films. Since they attracted a much larger audience to one venue, these corporate entities took over the first-run film industry.

The neighborhood theater struggled to survive. These establishments were often run by local people who knew darn well that they were never going to be rich from the endeavor but loved the theaters and the films. Their movie houses showed second-run films for lower prices, often filling auditoriums with screaming youngsters for Saturday matinees.

However, this could not sustain them for long. One by one, the beloved neighborhood movie houses fell. Sometimes they would struggle by, showing art films late at night, and in a few cases, such as Clifton's Esquire Theater, this did work. Sometimes the old neighborhood theaters were converted to churches. Sometimes they became completely unrelated businesses, with only the slightest hint that the building had ever shown movies. Sadly, sometimes they would fall to the wrecking ball. The Clovernook Theater in North College Hill, with its stunning Art Deco exterior, later housed a gymnasium for many years, then a pizza restaurant. Today, the Clovernook's former location is just an open field.

Even the grand movie palaces of downtown could not survive. The only hint that the Albee ever existed where the Westin Hotel now sits is its great classic portico that was, thankfully, preserved. This grand entranceway now sits a few blocks to the west, on Fifth Street, and serves as the decorative entryway to the Dr. Albert B. Sabin Convention Center. In a downtown that once boasted numerous theaters, ranging from opera houses to vaudeville stages to movie palaces, there are no cinemas in the area today.

While no one is showing films in the downtown area, this does not mean that film is entirely absent from the Queen City. With its old German heritage and architecture, the city has been a magnet for filmmakers, and a surprising number of motion pictures have been shot here.

Cincinnatians can delight in seeing Johnny Cash walk through Findlay Market in *The Pride of Jesse Hallam*, Tom Cruise and Dustin Hoffman drive over the Roebling Bridge or sit in Dixie Terminal in *Rain Man*, Jodie Foster standing in Government Square watching a bus pull off in *Little Man Tate*, and, of course, see the beloved Tyler Davidson Fountain in the opening credits of *WKRP in Cincinnati*. The extensive list of films shot here ranges from Disney's *A Mom For Christmas* to *Miles Ahead*. Scenes from the Queen City and northern Kentucky appear in films such as *A City of Hope*, *The Christmas Spirit*, *Airborne*, *Seabiscuit*, *Lost in Yonkers*, *Tango and Cash*, and others.

Not only does Cincinnati supply locations for Hollywood, it also supplies some very illustrious people. One of the earliest superstars of silent films, Theda Bara, known as "the Vamp," was from Avondale. Evelyn Venable, another Cincinnatian and Walnut Hills graduate, played the mother of Shirley Temple in *The Little Colonel*, the voice of the Blue Fairy in Disney's *Pinocchio*, and the bride of Death in *Death Takes a Holiday*; she will be forever enshrined as the lady holding the torch in the Columbia Pictures logo. George Clooney and Rosemary Clooney are from nearby Maysville, Kentucky. The great cowboy star Roy Rogers loved to brag that he was born at the location of what is now second base in the Cincinnati Reds' Great American Ball Park. One of Hollywood's greatest filmmakers, Steven Spielberg, was born in Cincinnati, although he moved to New Jersey when he was four years old.

Besides those who were born in the Cincinnati area, there are many more who spent part of their lives in the Queen City. The dashing leading man Tyrone Powers once worked as an usher in a Cincinnati theater. In the early days of television, a young writer from upstate New York named Rod Serling lived in the city, working for WLW television and later for WKRC. He often "commuted" to New York City before finally pulling up stakes and moving to the Big Apple.

From tree stump to multiplex, the theater has always held a beloved spot in the hearts of Cincinnatians. So, let us head on out to the lobby for a big bag of buttery popcorn and sit back to take a nostalgic look at the amazing story of Cincinnati's theaters.

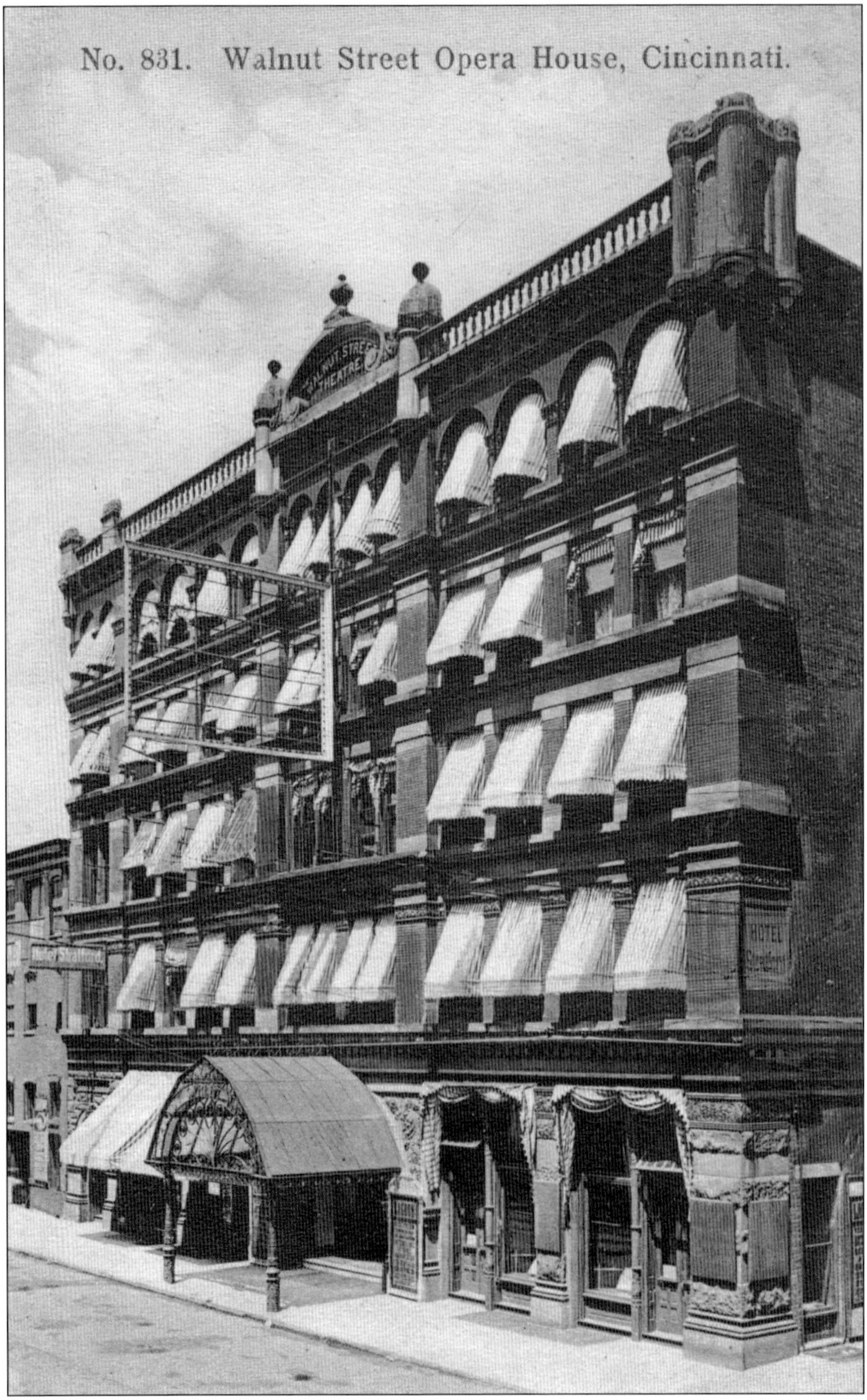

This old opera house was located on Walnut Street. Although this facility is long gone, the Aronoff Center for the Arts has once again revived Walnut Street as the center of Cincinnati's arts scene by serving as the venue for events such as performances by the Cincinnati Ballet and numerous Broadway productions. (Public Library of Cincinnati and Hamilton County.)

One

A Night at the Opera House

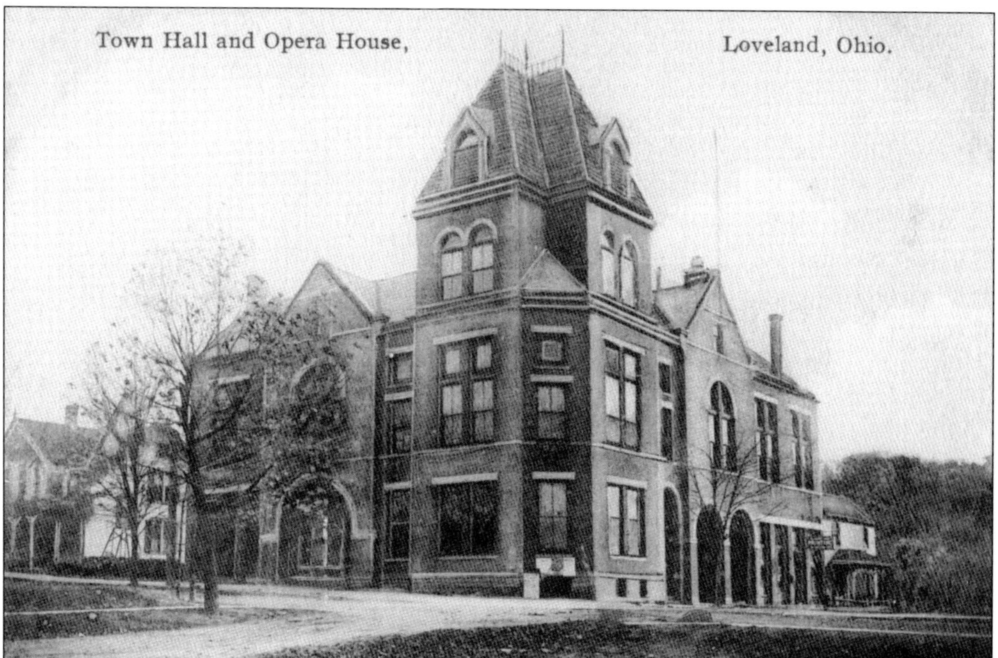

Just northeast of Cincinnati is the tiny city of Loveland. In the 19th century, the mostly rural community placed their local opera house in the town hall, putting politics and theater together in one building. By the late 19th century, the city had become a center of the temperance movement in Ohio. (Public Library of Cincinnati and Hamilton County.)

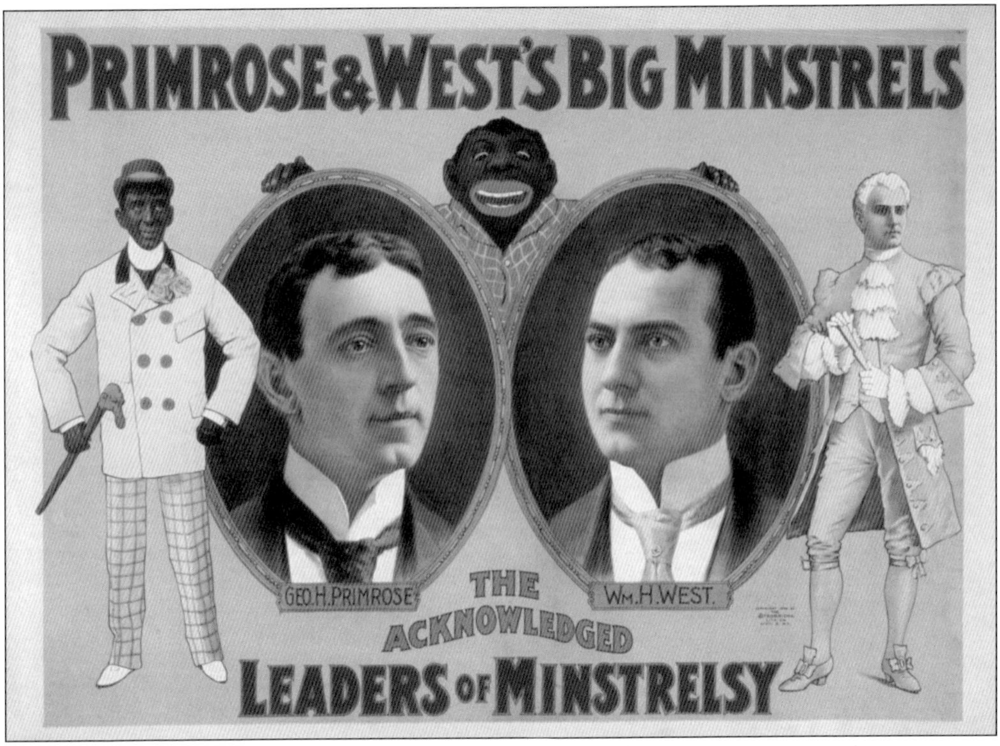

In 1834, Dan Emmett arrived in Cincinnati from central Ohio. Around the same time, Thomas Dartmouth "Daddy" Rice arrived from New York. Both men had heard the lively songs of African American laborers and formed the foundations of something that would become a popular form of American entertainment: the minstrel show. This poster from such a show reveals that the performers were almost always white people in blackface. (Library of Congress.)

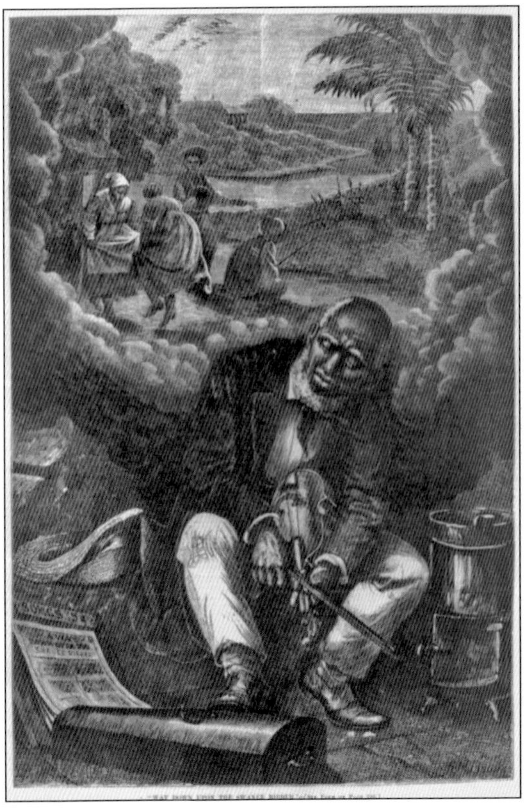

The image at left illustrates the true meaning of the minstrel show. Although minstrel shows presented an idealized, mythical depiction of black Americans enjoying a carefree life of ease, this was in direct conflict with reality, as shown by this downtrodden musician trying to earn money by playing a popular song that posits an existence about which he can only dream. (Library of Congress.)

One of the most famous songwriters in American history, Stephen Foster, of Pennsylvania, moved to Cincinnati in 1846 to become a bookkeeper for a steamship company owned by his brother. Foster's songs became favorites during the days of the gold rush and minstrel shows. (Public Library of Cincinnati and Hamilton County.)

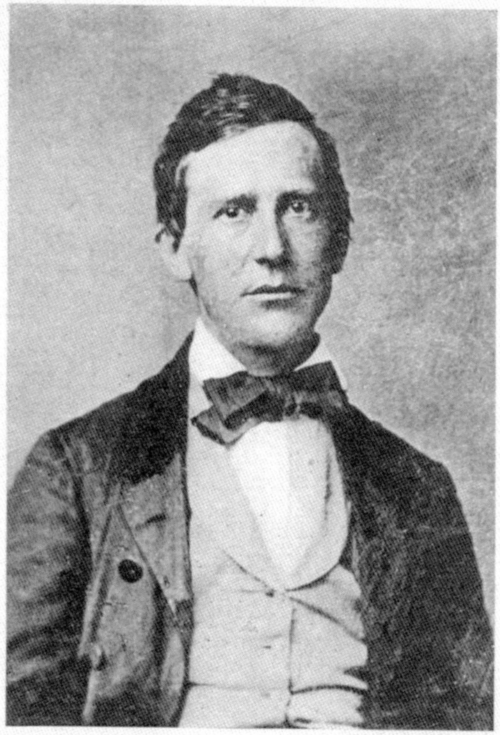

Stephen C. Foster

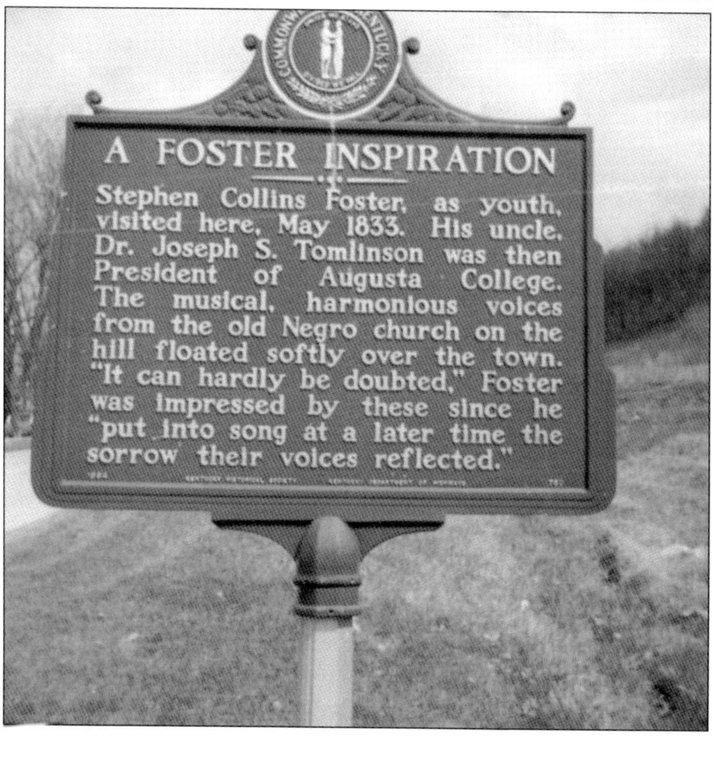

It should come as no surprise that the man who wrote "My Old Kentucky Home" would be honored in the Bluegrass State. Although Stephen Foster lived in Cincinnati, he is memorialized in towns across the river he loved so much. Here, the songwriter is memorialized by this historical marker in the small village of Bardstown. (Kenton County Public Library, Covington, Kentucky.)

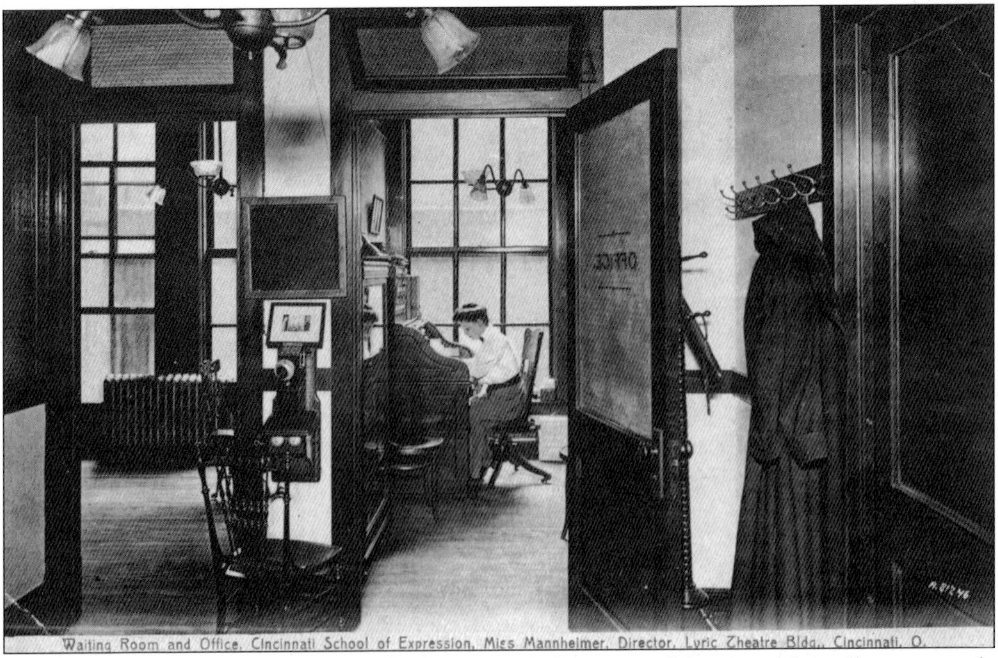

Those who wished to become the next Theda Bara might have started the journey by walking nervously into this room. The Cincinnati School of Expression was the creation of Jennie Mannheimer, daughter of a professor at Hebrew Union College. Born in New York in 1872, Mannheimer opened this school in 1894 and directed it until 1912. (Public Library of Cincinnati and Hamilton County.)

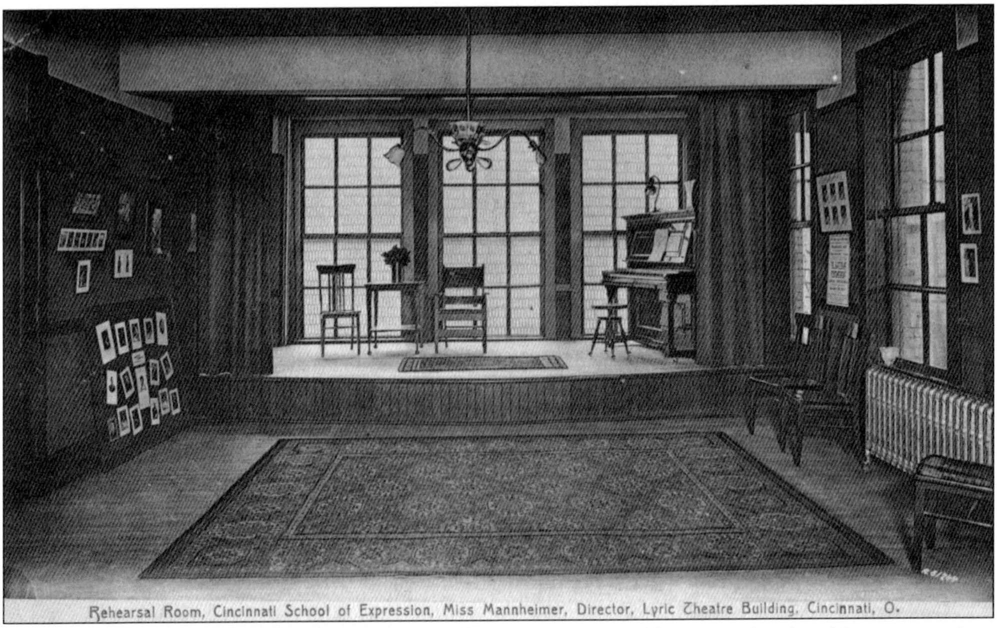

Although films were initially silent, actors and actresses were still expected to be able to enunciate correctly. From 1900 to 1907, Jennie Mannheimer served as the director of the drama department at the Cincinnati College of Music. She later changed her name to Jane Manner and returned to her native New York, where she appeared at Carnegie Hall. (Public Library of Cincinnati and Hamilton County.)

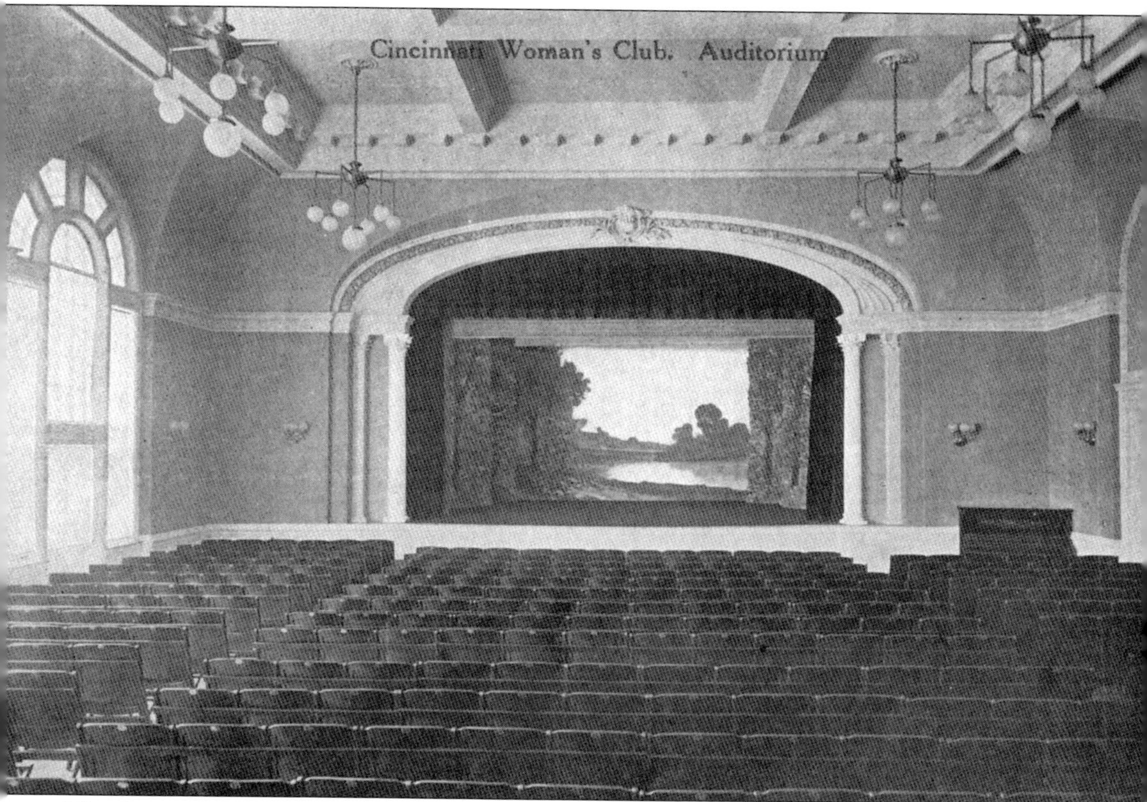

The Cincinnati Woman's Club has a proud past going back to 1894. Seven local women worked together on the 1893 Chicago World's Fair, then expanded their dream at home. The club's auditorium, located at 643 Oak Street, hosted musical and dramatic presentations, as well as guest speakers. (Public Library of Cincinnati and Hamilton County.)

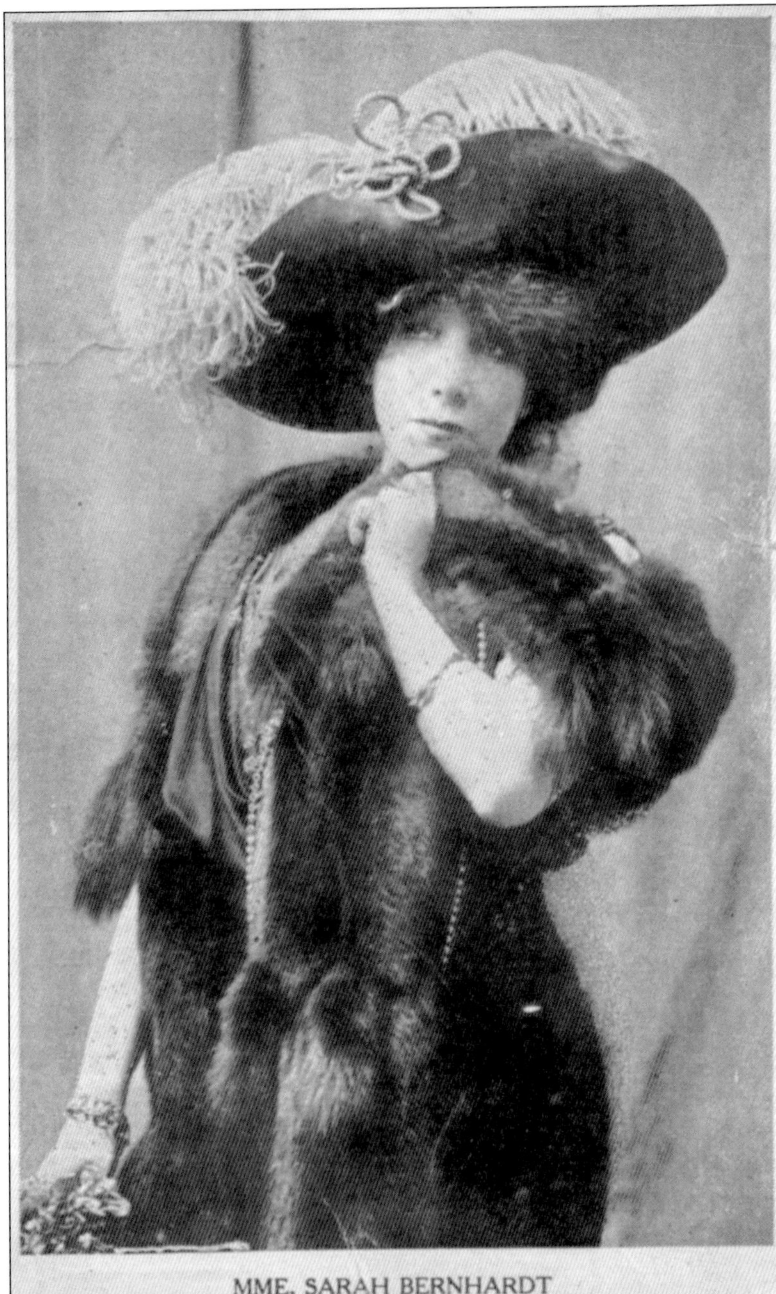

Known as "the most famous actress the world has ever known," French actress Sarah Bernhardt, often referred to simply as "the Divine Sarah," made many appearances in Cincinnati theaters in the Gilded Age. After starting her career in 1862, she became famous in both Europe and the United States. Among her idiosyncrasies was her habit of sleeping in a specially designed coffin as opposed to a bed. Her fame was so great that she was able to purchase her own theater in Paris, the celebrated Théâtre des Nations. In 1900, she expanded into the new medium of silent film. The Lyric Theatre produced this collector's postcard to advertise one of her many Cincinnati appearances. (Public Library of Cincinnati and Hamilton County.)

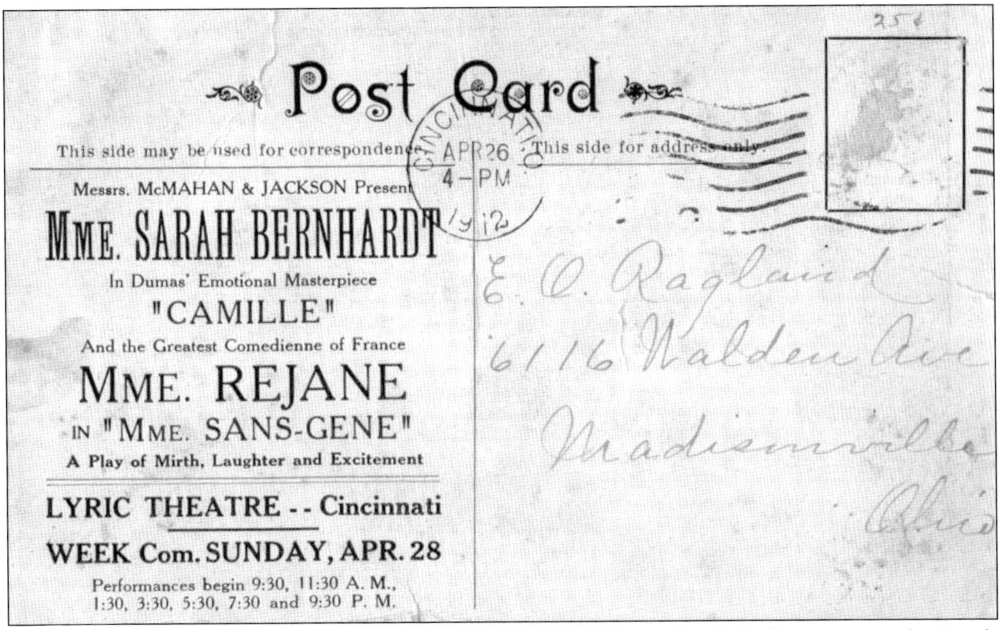

The reverse side of the postcard on the previous page featured a detailed advertisement for Sarah Bernhardt's appearance in Alexandre Dumas's classic *Camille*. Note the number of performances that the "Divine Sarah" would be presenting over the course of just one day. This would certainly encourage the addressee to make the long journey from Madisonville to downtown Cincinnati. (Public Library of Cincinnati and Hamilton County.)

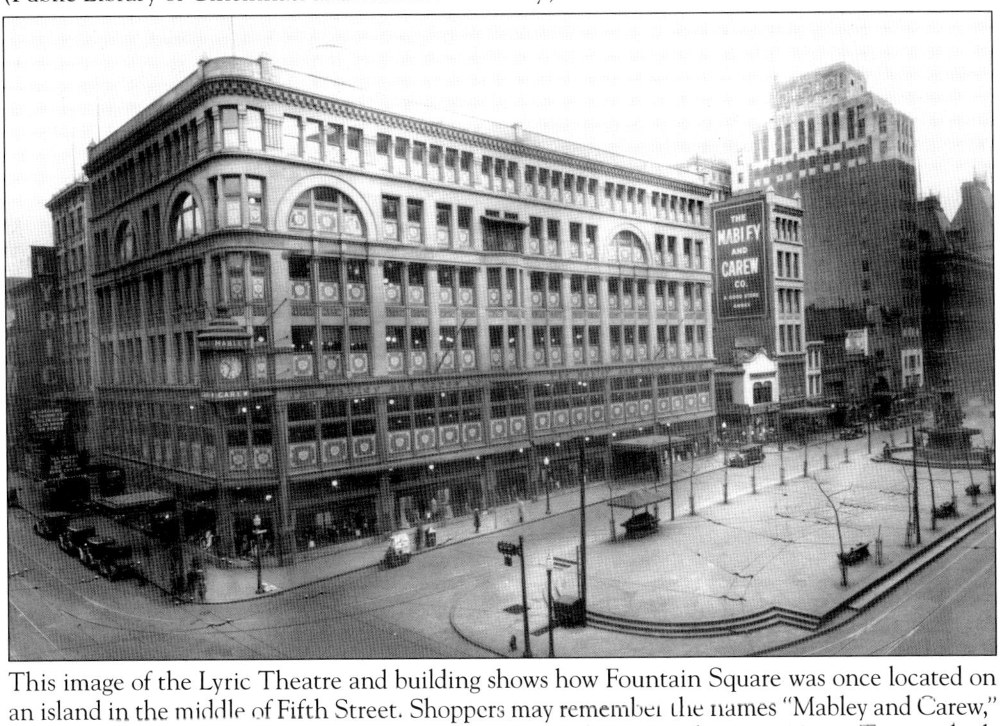

This image of the Lyric Theatre and building shows how Fountain Square was once located on an island in the middle of Fifth Street. Shoppers may remember the names "Mabley and Carew," which are prominently on display. Conspicuous for its absence is the great Carew Tower, which had not yet been constructed. (Kenton County Public Library, Covington, Kentucky.)

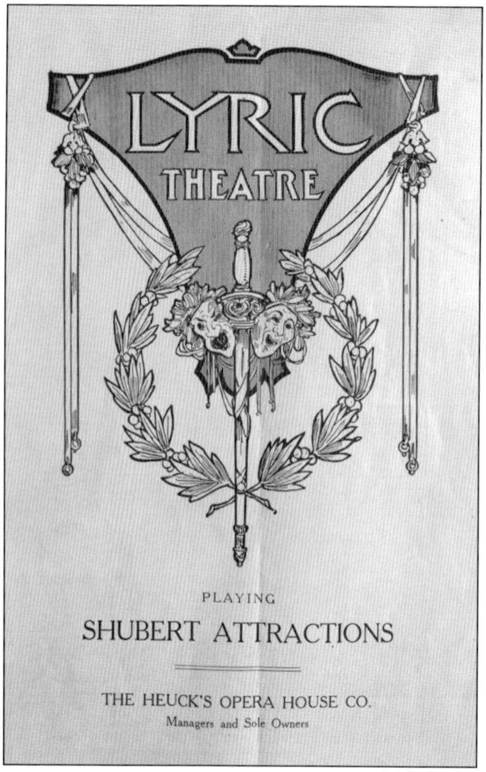

This old poster with a classical design advertises the Lyric Theatre while also mentioning its connection to the celebrated Heuck's Opera House. The Lyric, one of the first great downtown movie houses to fall to the wrecking ball, was demolished in 1958. (Phil Lind.)

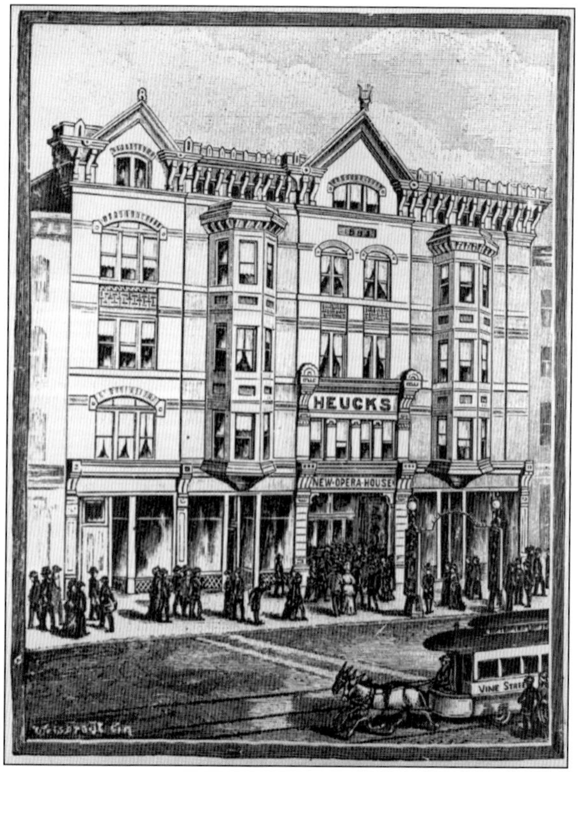

Heuck's Opera House, located on Vine Street in Over-the-Rhine, was named after owner Hubert Heuck, who also owned a biergarten across the street. In 1887, the opera house and garden was the meeting place for a political group known as the Stranglers, an organization connected to the up-and-coming George "Boss" Cox. (Cincinnati Museum Center, Cincinnati Historical Society Library.)

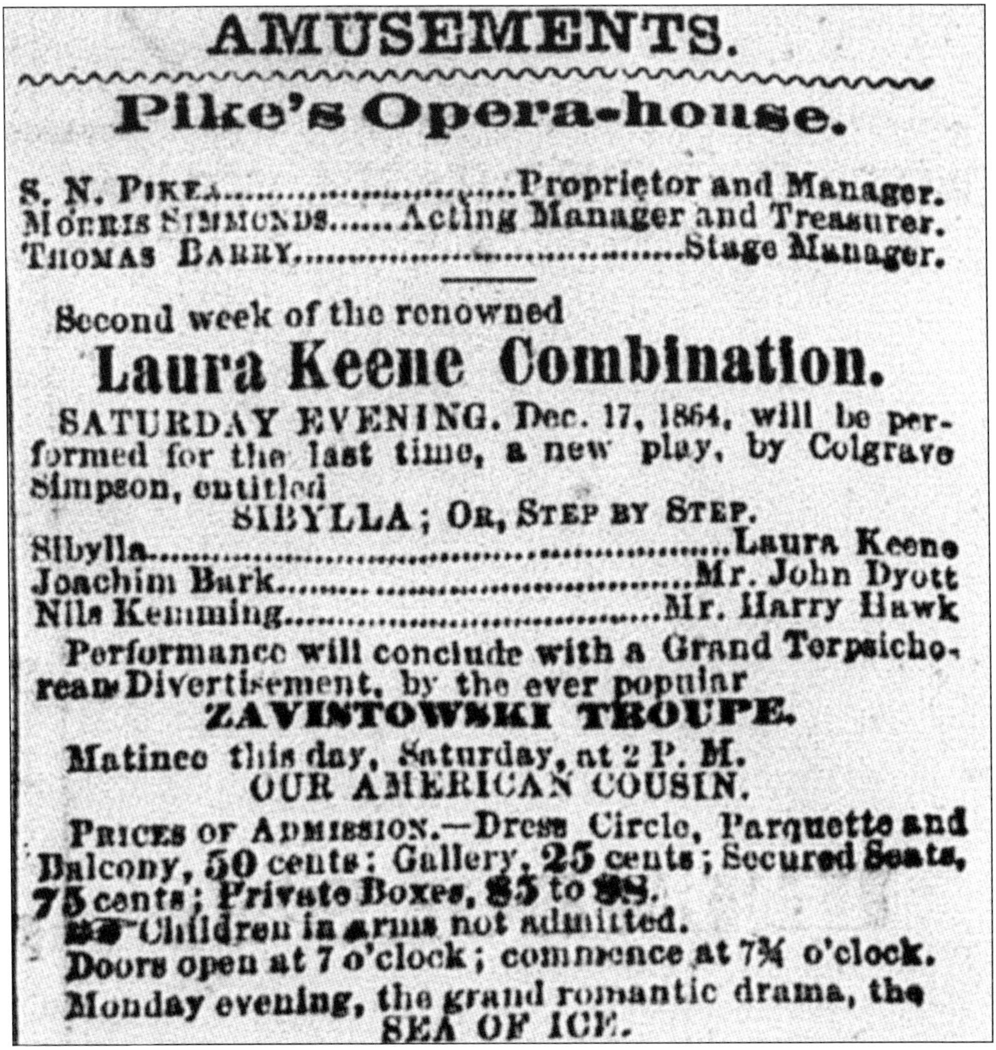

AMUSEMENTS.

Pike's Opera-house.

S. N. PIKE........................Proprietor and Manager.
MORRIS SIMMONDS......Acting Manager and Treasurer.
THOMAS BARRY.................................Stage Manager.

Second week of the renowned

Laura Keene Combination.

SATURDAY EVENING, Dec. 17, 1864, will be performed for the last time, a new play, by Colgrave Simpson, entitled

SIBYLLA; OR, STEP BY STEP.

Sibylla..Laura Keene
Joachim Bark.................................Mr. John Dyott
Nils Kemming.................................Mr. Harry Hawk

Performance will conclude with a Grand Terpsichorean Divertisement, by the ever popular

ZAVISTOWSKI TROUPE.

Matinee this day, Saturday, at 2 P. M.

OUR AMERICAN COUSIN.

PRICES OF ADMISSION.—Dress Circle, Parquette and Balcony, 50 cents; Gallery, 25 cents; Secured Seats, 75 cents; Private Boxes, $5 to $8.

☞ Children in arms not admitted.

Doors open at 7 o'clock; commence at 7¾ o'clock.

Monday evening, the grand romantic drama, the SEA OF ICE.

This advertisement for Pike's Opera House—from the December 1, 1864, edition of the *Cincinnati Volksblatt*—holds an unexpected bit of history. Laura Keene's production of Tom Taylor's play *Our American Cousin* was a comedy romp about an unsophisticated American visiting refined British relatives. A year later, during a performance on Good Friday in Washington, DC, when Asa Trenchard, the titular cousin, delivered the humorous line, "Don't know the manners of good society, eh? Well, I guess I know enough to turn you inside out, old gal—you sockdologizing old man-trap," John Wilkes Booth used the laughter to cover his gunshot that assassinated Pres. Abraham Lincoln. Note that in Cincinnati, the performance was to commence at "7¾ o'clock." (Public Library of Cincinnati and Hamilton County.)

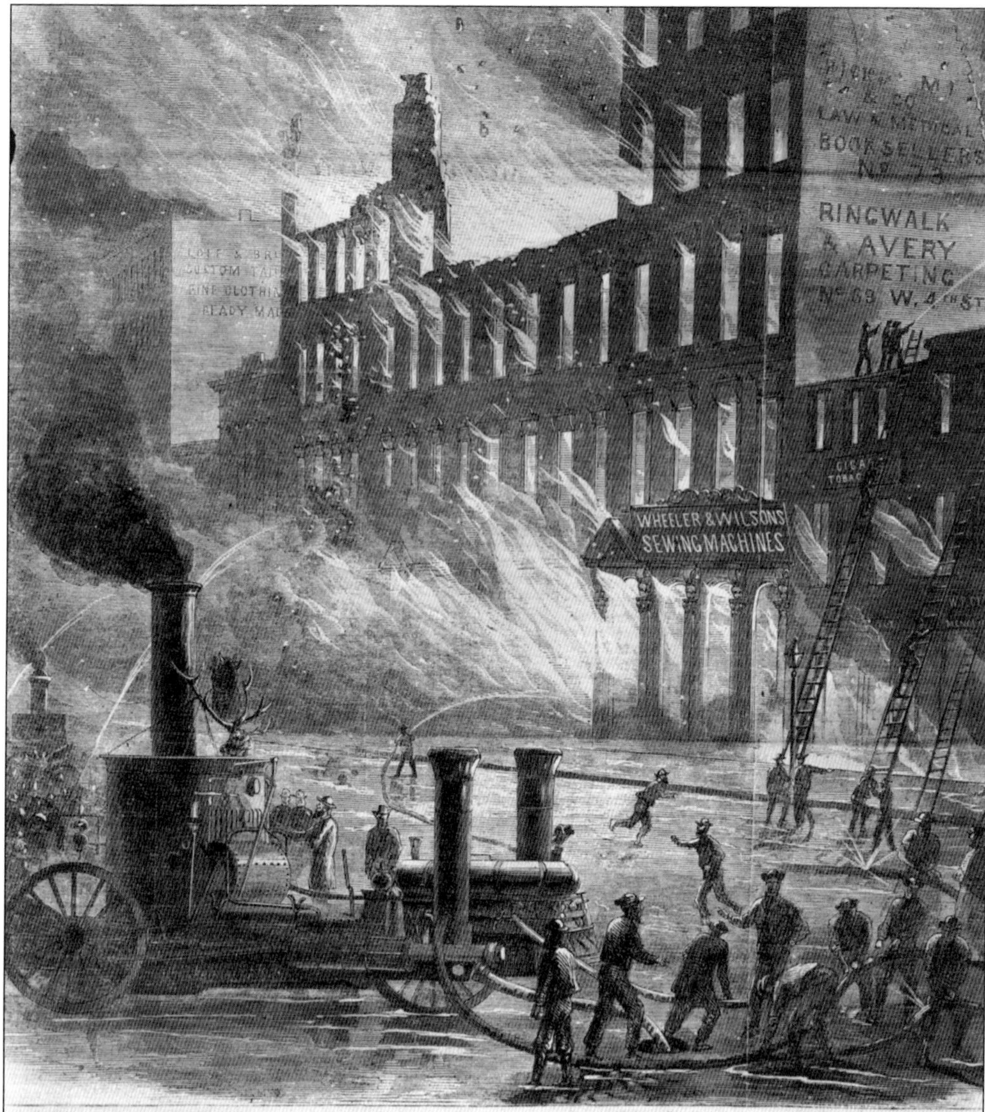

THE GREAT FIRE IN CINCINNATI, MARCH 22, 1866—BURNING OF PIKE'S OPERA-HOUSE.—SKETCHED BY A. R. WAUD.

After a performance of *A Midsummer's Night Dream* in April 1866, Pike's Opera House, located on Fourth Street, suffered the first of two devastating fires. The *Cincinnati Commercial* described the scene: "Flames had wrapped the whole magnificent interior of stage and auditorium, and burst through the rear portion of the roof. On the wings . . . the flames shot up to a great height and lapped over upon adjoining buildings . . . Soon huge masses of black smoke burst from the cornice of the Fourth Street front windows. The half square bounded by Fourth, Vine, Baker and Walnut streets had a dome of luridly gleaming flames, through which columns of smoke shot up, and from which showers of sparks and bunches of flames floated upwards and then descended upon the burning mass below." (Cincinnati Museum Center, Cincinnati Historical Society Library.)

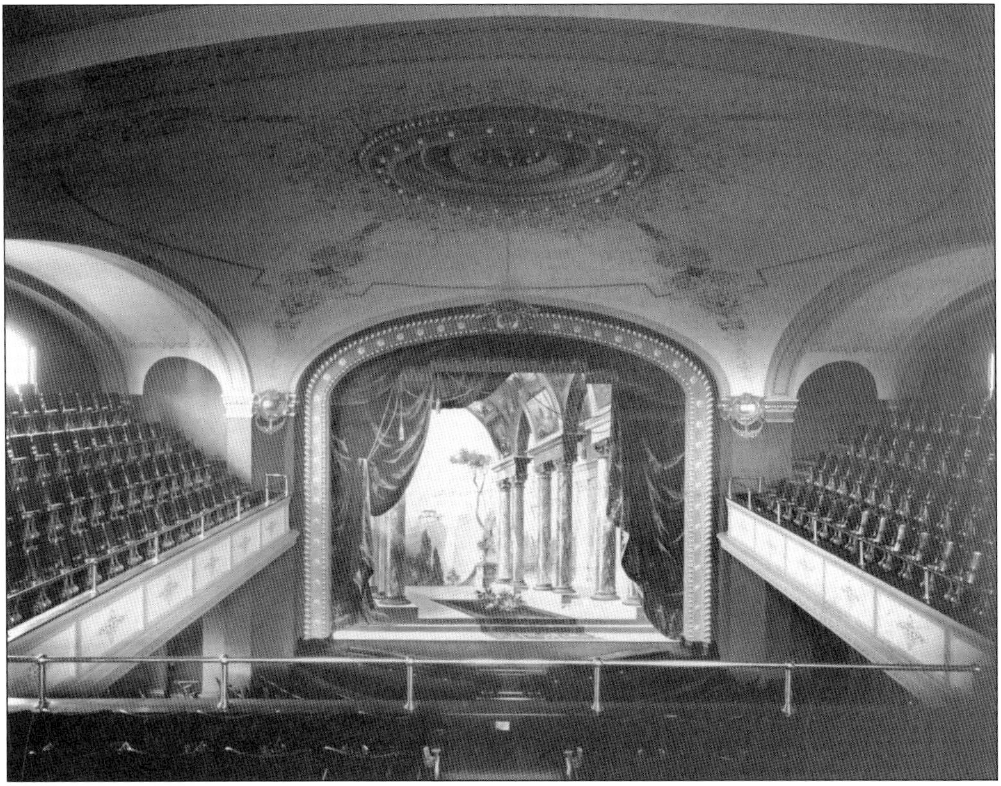

This 1909 photograph of the Carnegie, located in Covington, Kentucky, is a good representation of the elegance found in the turn-of-the-century opera houses. Some might say that this is the way a theater should look. (Kenton County Public Library, Covington, Kentucky.)

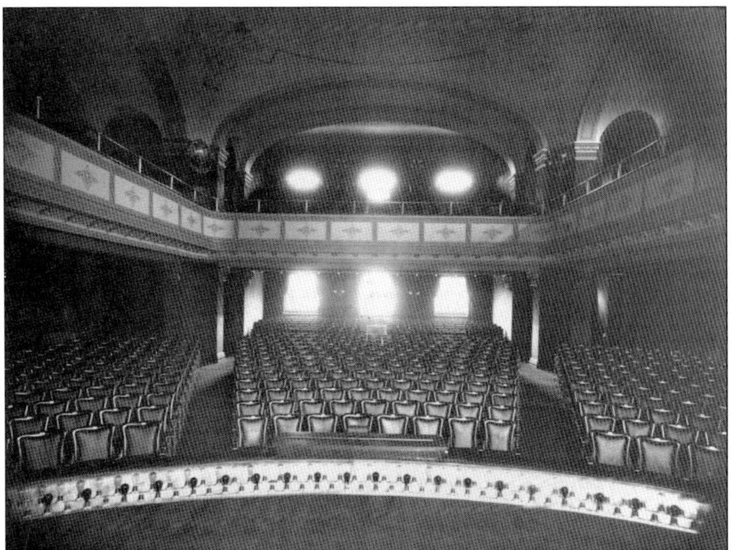

Another image of the Carnegie theater offers a view from the actor's perspective. Note the elegant padding on the seats and the early footlights. The audience would certainly be comfortable during their evening out at the theater. (Kenton County Public Library, Covington, Kentucky.)

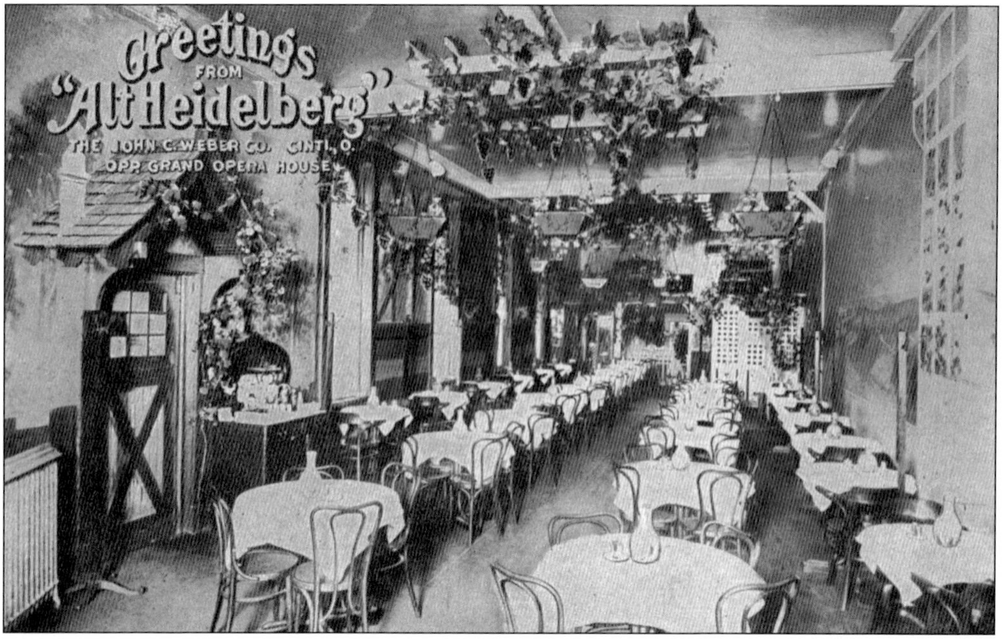

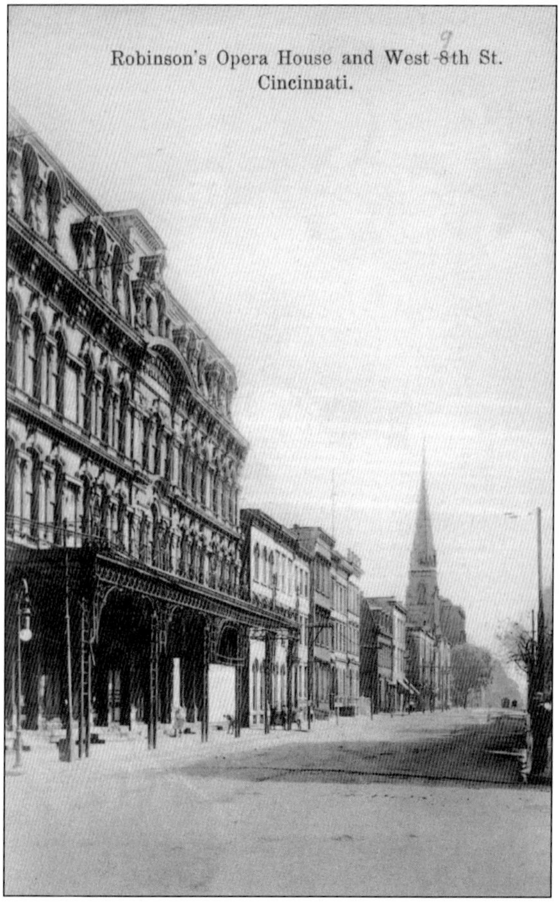

An evening at the theater has long been preceded by a meal in a restaurant. Thus, it comes as no surprise that the area around today's Fountain Square was filled with popular restaurants, such as the Alt Heidelberg Cafe, that catered to patrons of the nearby opera houses. (Public Library of Cincinnati and Hamilton County.)

Robinson's Opera House was located on Ninth Street, near city hall. In 1876, a boy thought it would be funny to shout "fire" even though there was no danger. In the ensuing panic, 10 people died and numerous others were injured. (Public Library of Cincinnati and Hamilton County.)

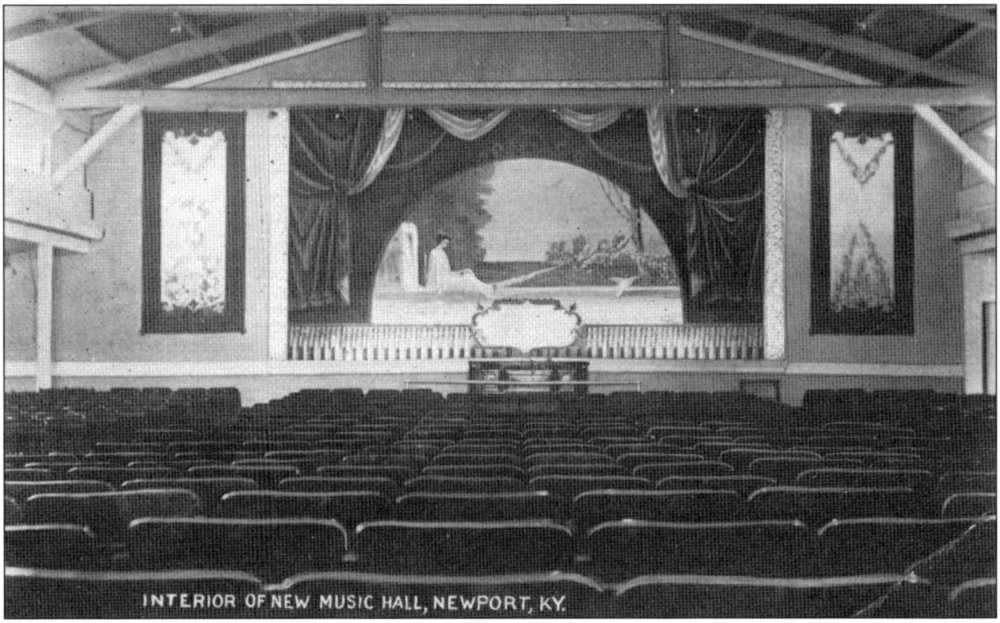

This 1910 photograph clearly shows the elegance of the old-time opera houses (despite the exposed beams in the ceiling). This venue, the Music Hall in Newport, Kentucky, was located at Eleventh and York Streets. Sadly, it has long since been torn down. (Kenton County Public Library, Covington, Kentucky.)

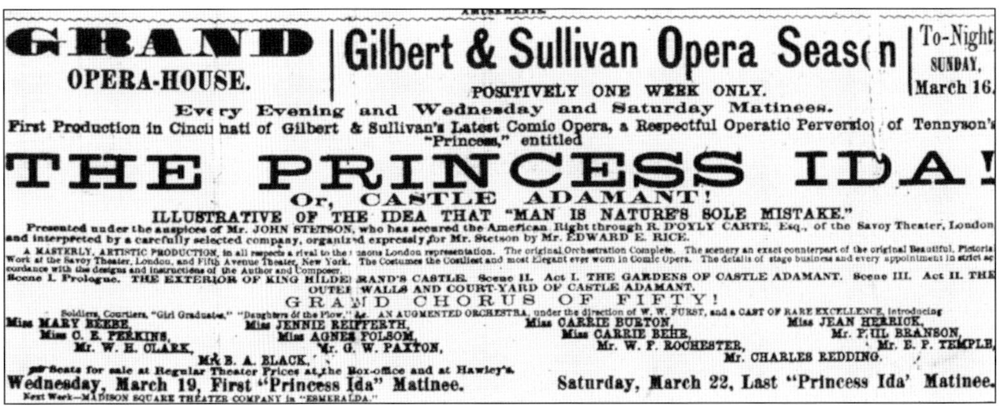

GRAND OPERA-HOUSE.

Gilbert & Sullivan Opera Season

POSITIVELY ONE WEEK ONLY.

To-Night SUNDAY, March 16,

Every Evening and Wednesday and Saturday Matinees.

First Production in Cincinnati of Gilbert & Sullivan's Latest Comic Opera, a Respectful Operatic Perversion of Tennyson's "Princess," entitled

THE PRINCESS IDA!

Or, CASTLE ADAMANT!

ILLUSTRATIVE OF THE IDEA THAT "MAN IS NATURE'S SOLE MISTAKE."

Presented under the auspices of Mr. JOHN STETSON, who has secured the American Right through R. D'OYLY CARTE, Esq., of the Savoy Theater, London and interpreted by a carefully selected company, organized expressly for Mr. Stetson by Mr. EDWARD E. RICE.

A MASTERLY, ARTISTIC PRODUCTION, in all respects a rival to the famous London representation. The original Orchestration Complete. The scenery an exact counterpart of the original Beautiful, Pictorial Work at the Savoy Theater, London, and Fifth Avenue Theater, New York. The Costumes the Costliest and most Elegant ever worn in Comic Opera. The details of stage business and every appointment in strict accordance with the designs and instructions of the Author and Composer.

Scene I. Prologue. THE EXTERIOR OF KING HILDEBRAND'S CASTLE. Scene II. Act I. THE GARDENS OF CASTLE ADAMANT. Scene III. Act II. THE OUTER WALLS AND COURT-YARD OF CASTLE ADAMANT.

GRAND CHORUS OF FIFTY!

Soldiers, Courtiers, "Girl Graduates," "Daughters of the Plow," &c. AN AUGMENTED ORCHESTRA, under the direction of W. W. FURST, and a CAST OF RARE EXCELLENCE, introducing

Miss MARY BEEBE, Miss C. E. PERKINS, Mr. W. H. CLARK, Mr. B. A. BLACK, Miss JENNIE REIFFERTH, Miss AGNES FOLSOM, Mr. G. W. PAXTON, Miss CARRIE BURTON, Miss CARRIE BEHR, Mr. W. F. ROCHESTER, Mr. CHARLES REDDING, Miss JEAN HERRICK, Mr. PHIL BRANSON, Mr. E. P. TEMPLE,

Seats for sale at Regular Theater Prices at the Box-office and at Hawley's.

Wednesday, March 19, First "Princess Ida" Matinee. Saturday, March 22, Last "Princess Ida' Matinee.

Next Week—MADISON SQUARE THEATER COMPANY in "ESMERALDA."

Published in the *Cincinnati Commercial* on March 18, 1884, this advertisement for a production at the Grand Opera House on Vine Street that assures the Gilded Age audience that "man is nature's sole mistake." Patrons would hopefully be induced to spend their admission money with the promise of a 50-voice choir and the dreamy gardens of Castle Adamant. (Public Library of Cincinnati and Hamilton County.)

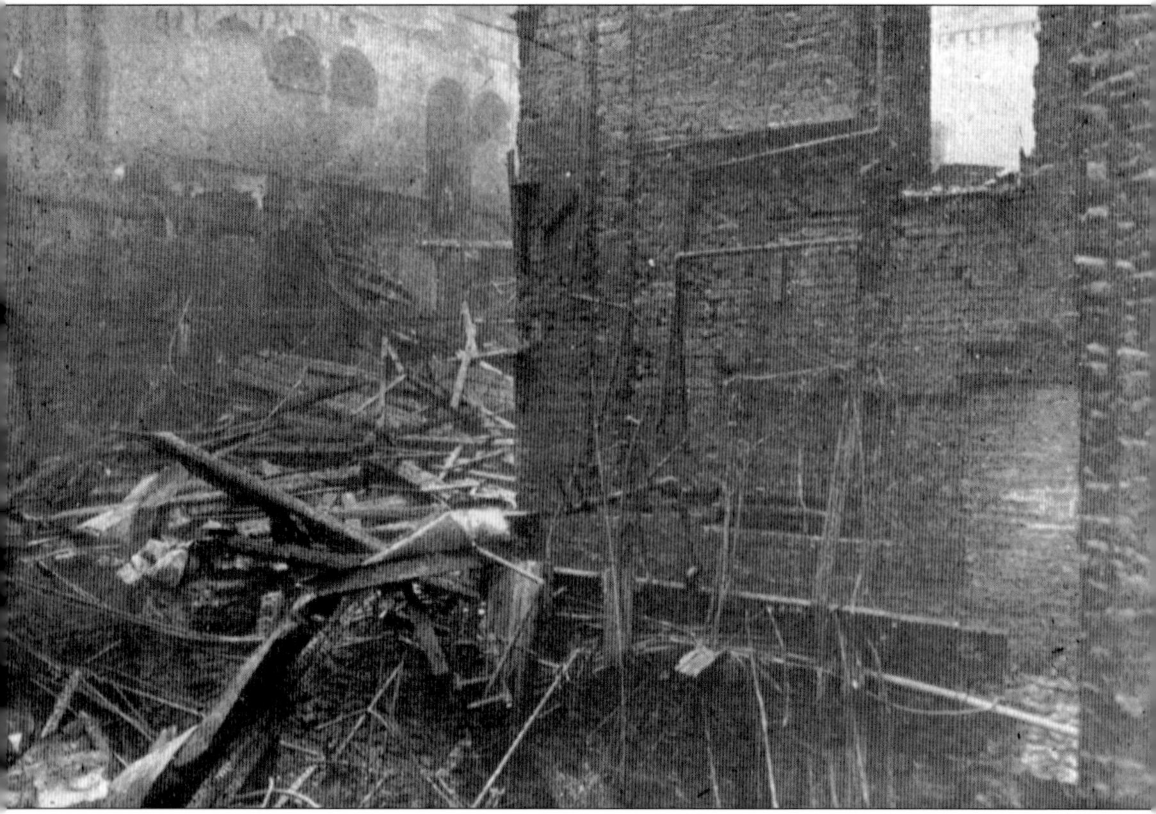

This dreadful fire occurred in the midst of a packed house, yet every person in the theater escaped safely. In January 1901, the prestigious E.H. Sothern Company was at the Grand Opera House performing their traveling production of *Hamlet*. Shortly after 8:00 p.m., this blaze erupted, apparently in the dressing rooms. Sothern personally directed the evacuation, keeping people calm as smoke filled the auditorium. The flames spread to nearby buildings. The Butler Building was heavily damaged; however, thanks to the quick work of the firefighters, the Mechanics Institute was spared. David Sinton, a very famous name in Cincinnati, was a multimillionaire. Among his holdings was the elegant Sinton Hotel, and it was Sinton who purchased the auditorium to erect his opera house. Charles P. Taft, executor of the David Sinton estate, viewed the scene the next morning. Although the building was uninsured, Taft stated that he was thankful that everyone had escaped unharmed. (Public Library of Cincinnati and Hamilton County.)

Two

Downtown Theaters

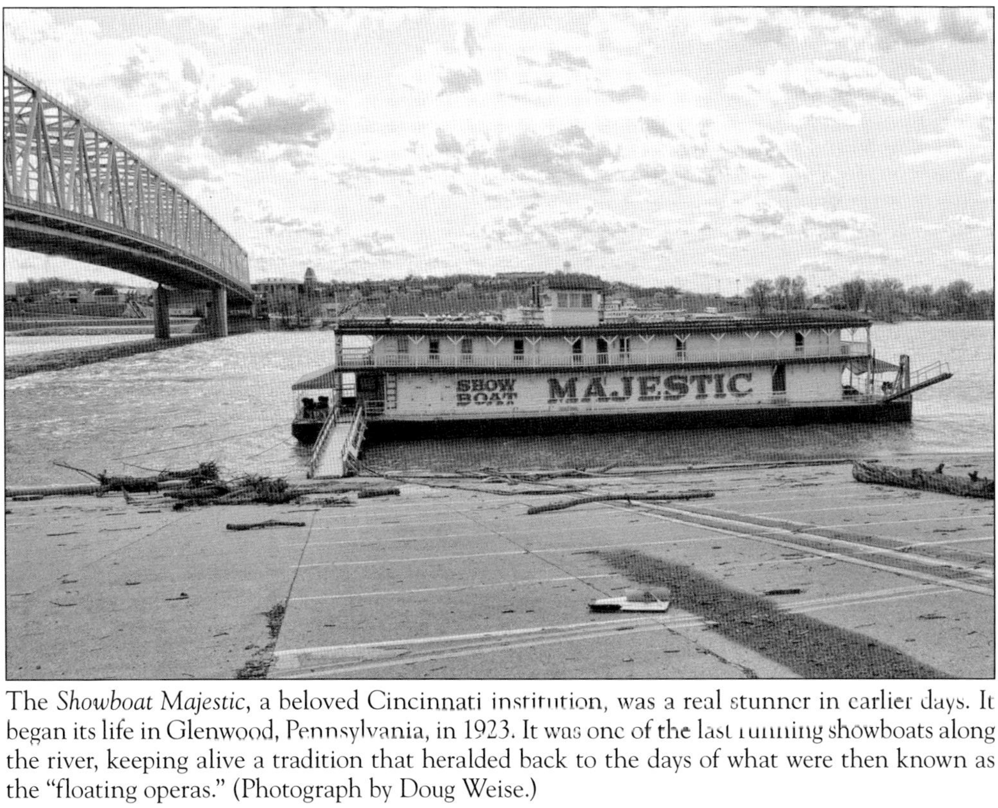

The *Showboat Majestic*, a beloved Cincinnati institution, was a real stunner in earlier days. It began its life in Glenwood, Pennsylvania, in 1923. It was one of the last running showboats along the river, keeping alive a tradition that heralded back to the days of what were then known as the "floating operas." (Photograph by Doug Weise.)

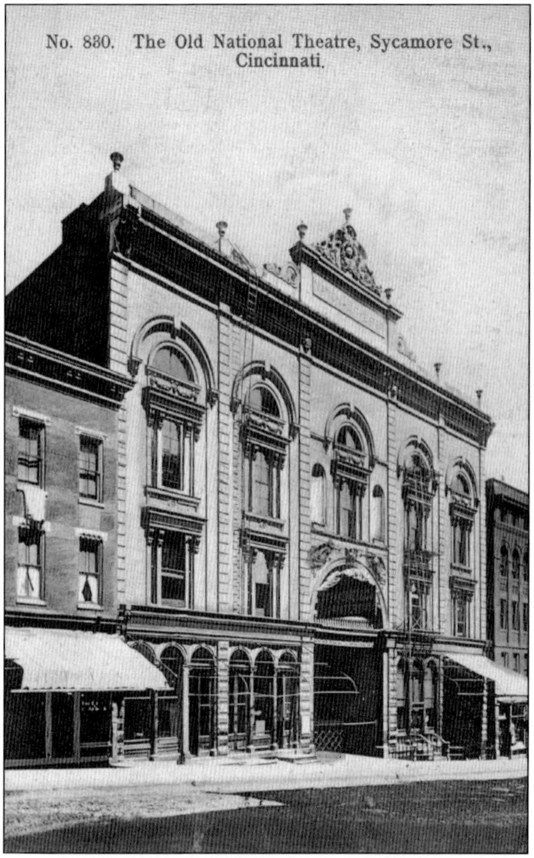

This ornate theater was often referred to as "Old Drury" after the famous Drury Lane showplace in London. It featured live performances, attracting talent such as Jenny Lind and Junius Booth Jr. Over the years, it was neglected and eventually turned into what must have been the world's most opulent tobacco warehouse. It was razed in 1940. (Public Library of Cincinnati and Hamilton County.)

This theater's name—"Columbia"—stemmed from the fact that Second Street was originally known as Columbia Street. Located in the southeastern part of downtown, this was the second theater in Cincinnati named "Columbia." (Public Library of Cincinnati and Hamilton County.)

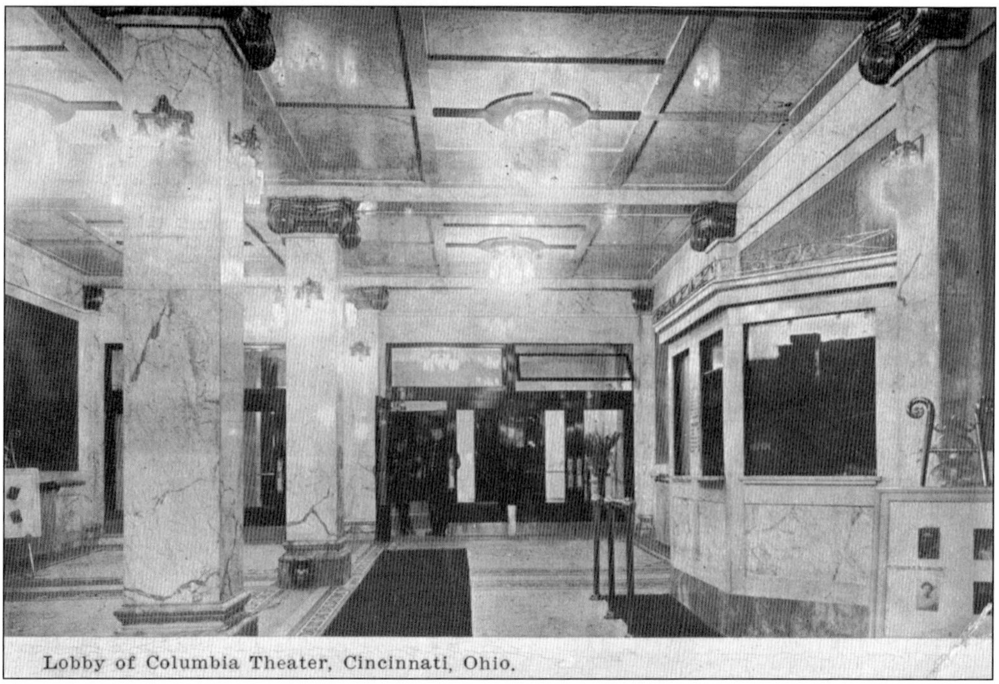

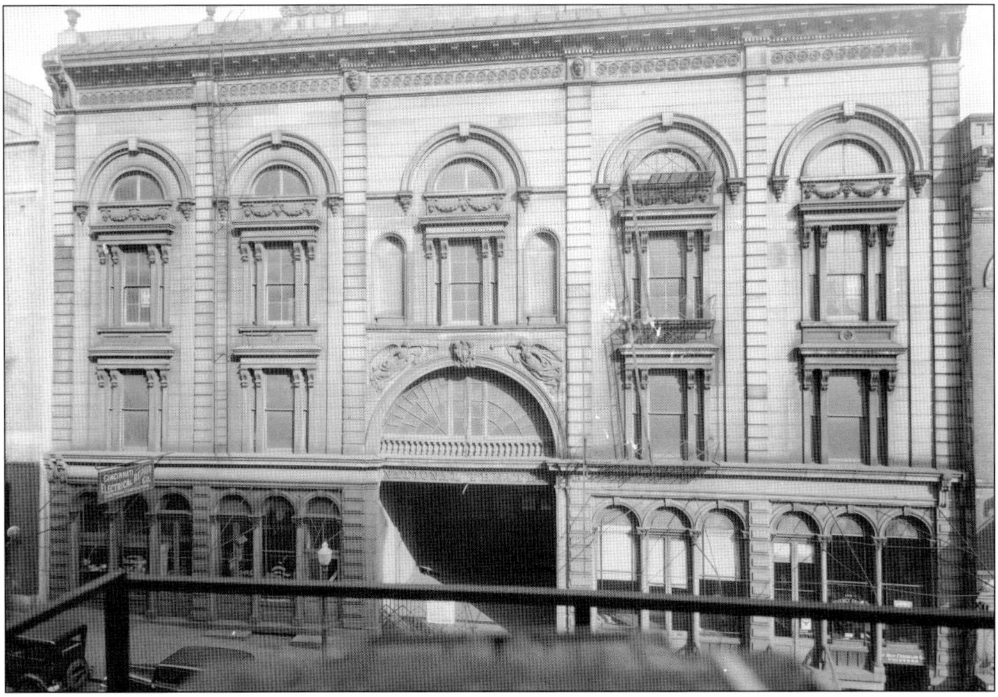

The National Theatre on Sycamore Street stood out from its surroundings. It was located three blocks uphill from the spot where the first permanent settlers landed in flatboats in 1788. Fort Washington was located one block to the east. (Library of Congress.)

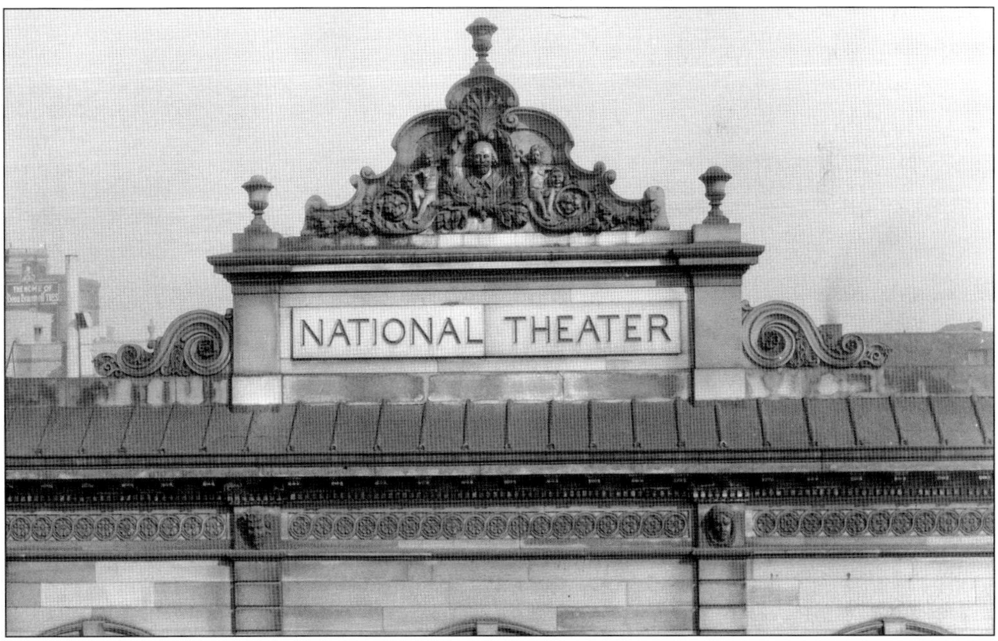

This detailed close-up of the National Theatre provides an interesting contrast. The top of the front facade was extremely ornate, ushering patrons into another world of culture and beauty with a bust of William Shakespeare. In the background at left is the far more mundane facade of a warehouse being advertised as "the Home of Beau Brummell Ties." (Library of Congress.)

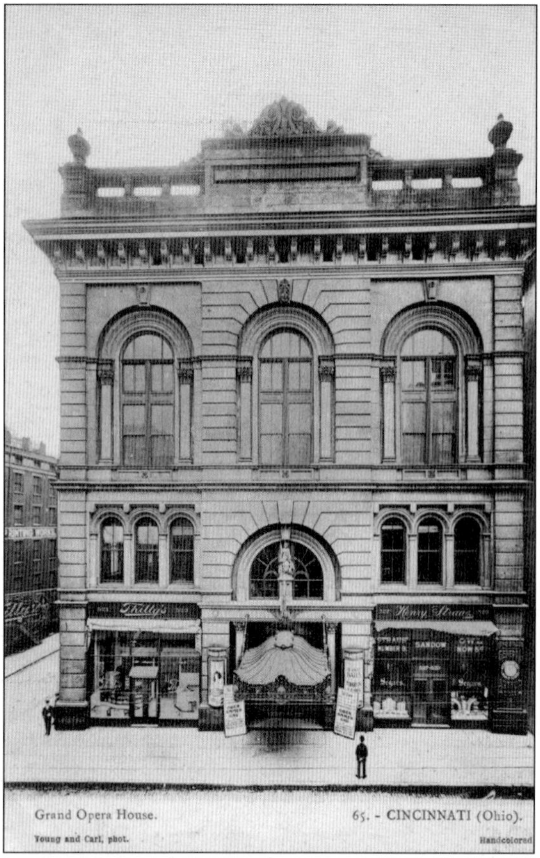

The location of the Grand Opera House building, on Vine Street across from the current Fountain Square, was once home to an auditorium owned by the Catholic Archdiocese of Cincinnati. After an atheist gave a disrespectful presentation, Archbishop John Baptist Purcell sold the establishment to David Sinton, who had made a fortune selling iron to the Union army for use in the Civil War. The opera house, owned by Sinton, opened in 1875. It ceased operation as a live theater venue in 1932 and closed for good in 1939. (Public Library of Cincinnati and Hamilton County.)

The small Lubin Theatre was located on Fifth Street between Race and Elm Streets. It was run by the Hennegan brothers, who also printed movie posters for Hollywood studios. As time went on, the establishment played African American films. The area around the theater had numerous nickelodeons and arcades. Note the decorative metalwork on the sides of the seats. (Public Library of Cincinnati and Hamilton County.)

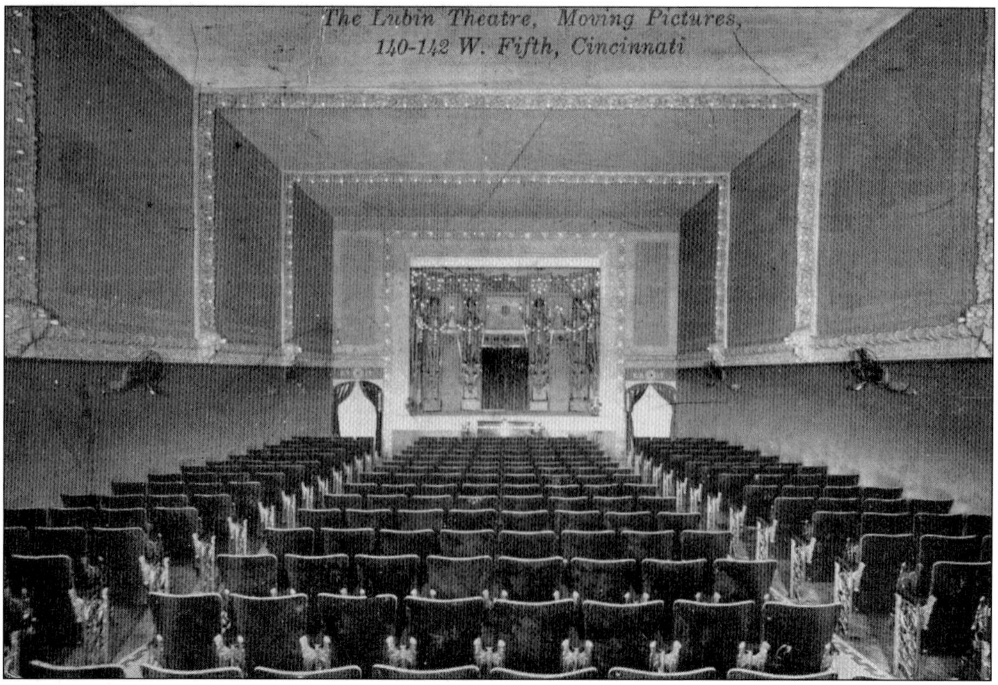

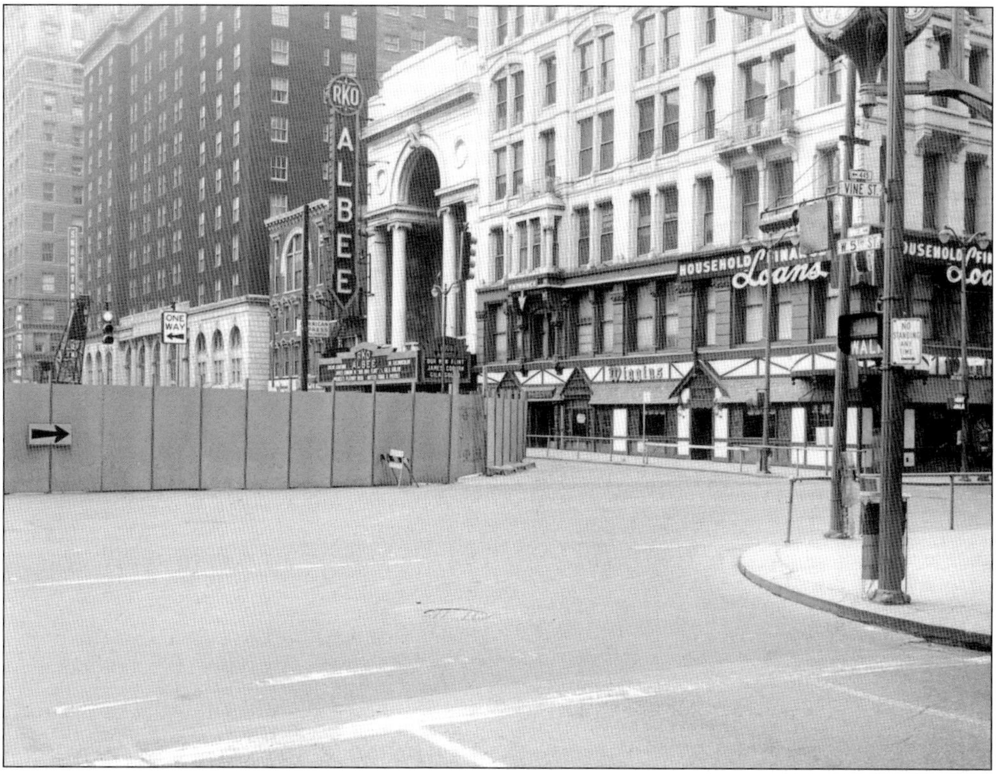

This picture of the RKO Albee at Fifth and Vine Streets shows the construction fence surrounding Fountain Square as it receives a facelift. The most curious feature of this view, however, is the complete lack of people and cars, although this photograph was taken in the very center of Cincinnati during the middle of the day. (Phil Lind.)

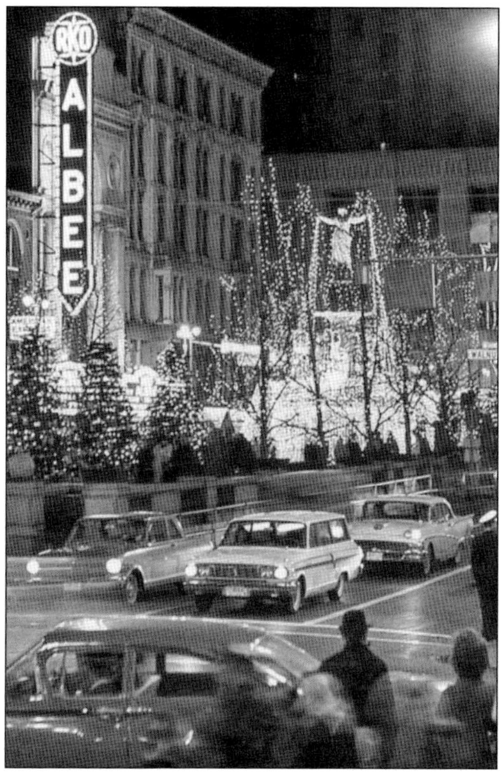

This enchanting image from the 1950s shows the marquee of the RKO Albee movie palace and Fountain Square decorated for Christmas. Note how the square is situated amid the traffic. The monument once occupied an island in the middle of Fifth Street. In 1971, the site was renovated into a modern plaza, and the traffic pattern was altered to flow only east. (Phil Lind.)

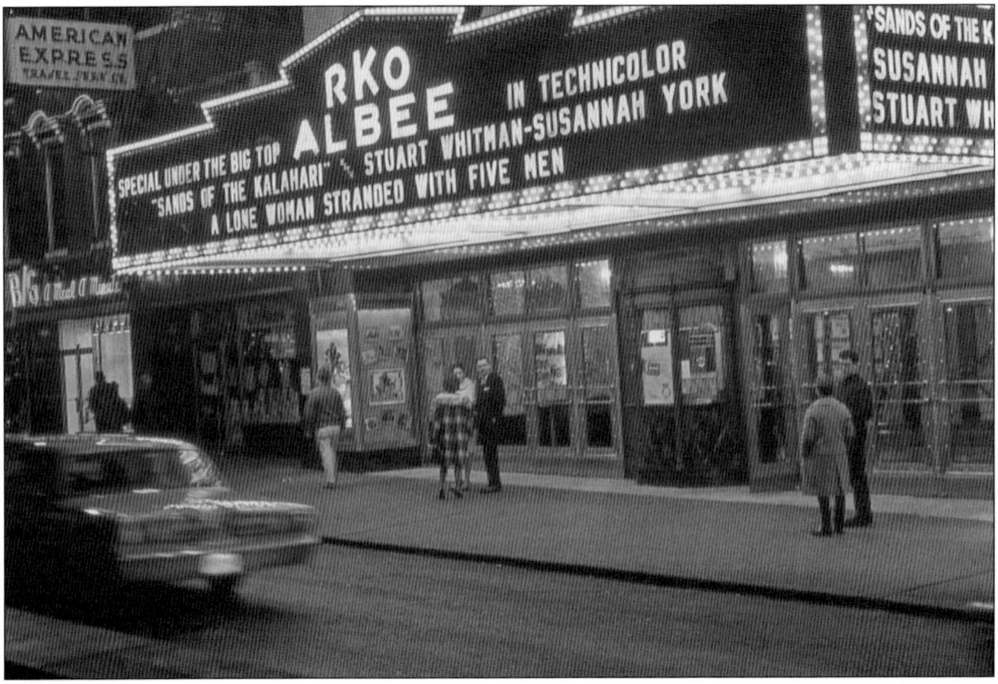

This 1965 photograph shows the RKO Albee, the grandest movie palace in Cincinnati, in its heyday. The name of this Fifth Street cinema was derived from E.F. Albee, who built the theater in 1927 for the astronomical cost of $4 million. Albee had previously owned vaudeville showplaces. (Joe Raphael.)

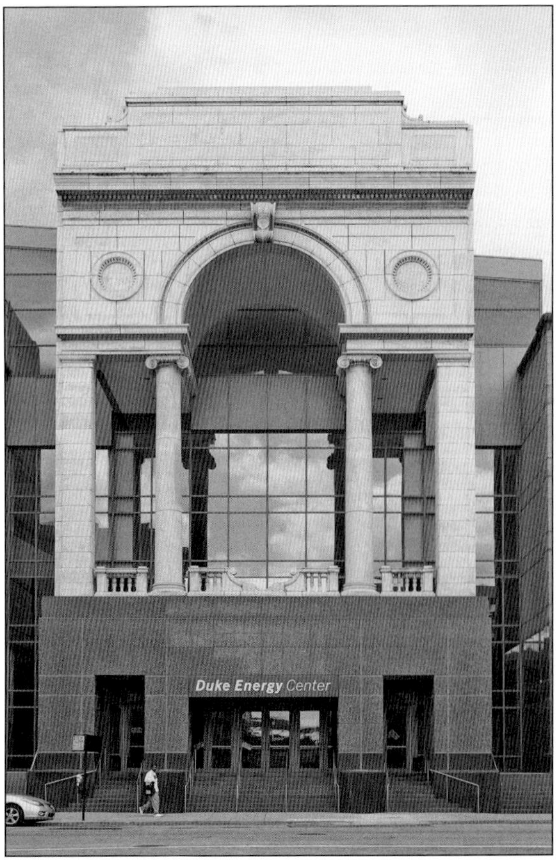

While the Albee movie palace is now gone, it is heartening to know that pieces of the elegant architecture have been preserved, with some becoming part of such buildings as the Music Hall and the public library. The magnificent facade, with its great pillars, was moved a few blocks west to crown the Albert B. Sabin Convention Center, now known as the Duke Energy Center. (Photograph by Doug Weise.)

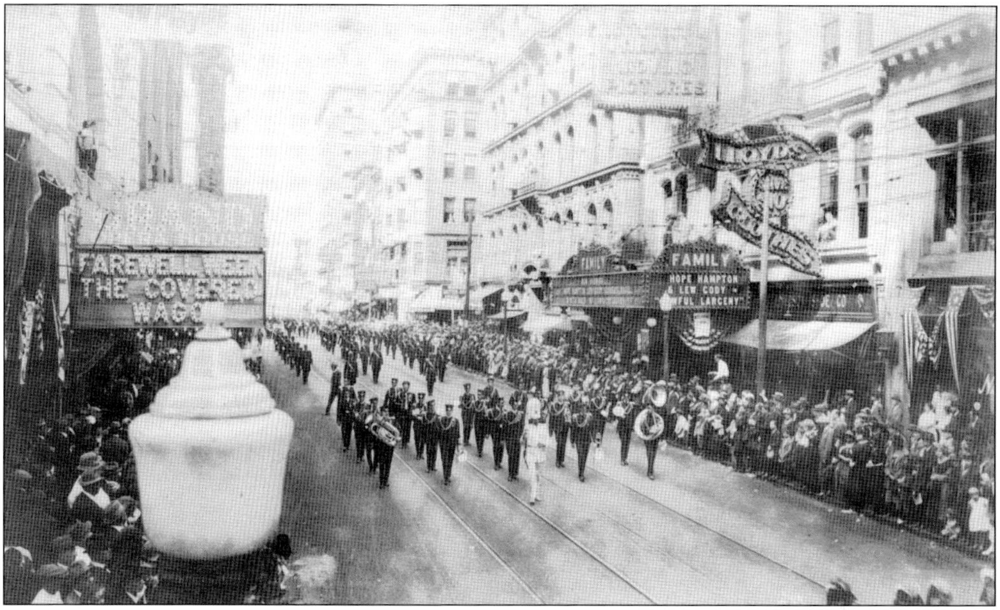

This picture from 1923 shows a parade making its way between two popular theatrical venues on Vine Street, near the site of the modern Fountain Square. At left is the Grand Opera House, and at right is the Family Theater. (Phil Lind.)

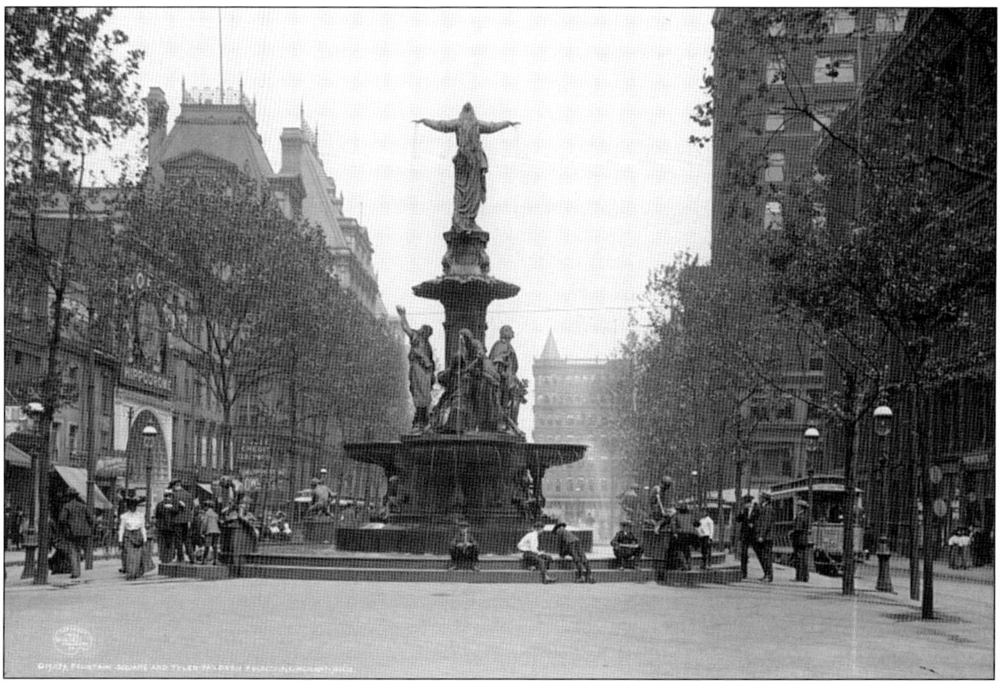

This delightful picture of vintage Fountain Square contains a rare sight—at left, just above the second gaslight, is the front of the elaborate Hippodrome Theater. (Library of Congress.)

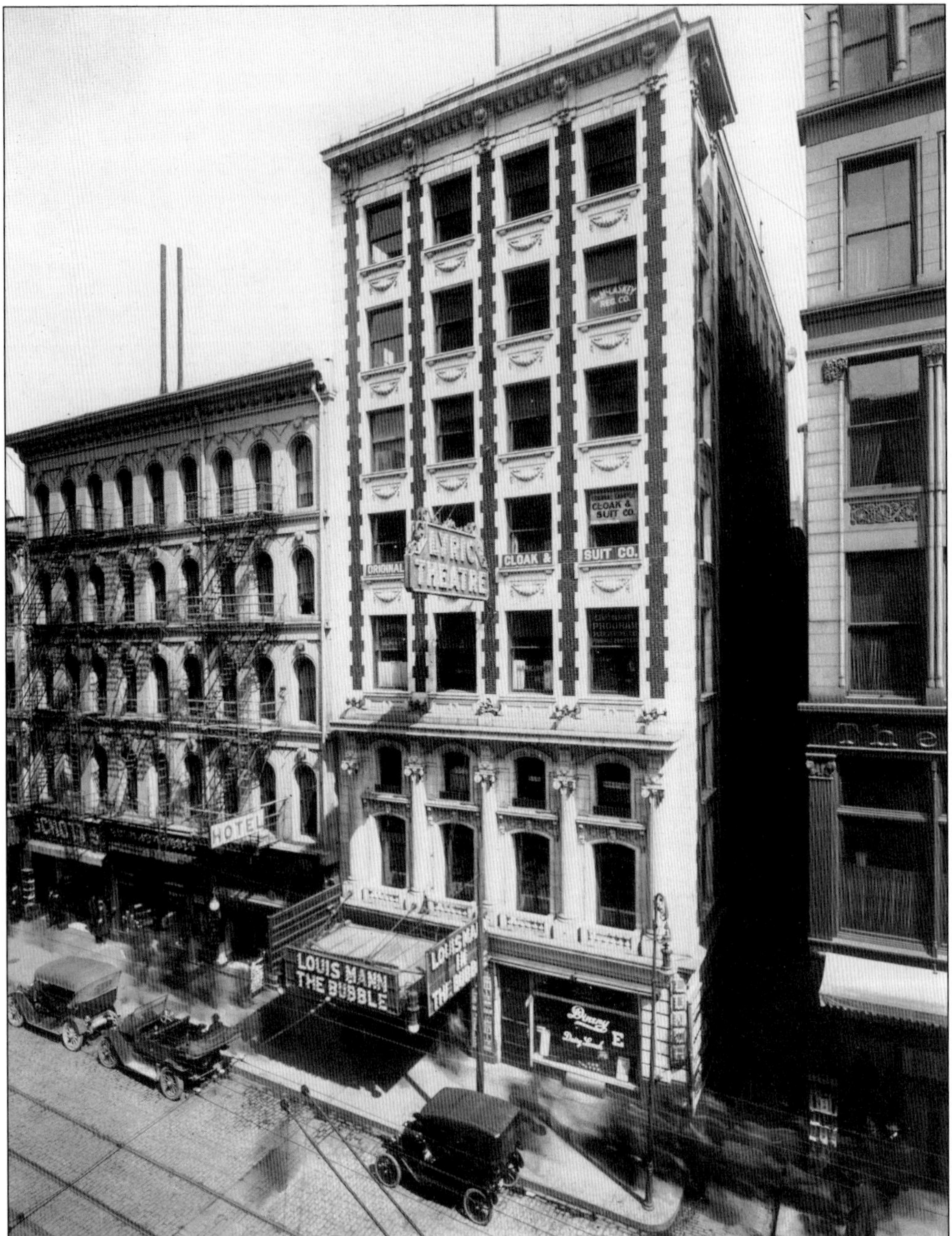

This 1915 image shows not only the popular Lyric Theatre, then featuring Louis Mann performing in *The Bubble*, but also such local landmarks as Schott's Shoes (left) and the Queen City College of Pharmacy (right). The Cincinnati Program Publishing Company was located in the Lyric Building, as shown on the window. The Lyric opened in 1906. Six years after this photograph was taken, the Lyric ended its run of live stage performances. Soon after, it became a major vaudeville house. The building was torn down in 1952. (Kenton County Public Library, Covington, Kentucky.)

This venerable theater, which had a busy history, first opened its doors in 1892 as the Fountain Square Theater. It closed in 1899 but reopened a decade later as the Columbia. By 1910, it had been purchased by vaudeville entrepreneur B.F. Keith. The Keith Theater became a major stop for vaudeville artists. (Kenton County Public Library, Covington, Kentucky.)

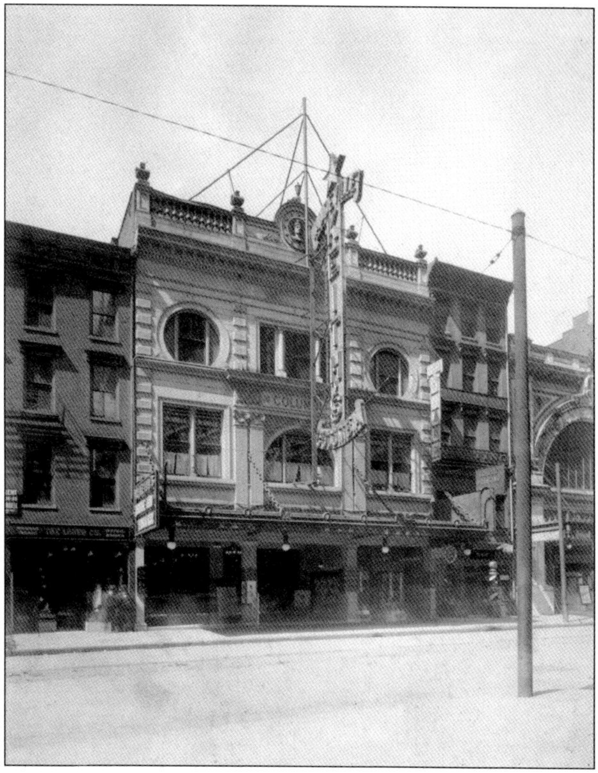

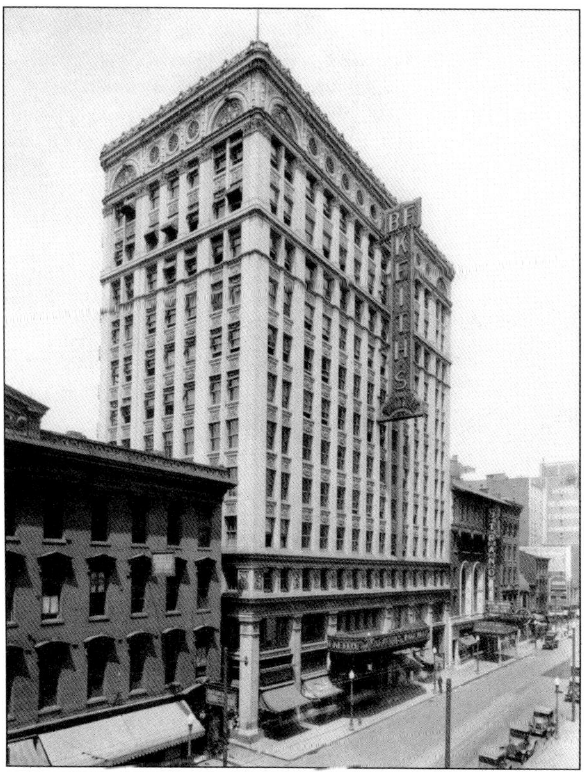

This 1925 image shows the Keith Theater on Walnut Street in all its glory. Note the size of the sign—nearly six stories tall. The beloved Cincinnati landmark was torn down in 1964 to make room for renovations of Fountain Square. (Kenton County Public Library, Covington, Kentucky.)

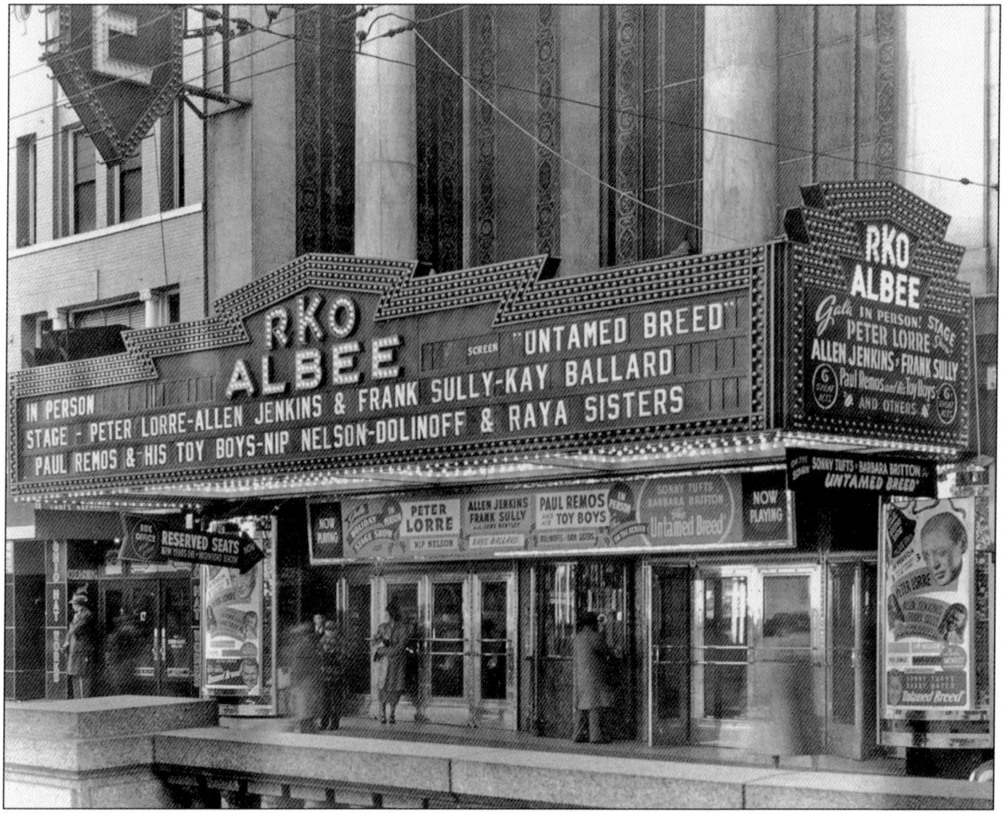

This 1948 image of the marquee at the RKO Albee lists the western *The Untamed Breed* as appearing on screen and also promises "in person" appearances by big stars promoting their films. One wonders exactly what Peter Lorre did on stage—hopefully he did not sing and dance! (Kenton County Public Library, Covington, Kentucky.)

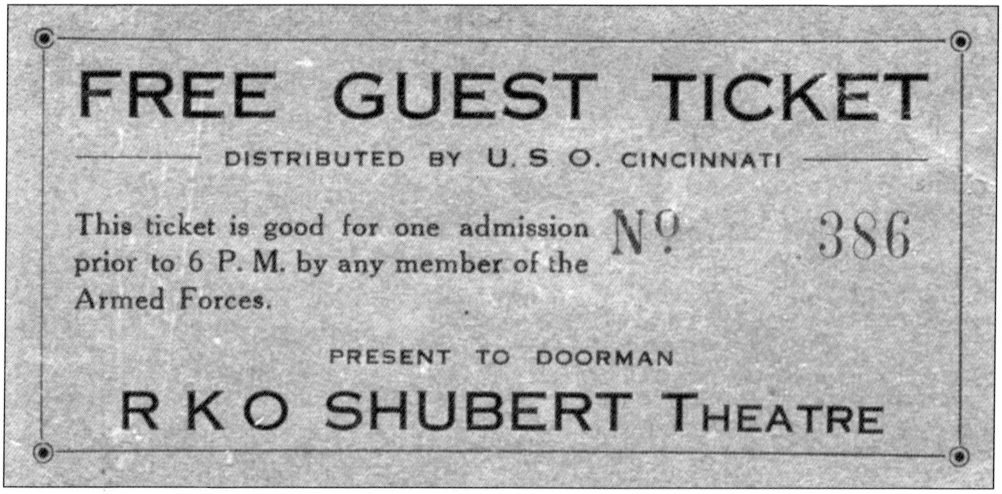
FREE GUEST TICKET

DISTRIBUTED BY U. S. O. CINCINNATI

This ticket is good for one admission prior to 6 P. M. by any member of the Armed Forces.

Nº 386

PRESENT TO DOORMAN

R K O SHUBERT THEATRE

During the Second World War, the downtown movie palaces helped to make life as enjoyable as possible for the many young men in uniform who passed through the Queen City. The USO distributed free tickets for a number of downtown theaters; the servicemen merely had to give the tickets to the doorman for free admission. (Phil Lind.)

When the popularity of vaudeville waned, many theaters converted to the new technology of motion pictures. The Lyric was one of the most popular venues in the downtown area. It began as a live theater in 1906, and 15 years later, it began showing motion pictures. In 1950, it closed its doors forever. (Public Library of Cincinnati and Hamilton County.)

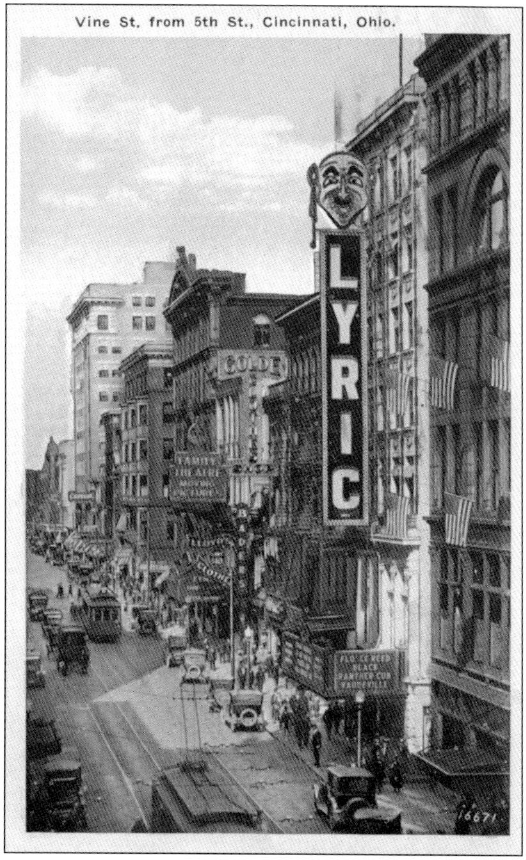

This view, looking down on old Cincinnati in 1925, shows just how many theaters were crammed together in the small area around Fifth and Vine Streets. The Duncan Sisters are performing at the Grand Opera House (at left), and *The Lost World* is showing at the Lyric (at right). The steeple of the Capitol is in the background. (Phil Lind.)

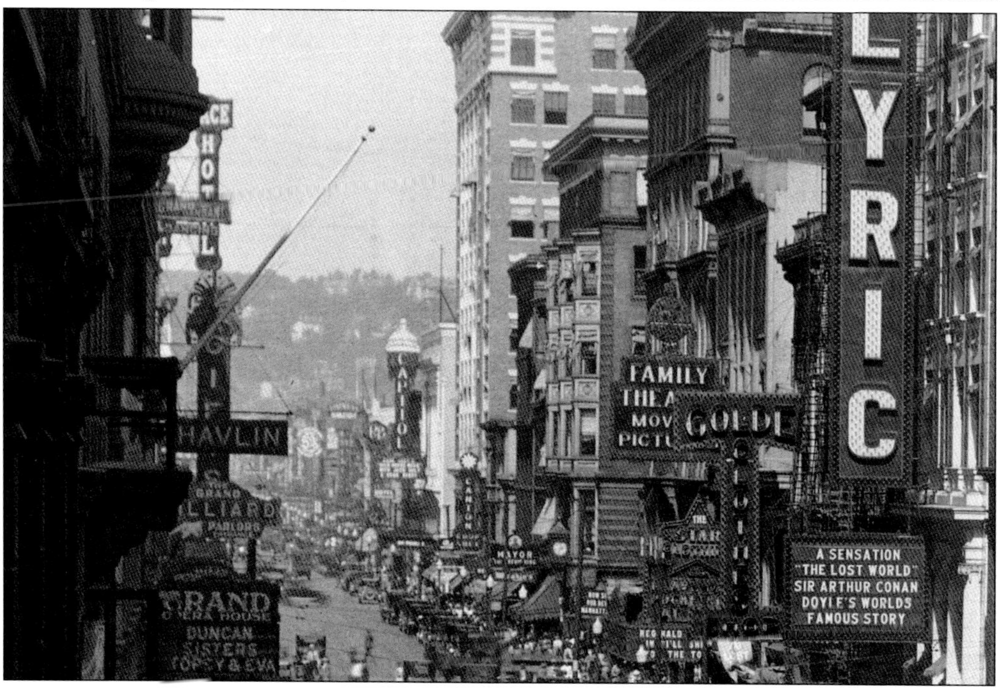

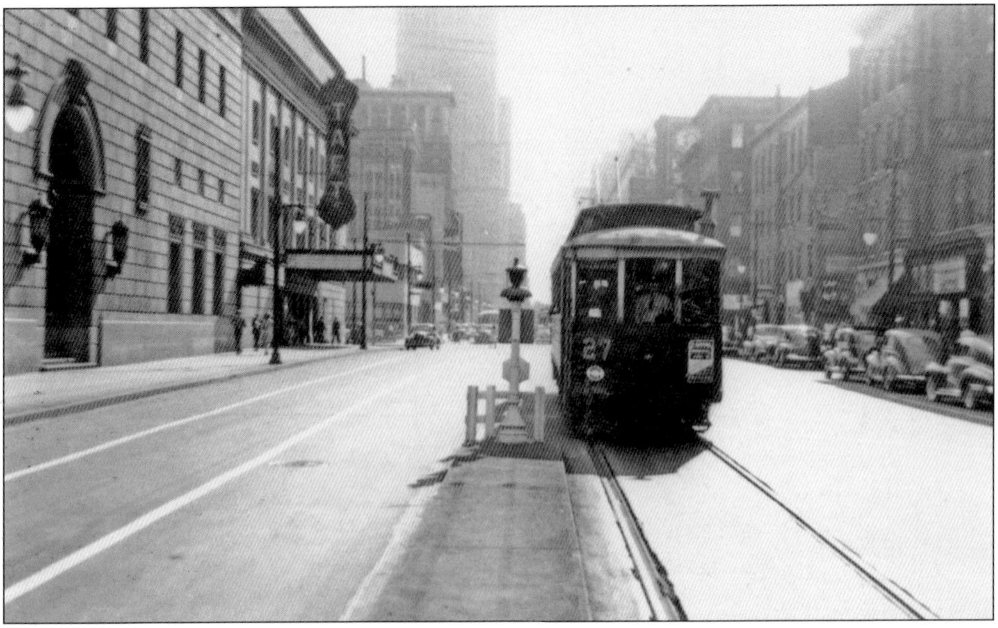

Built in 1928, the Taft Theatre is located at the eastern end of Fifth Street between Sycamore Street and Broadway. The building, a fascinating combination of both Art Deco and classical design, was part of the Cincinnati Masonic Temple. The theater is owned by the Scottish Rite of Freemasonry. (Phil Lind.)

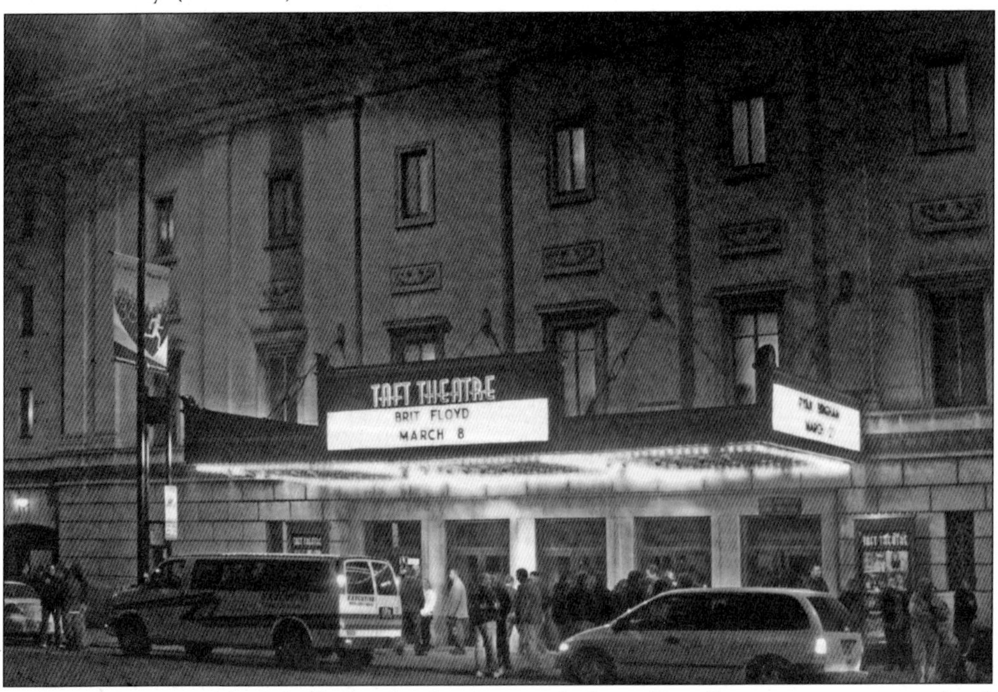

Recently, the venerable Taft Theatre has been revived after a $3 million renovation, completed in 2011, that made it one of the two most popular venues in the downtown area. Major acts such as Jay Leno, Bonnie Raitt, and Jackson Browne have recently appeared at this classic theater. (Photograph by Jordan Rolfes.)

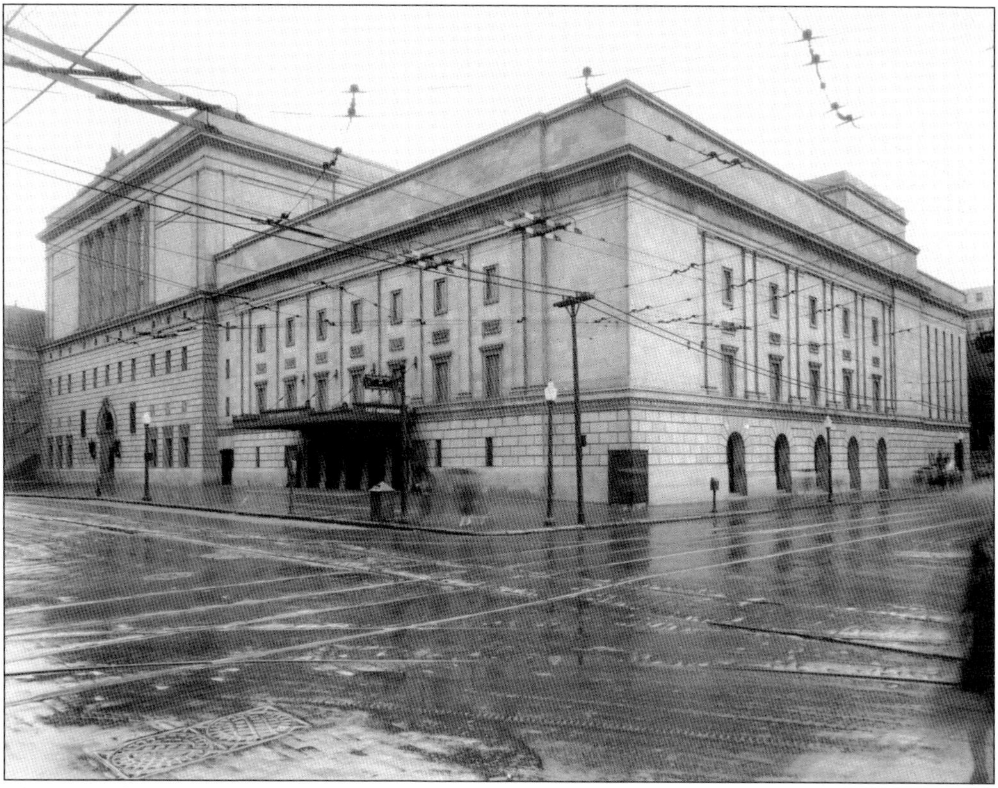

This rainy-day photograph of the Taft Theatre on Fifth Street also provides a view of the Masonic Temple next to it. Both use the curious combination of classical design and modern Art Deco. Note the streetcars wires strung overhead. (Kenton County Public Library, Covington, Kentucky.)

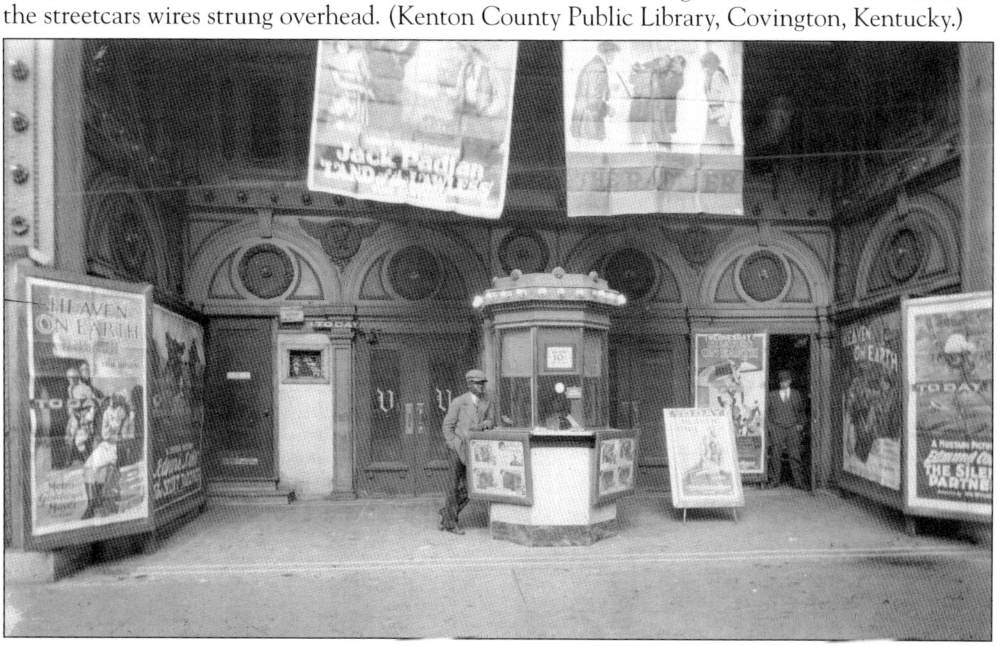

This 1927 photograph shows the ticket booth at the Victorian Theater on Fifth Street in the West End. (Cincinnati Museum Center, Cincinnati Historical Society Library.)

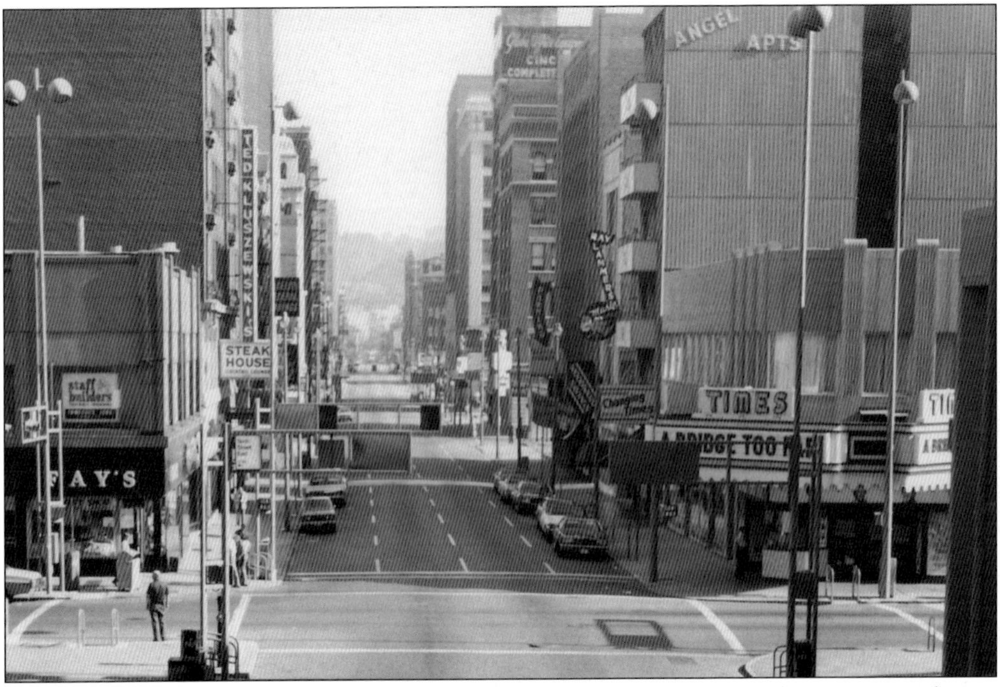

Those who experienced downtown Cincinnati in the 1960s and 1970s may appreciate this picture of Sixth and Walnut Streets. Not only does it show the Times Theater on the corner, but the popular Fay's Gifts, Ray Lammer's Music, and even Ted Kluszewski's Steakhouse are also visible. (Photograph by Vern Oliver.)

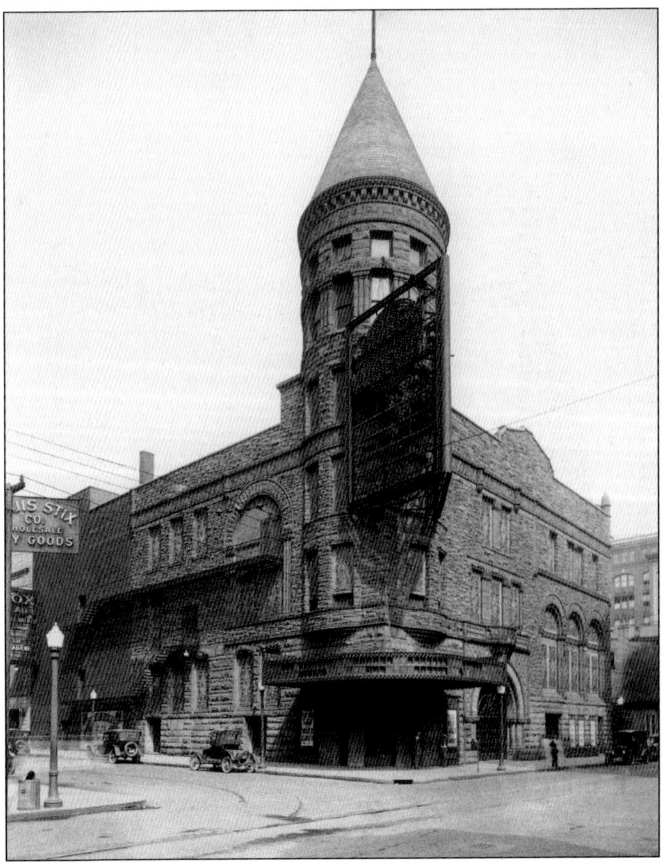

Downtown's magnificent Shubert Theater has had an interesting history. The Gothic building was constructed in 1848 to house the first YMCA in Cincinnati. By 1921, it had become a vaudeville theater; a decade later, it featured films and live performances. Like many theaters, this one became a church. In 1955, however, it returned to its former designation as a theater. (Kenton County Public Library, Covington, Kentucky.)

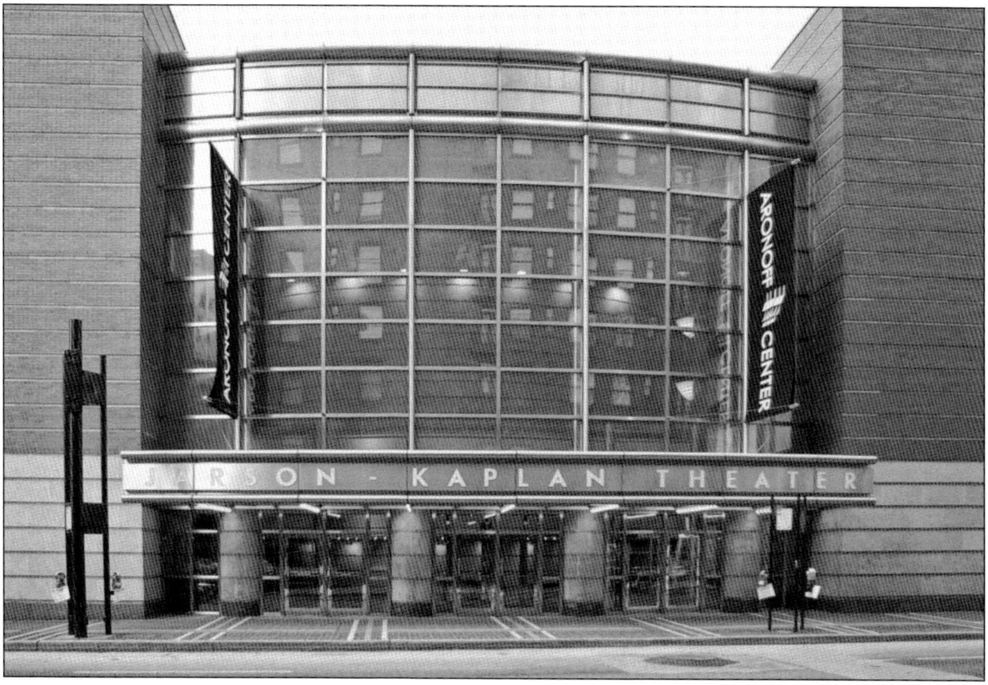

Downtown Cincinnati has two major venues for live theater: the Taft and the Aronoff Center, located at Walnut and Sixth Streets. Just as in the old days of the opera houses, the Aronoff, which opened in 1995, hosts major Broadway productions and is surrounded by upscale restaurants to make for a perfect evening out. (Photograph by Doug Weise.)

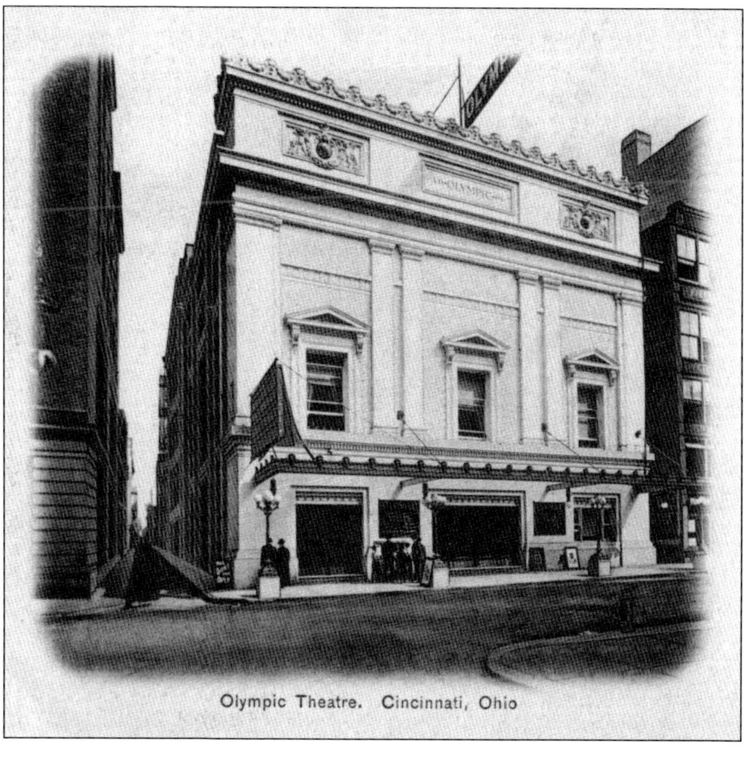

The Olympic Theatre, yet another stage establishment on Seventh Street, was located between Main and Walnut Streets. Like many of the old theaters, it began its life as a venue for live performances, moving from standard vaudeville to burlesque. (Public Library of Cincinnati and Hamilton County.)

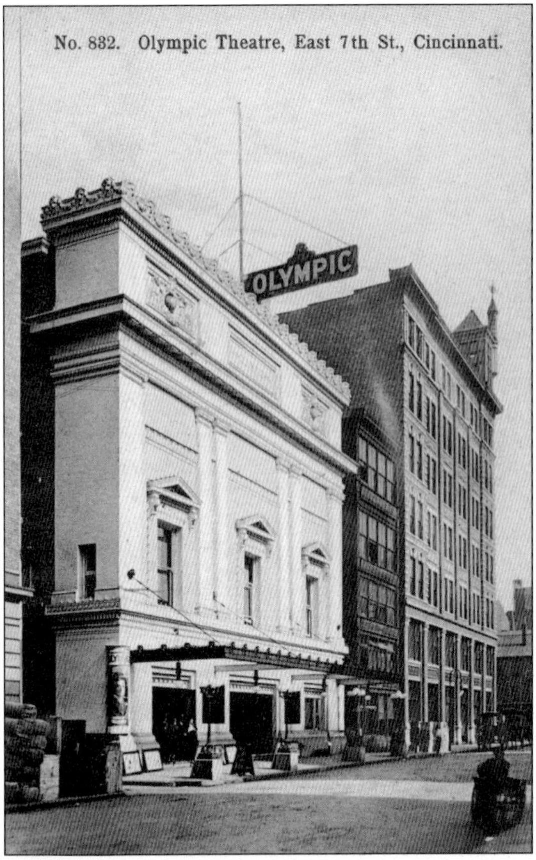

If the name "Olympic" sounds familiar, it may be because the theater was razed to make way for a parking garage named—of course—the Olympic. Ironically, people park there to attend the Aronoff Center across the street; thus, what was once a burlesque house has become a parking garage for a theater. (Public Library of Cincinnati and Hamilton County.)

This marvelous close-up of the detailed stonework on the facade of the Bijou Theater on Vine Street offers a good idea of just how fancy the outside of a downtown theater could be. However, despite how beautiful the facade was, failure to keep up with technology and the desires of its clientele spelled doom for the Bijou. (Library of Congress.)

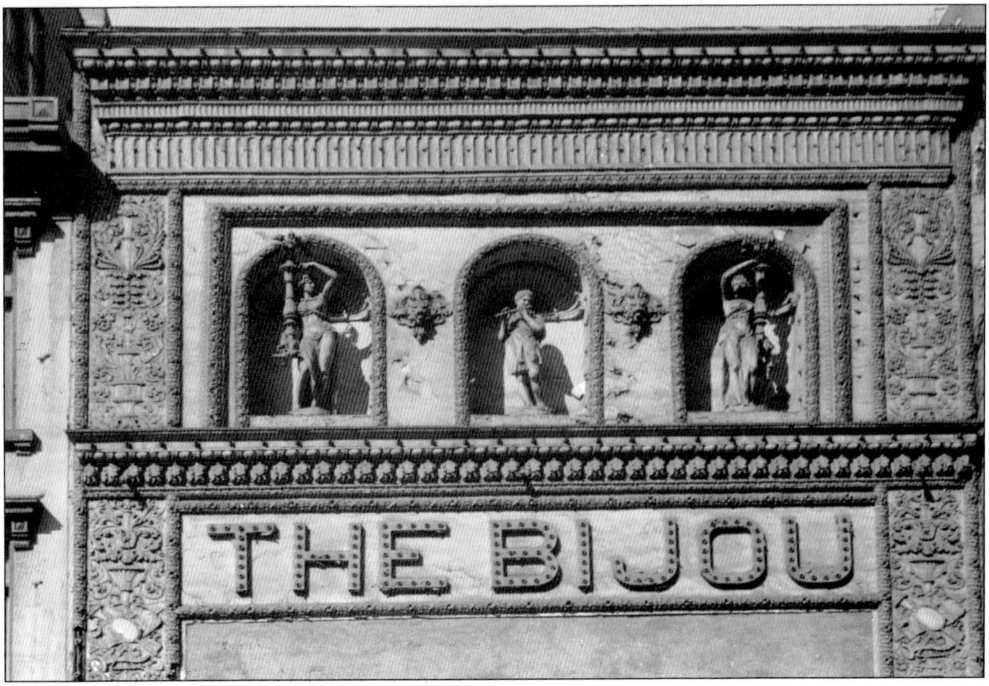

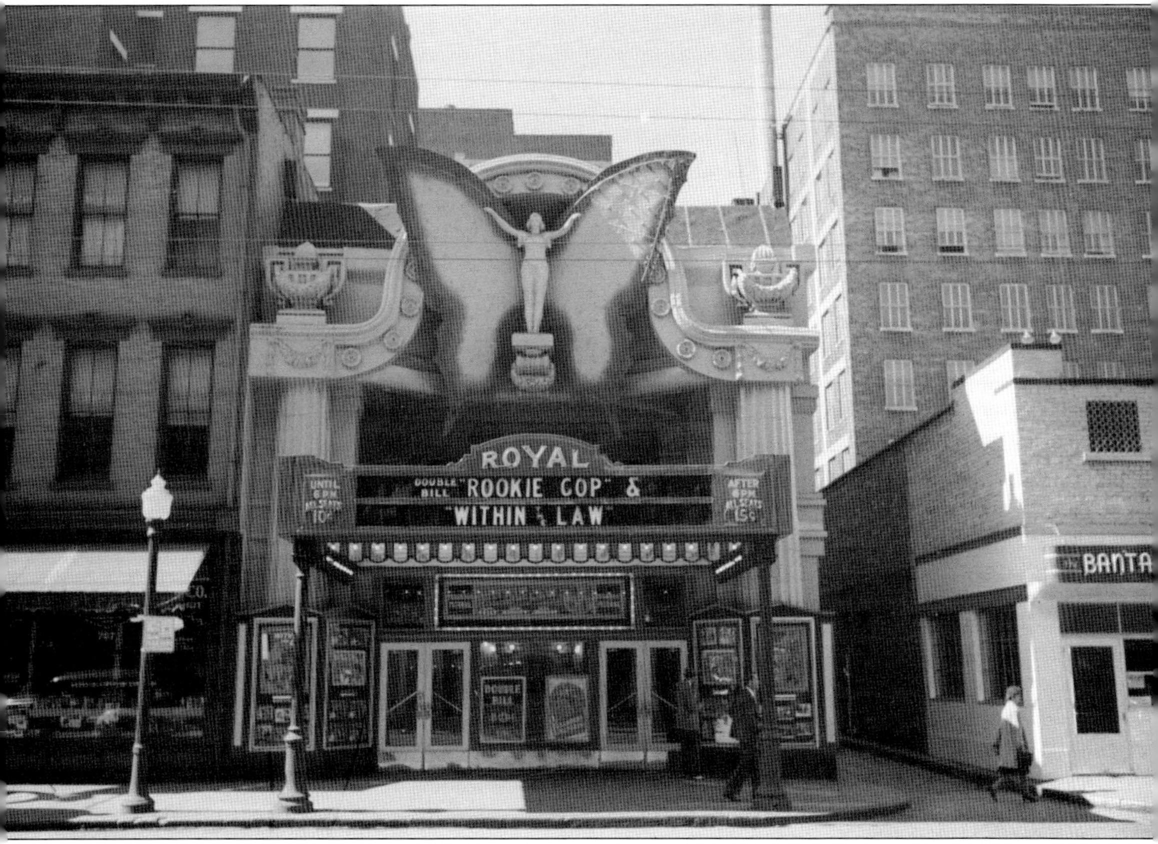

Theaters would often use extravagant architecture or ornamentation to attract attention. Some used Art Deco modernist designs; others went for a classical theme. The Royal Theater, however, opted for a design all its own. The motif was pure kitsch, including a massive fairy certain to pique interest. Located on Vine Street near the Gayety Burlesque House, this tiny cinema opened in 1910 and, for all its low-class glitter, became the longest continuously running theater in downtown Cincinnati. The fairy eventually flew away, and the Royal began showing soft-core pornography in 1964. In 1978, it attracted the attention of the vice squad, and the Royal closed its doors forever in 1979. (Library of Congress.)

Not all of the great downtown theaters were located on Vine Street. On the other side of Fountain Square on Walnut Street, between Fifth and Sixth Streets, was the old American Theater. Note the proud eagle beckoning entertainment-seekers to come in and enjoy a film. (Phil Lind.)

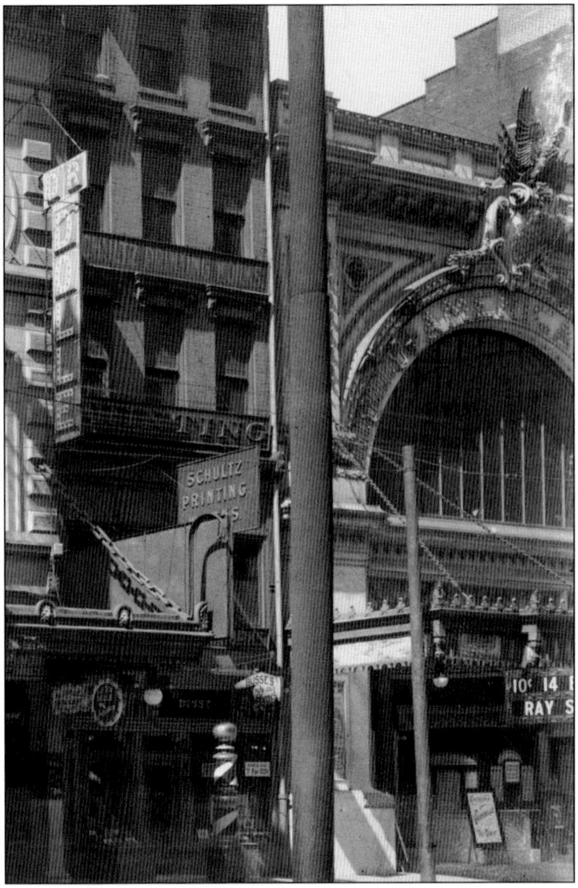

Some feared that motion pictures would destroy the art of theatrical performances. In the early 20th century, the Taft Theatre (built in 1928) and the Cox Memorial Theatre (built in 1920) were constructed to refute this notion. The men for whom these theaters were named—one a president and chief justice (Taft), the other a powerful political boss (Cox)—were bitter rivals. (Public Library of Cincinnati and Hamilton County.)

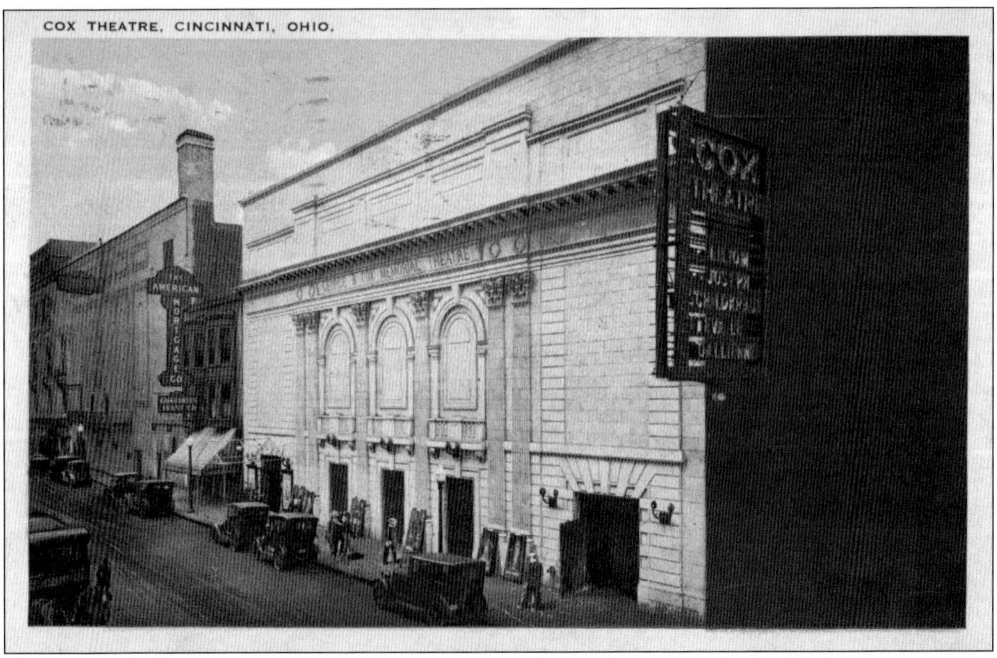

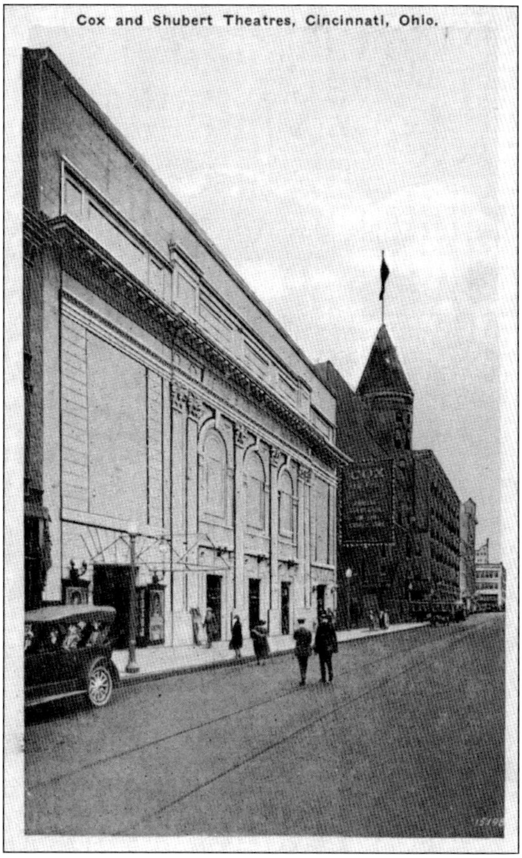

The intense competition between newfangled motion pictures and traditional stage performances is exemplified in this vintage postcard. On Seventh Street, the Cox Memorial Theatre, which hosted live productions, literally bumped up against the new movie theater, the Shubert. (Public Library of Cincinnati and Hamilton County.)

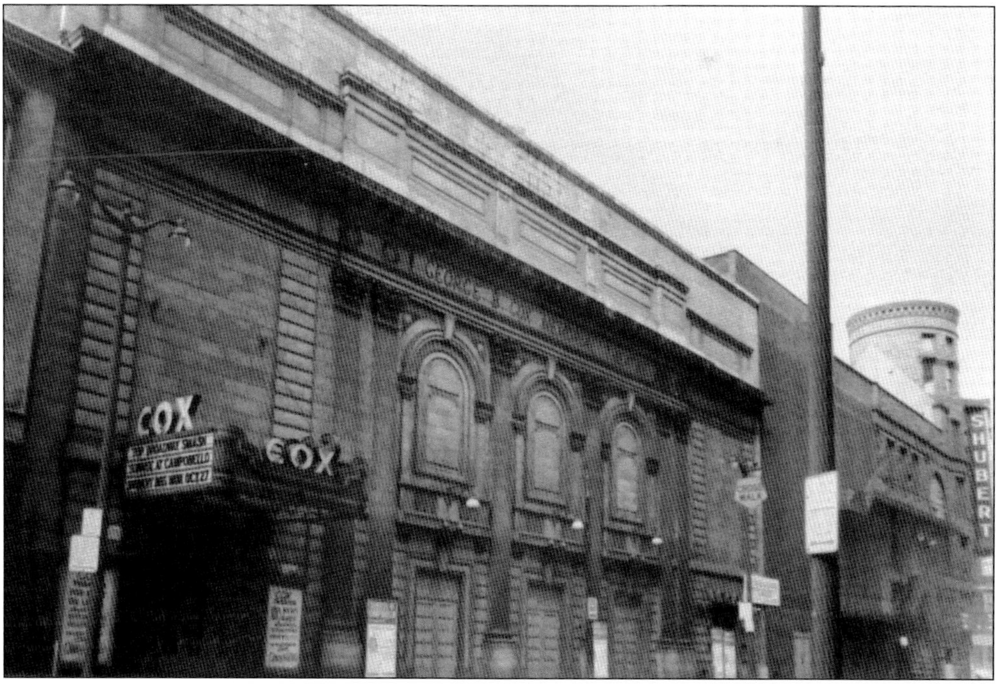

Three of the top members of the George "Boss" Cox machine were connected to Cincinnati entertainment. Cox died in 1916, and his widow, Caroline, later built this theater in his honor. Cox's right-hand man, Rudolph Hynicka, owned Coney Island for a short time. His other confidante, August Hermann, briefly owned the Cincinnati Reds. (Phil Lind.)

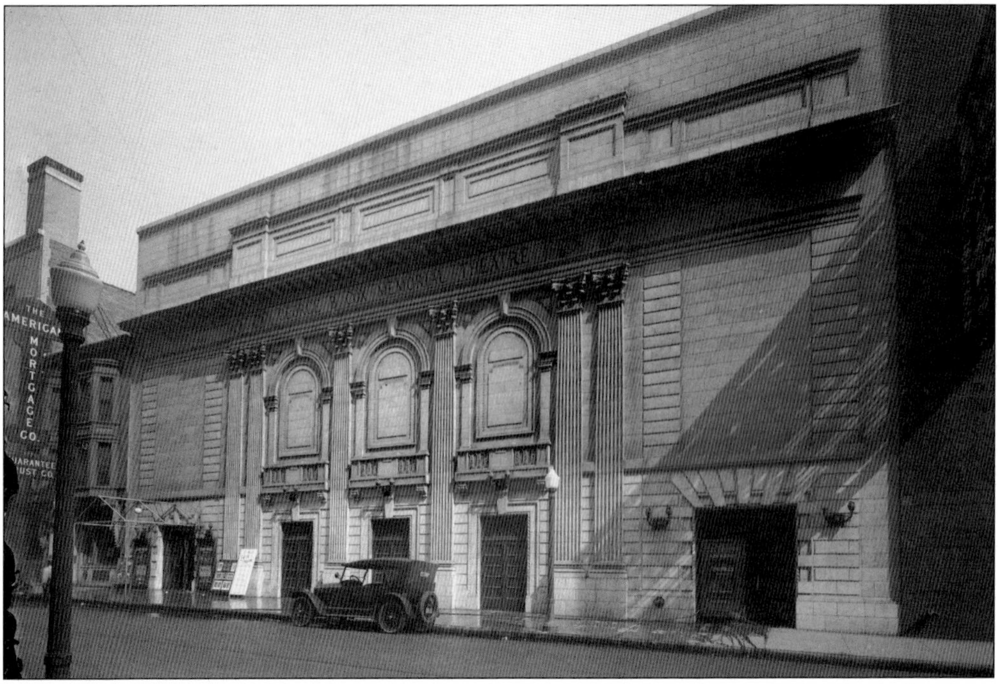

This motorist secured a fine parking space directly in front of the Cox Memorial Theatre. Note how the ornamentation of the building's architecture is recessed into the structure. It is also interesting to note the absence of parking meters. (Kenton County Public Library, Covington, Kentucky.)

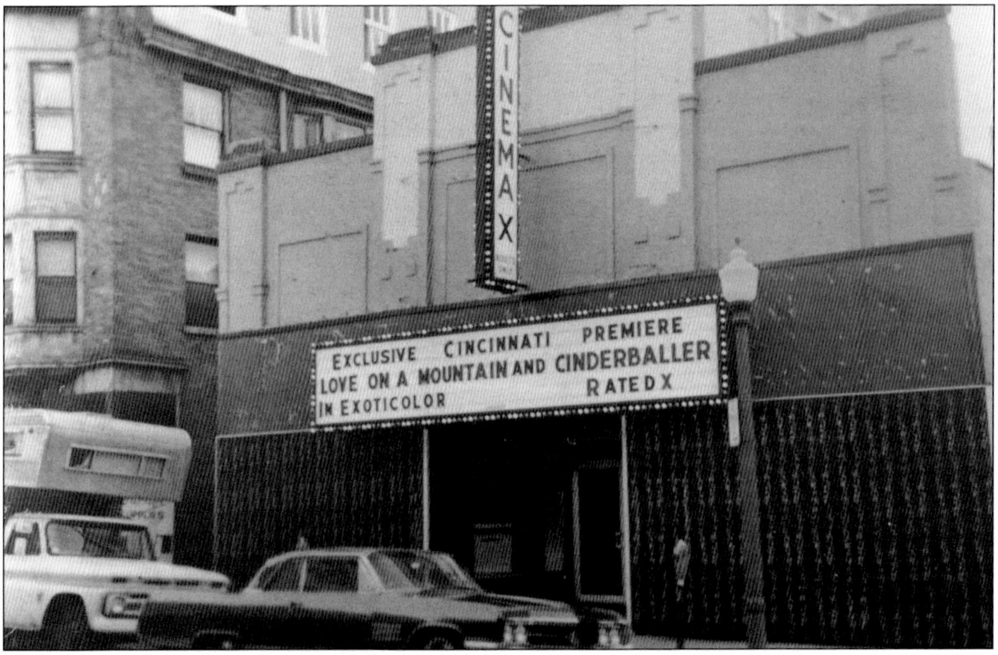

In the late 1960s and into the early 1970s, a small number of adult bookstores operated in Cincinnati. In 1971, this Art Deco building on Race Street housed an adult theater, Cinema X. It was immediately embroiled in legal problems and eventually closed in 1973. However, the real Cinema X battle was fought across the river in wide-open Newport. (Greater Cincinnati Police Historical Society.)

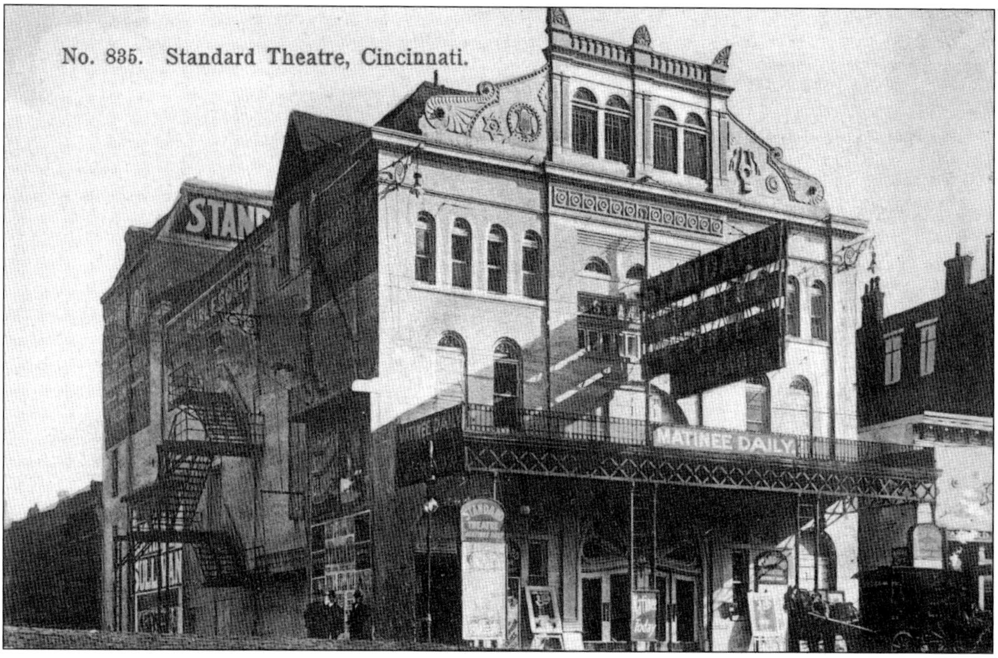

Moviegoers may have wanted to brush up on their German before seeing the promised daily matinee at the Standard Theatre, which bordered on being a downtown showplace and a neighborhood movie house. It was located on Vine and Canal Streets, across the Miami-Erie Canal from the downtown area, in the German neighborhood of Over-the-Rhine. (Public Library of Cincinnati and Hamilton County.)

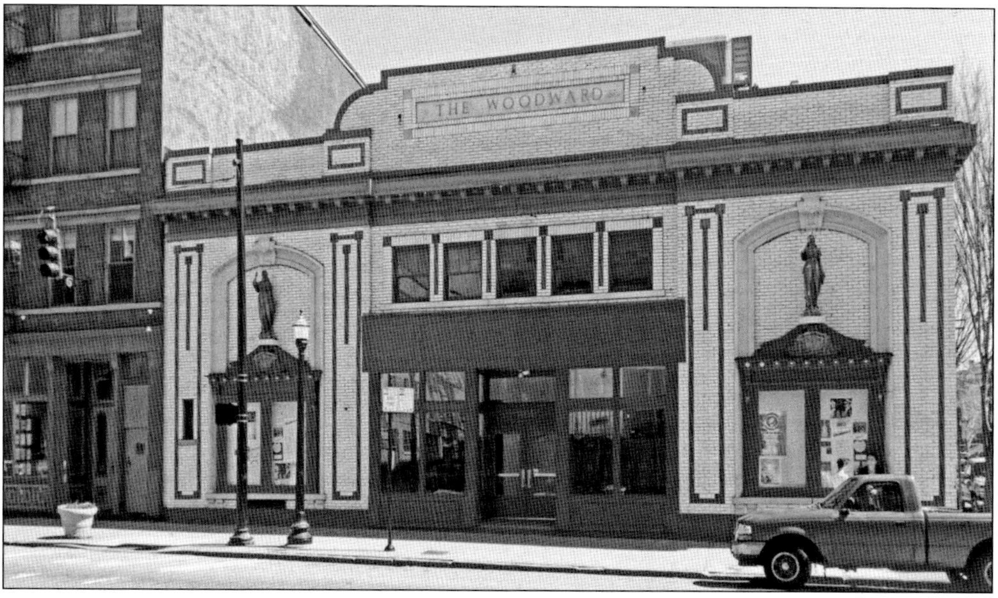

One of the most amazing transformations in Cincinnati's history is the unexpected revitalization of Over-the-Rhine. It began as a German enclave and was a low-income slum throughout much of the 20th century. Today, the area, filled with art galleries and trendy restaurants, attracts young professionals. Even the abandoned Woodward Theater has been revived as a venue for live entertainment. (Photograph by Doug Weise.)

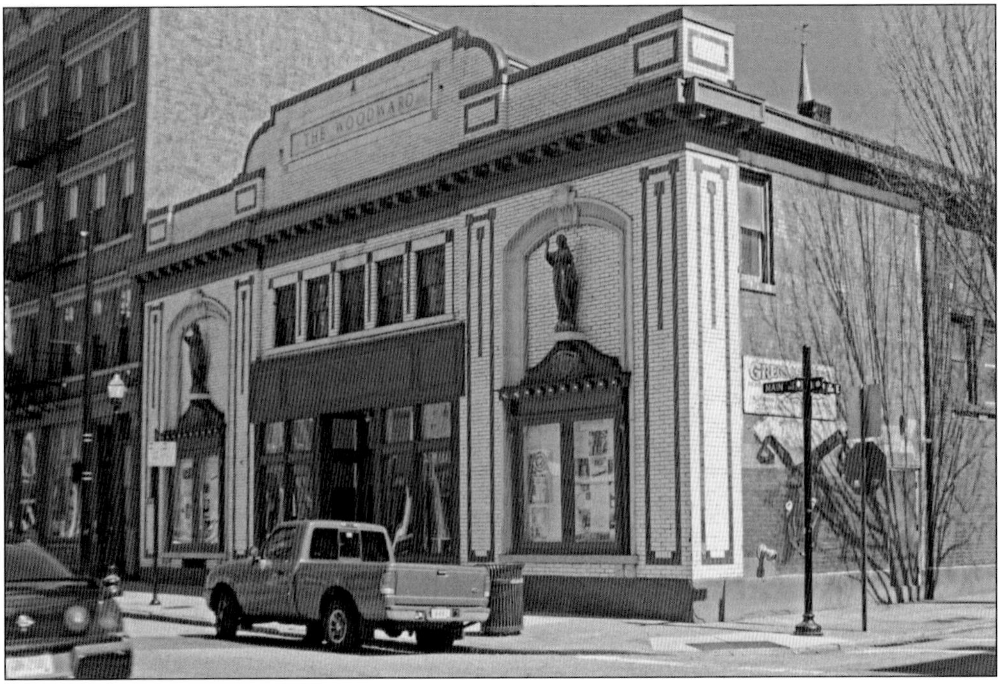

Another view of the Woodward Theater shows off the unique Beaux Arts style of its facade. This venue began by showing silent films in 1913. As the neighborhood around it changed, it closed its doors in 1933 amid the trials of the Great Depression. (Photograph by Doug Weise.)

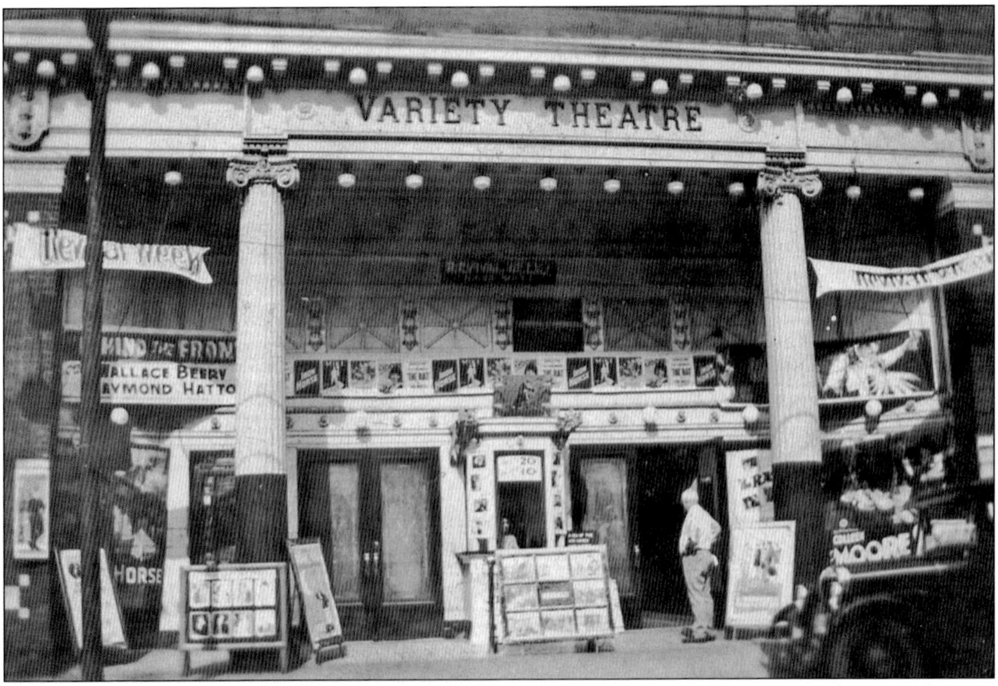

The Variety Theatre was among the neighborhood theaters in the old German district of Over-the-Rhine. By the 1930s, its name had changed to the Uptown. It was located on East McMicken Avenue, close to the bottom of the hill leading up to Clifton Heights. (Pat Kelly.)

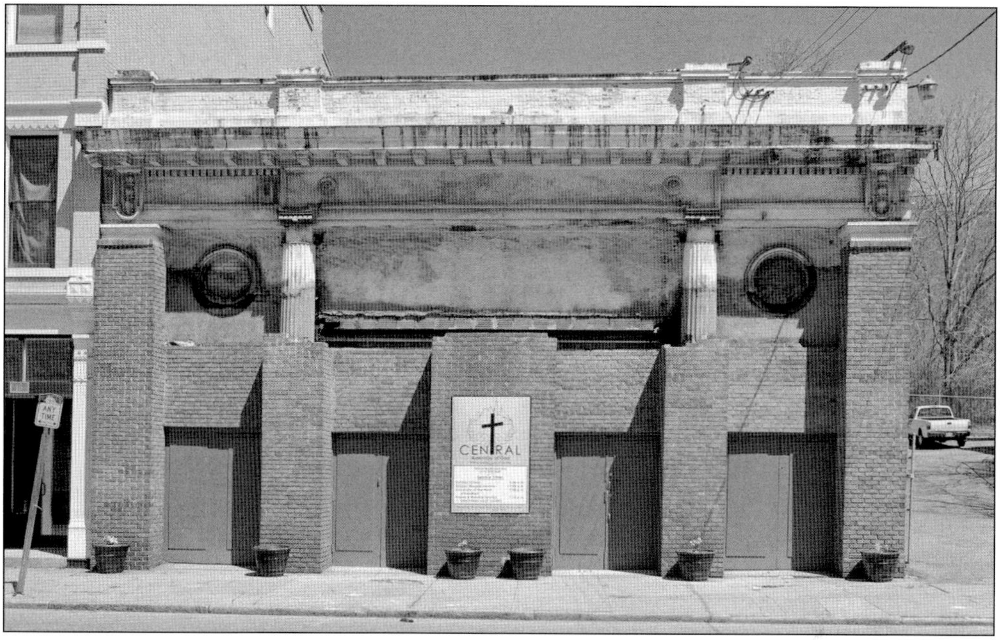

As noted on the sign out front, this building has joined other neighborhood theaters that have now become churches. This theater was originally the Variety and then became the Uptown in 1931/1932. It was unique in that it did not have a marquee. Sometimes there were posters outside, but many longtime residents remember paying 75¢ on a Saturday afternoon with no idea what film they would see. (Photograph by Doug Weise.)

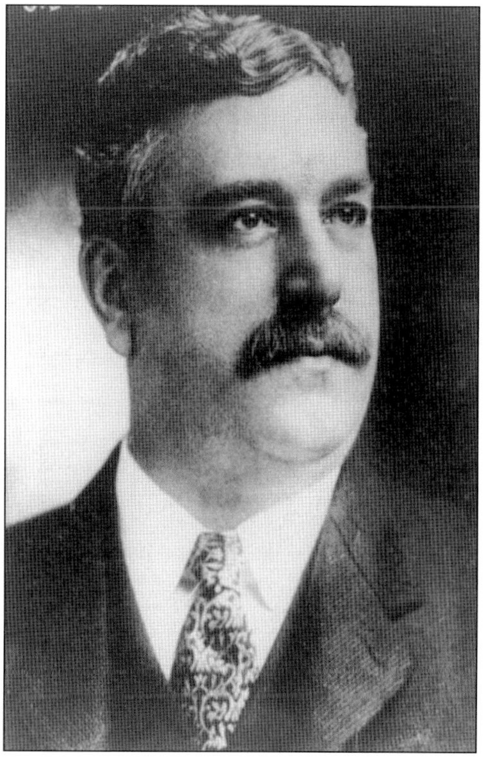

George Barnsdale "Boss" Cox (1853–1916) is the man for whom the Cox Memorial Theatre on Seventh Street was named. Unlike others mentioned in this book, Cox was not in show business but rather in politics. Rising to fill a vacuum after the 1884 Courthouse Riot, this self-made man consolidated power, playing local politics like a chess master. What went on in city hall was merely for show; the real decisions that dictated how the city ran were made by this man and his close associates around a large table at Weilert's Biergarten in Over-the-Rhine. While Cox thrived in a fascinating world of backroom deals, he made appearances in the theaters and the taverns around them. The theater named after him was in some ways an act of defiance against those who eventually supplanted his political machine. (Library of Congress.)

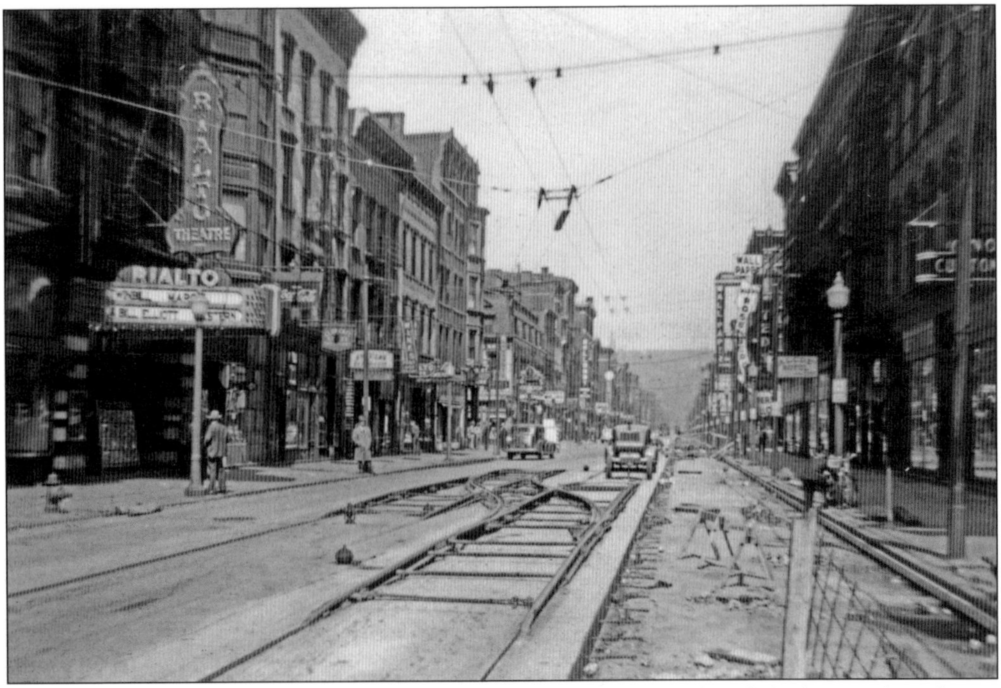

This image from 1946, about a decade before the old Rialto was demolished, provides a better view of the Over-the-Rhine neighborhood. By this time, the Germans had, for the most part, completed their migration to the suburbs. The days of George "Boss" Cox running the city from his favorite table at Weilert's Biergarten were long gone. (Phil Lind.)

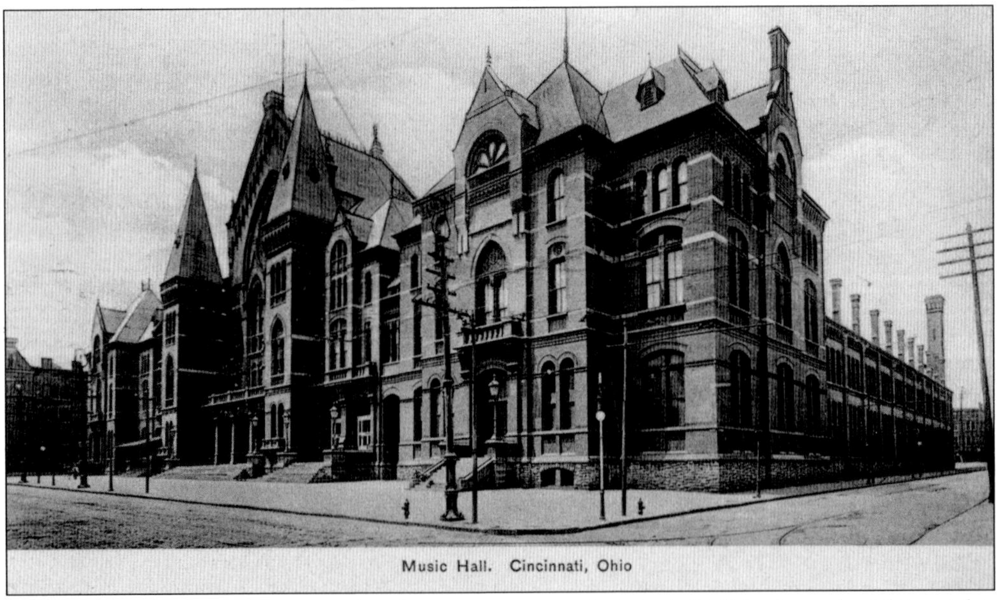

Music Hall. Cincinnati, Ohio

The most magnificent theater in the Cincinnati area is the Music Hall in Over-the-Rhine. This Venetian Gothic structure was built by renowned architect Samuel Hannaford in 1878. Its original purpose was to house the German singing festival, the Saengerfest. Situated over a potter's field, it is reputedly one of the most haunted locations in the country. (Public Library of Cincinnati and Hamilton County.)

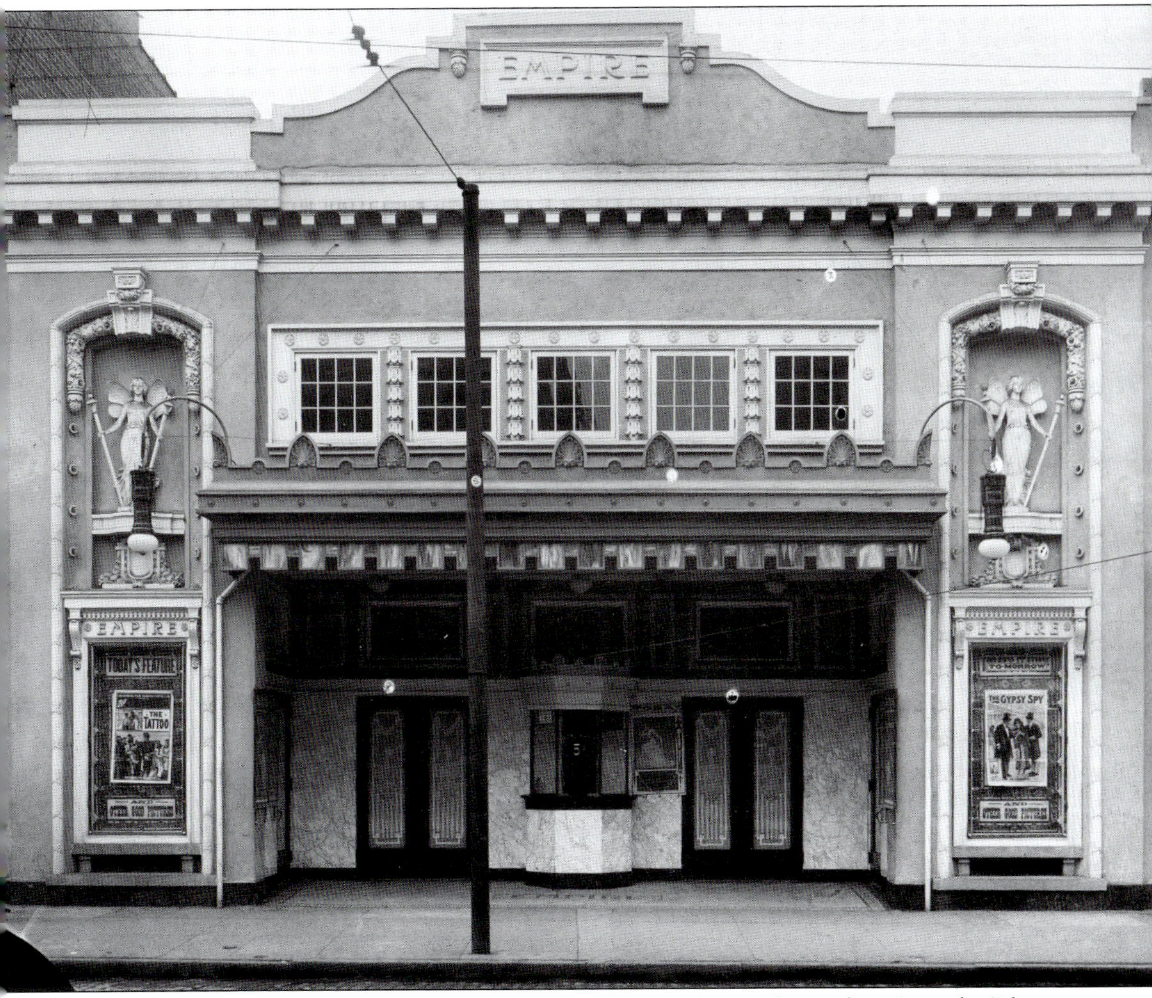

This rare 1912 photograph shows the venerable Empire Theater, located in Over-the-Rhine, before the Art Deco facade was added. At this time, it was still covered in Gilded Age elegance, ready to show a mostly German audience the latest silent films. (Cincinnati Museum Center, Cincinnati Historical Society Library.)

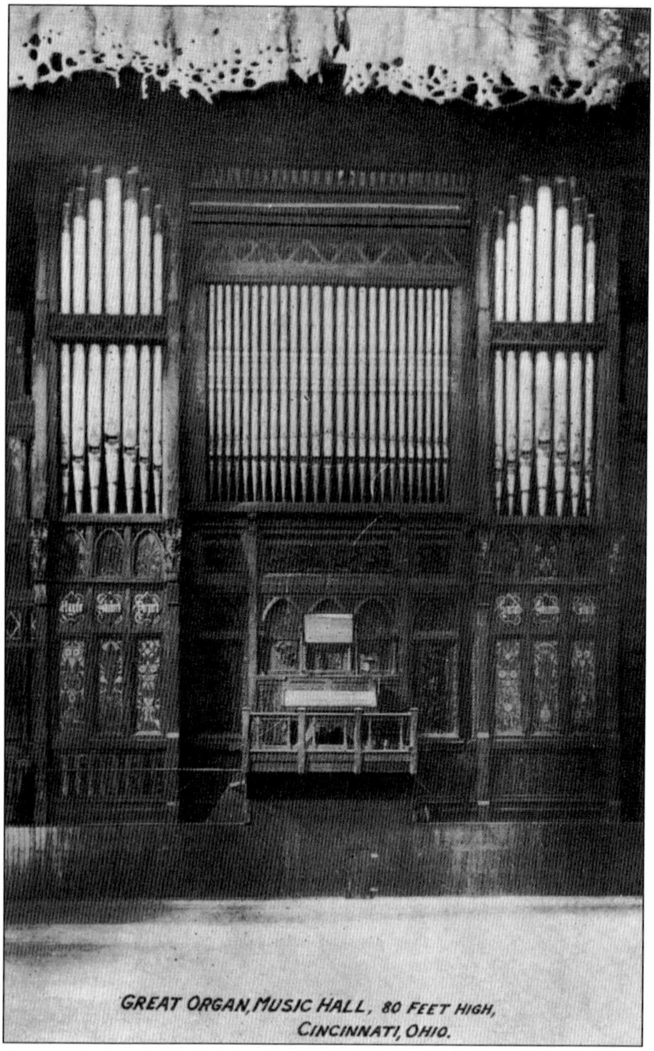

In 1878, the Music Hall's grand opening featured music from this magnificent organ. Built by Hook & Hastings in Boston, it had over 6,000 pipes and was 50 feet wide and 60 feet tall. Astonishingly, this great masterpiece was disassembled and thrown away for scrap to provide more room during a renovation in the 1970s. (Public Library of Cincinnati and Hamilton County.)

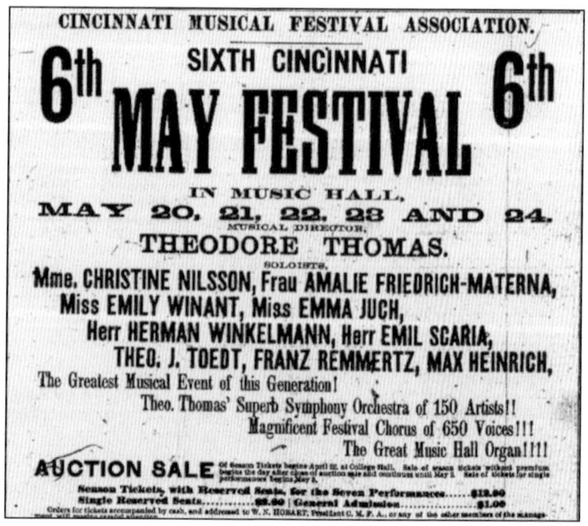

A direct descendant of the traditional Saengerfest is the beloved May Festival, which started in 1873. Since it is reminiscent of the singing competition in *Die Meistersinger von Nürnberg*, many famed Wagnerian singers have performed at this festival over the years, including the immortal Kirsten Flagstad in 1937 and 1939 and James Morris in 1986, 2003, and 2004. (Public Library of Cincinnati and Hamilton County.)

Here is the marvelous facade of Cincinnati's greatest movie palace, the Albee, as shown through the silhouette of the Genius of Water on Fountain Square. (Environmental Protection Agency, Digital Public Library of America.)

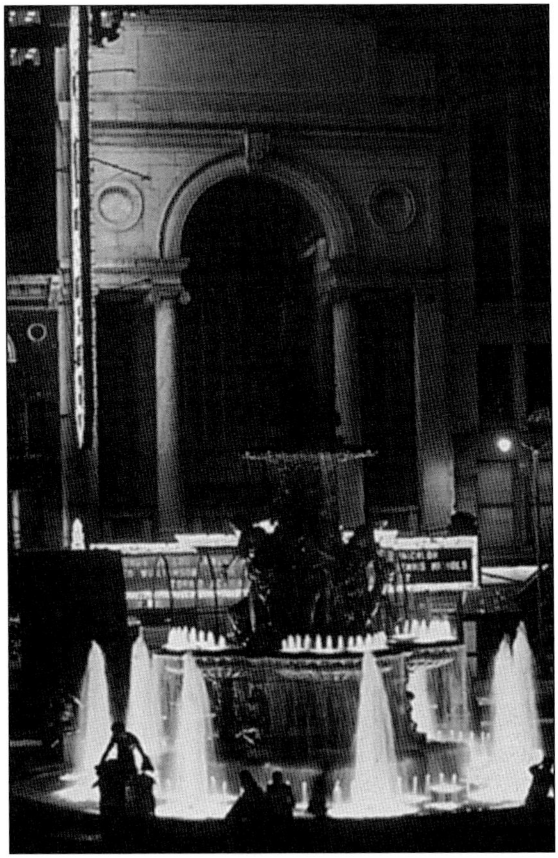

This vintage aerial photograph of Walnut Street shows the delightful Bijou Theater and the famed Gayety burlesque house. It was near this location that one of the greatest products of the Queen City was created—Cincinnati chili. Custom-made for hungry theatergoers, it is now an integral part of the tristate area. (Phil Lind.)

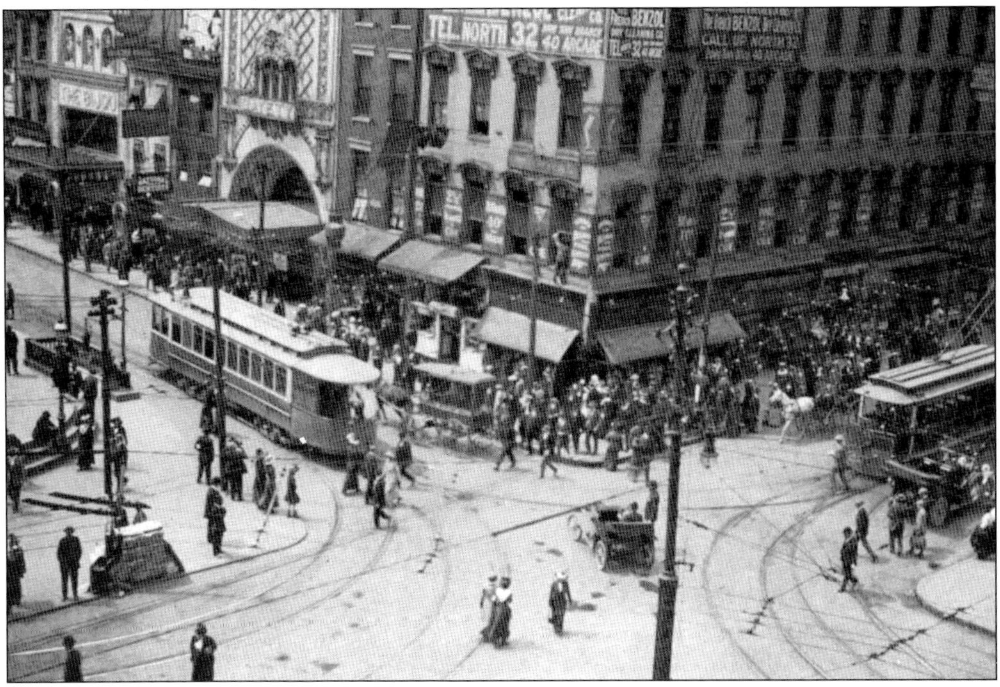

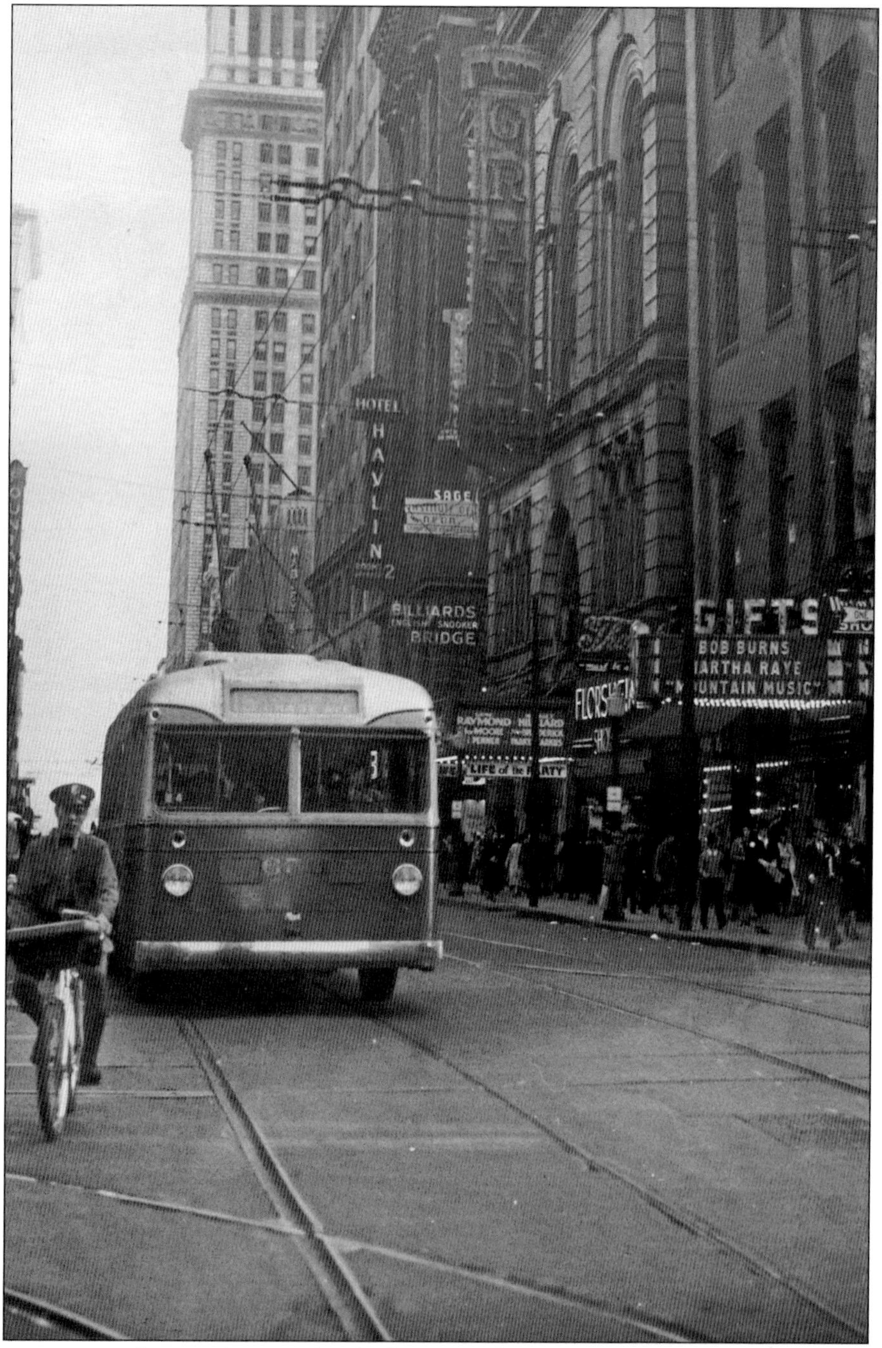

This is an extremely rare photograph of a forgotten theater at the center of the entertainment district in the heart of downtown. Hidden near the Grand Opera House, the Gifts was located on the west side of Vine Street. It was unique in that it featured two separate entrances on different streets. Its curious name came from the fact that the movie house was located on a site that formerly contained a firehouse that was labeled as being a gift from the people of Cincinnati; when the theater was built, it simply picked up the title from the previous owners. (Phil Lind and the McNamara Collection.)

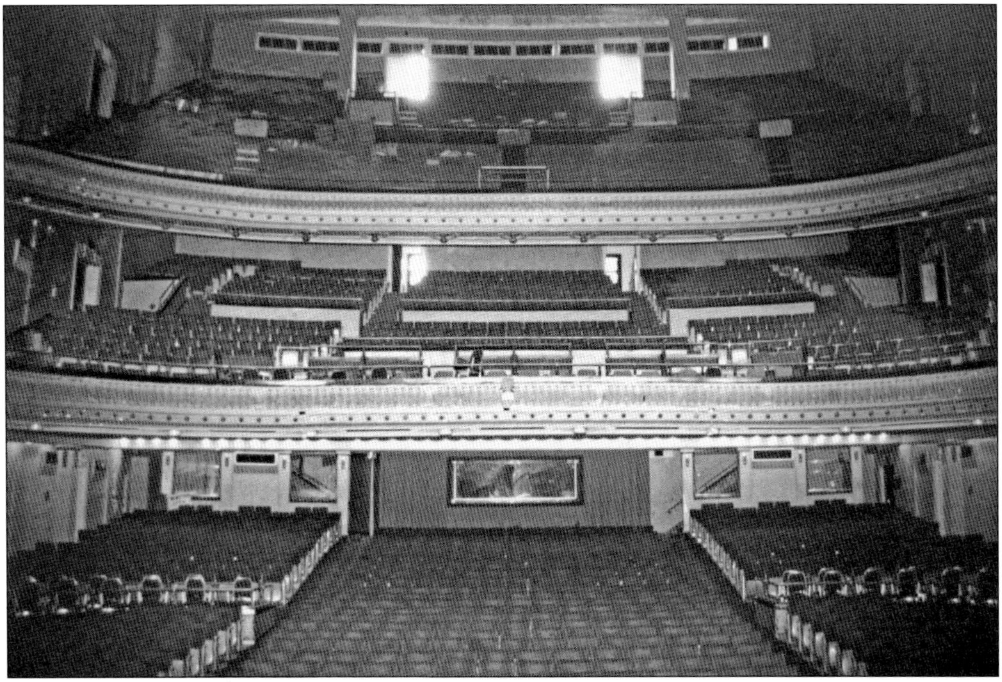

Welcome to a true palace of entertainment, the marvelous Emery Theatre. Famous for its massive organ, the Emery was located just across the Miami-Erie Canal in the German neighborhood of Over-the-Rhine. It is quite rare to find a theater that features three levels. The future of the venerable Emery Theater is up in the air. As Over-the-Rhine has been revitalized, efforts have been made to renovate the theater. Much of the upper part of the building has been converted to apartments. Its future as a working theater is uncertain. (Phil Lind and the Grothaus Collection.)

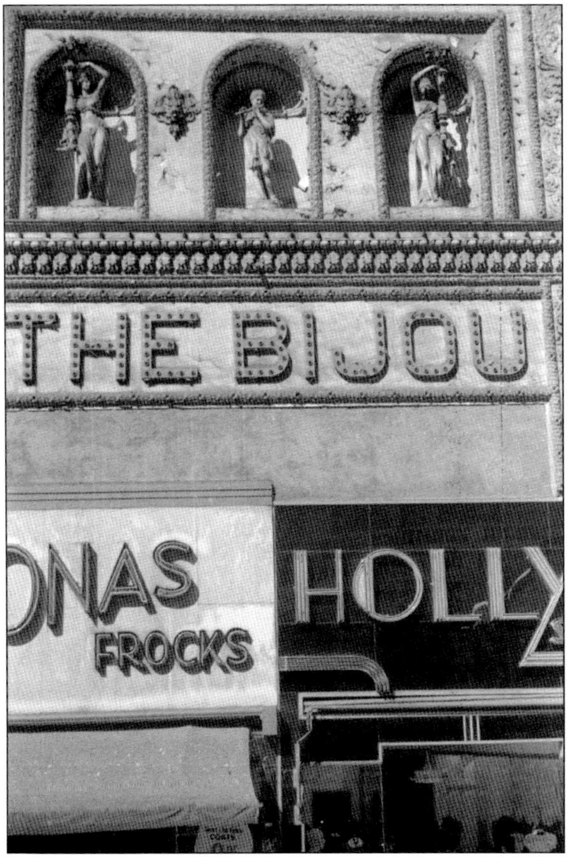

The Bijou Theater was located on Vine Street across from the Grand Opera House, where Fountain Square sits today. The Bijou was one of the houses that did not make the transition to talkies. Ike Libson began operation of the Bijou in 1908. It was originally a nickelodeon, later switching to silent films. The Bijou closed in 1934, when it became clear that soundtracked films were here to stay. (Library of Congress.)

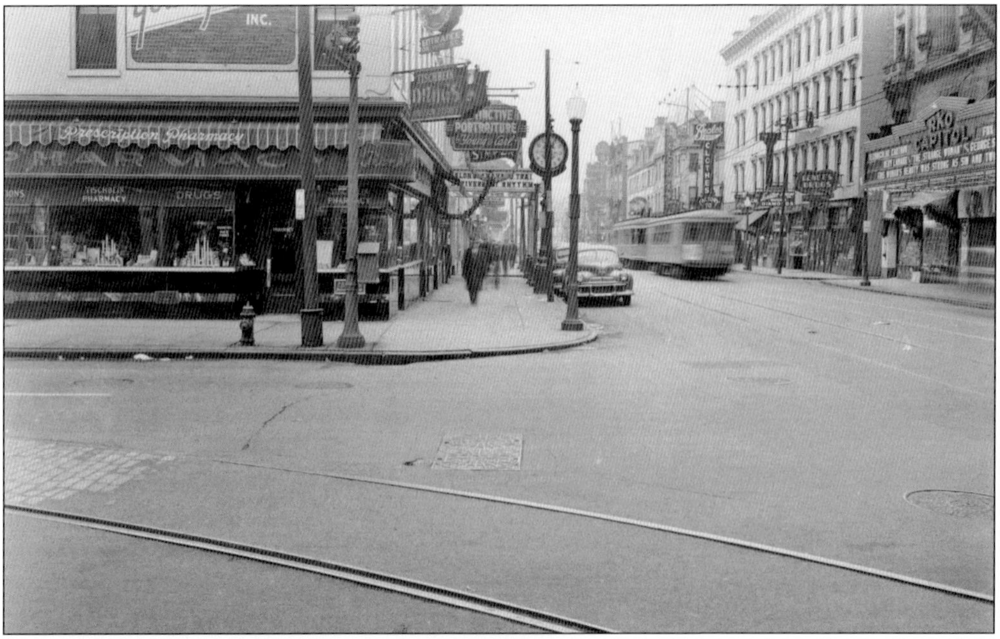

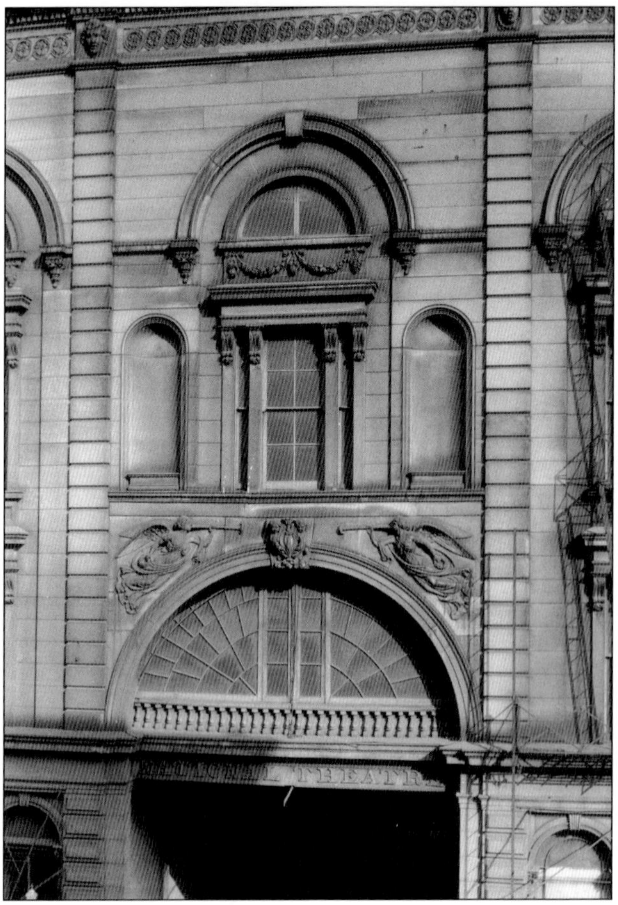

This 1946 photograph shows the RKO Capitol Theater (at far right) at Seventh and Vine Streets. A decade later, it became one of the most popular movie palaces in downtown Cincinnati as the home of Cinerama films. The new technology did not catch on, however. The theater closed its doors in 1967; three years later, the wrecking ball swept it away to make space for a parking lot. (Phil Lind.)

Before moving on to the suburbs, one last look at the downtown palaces offers a closer view of the National Theatre on Sycamore Street. This classical structure bears little resemblance to the theaters of today. Note the angel Gabriel figures positioned over the front door and tooting their horns to welcome patrons. (Library of Congress.)

Three

Out in the Suburbs

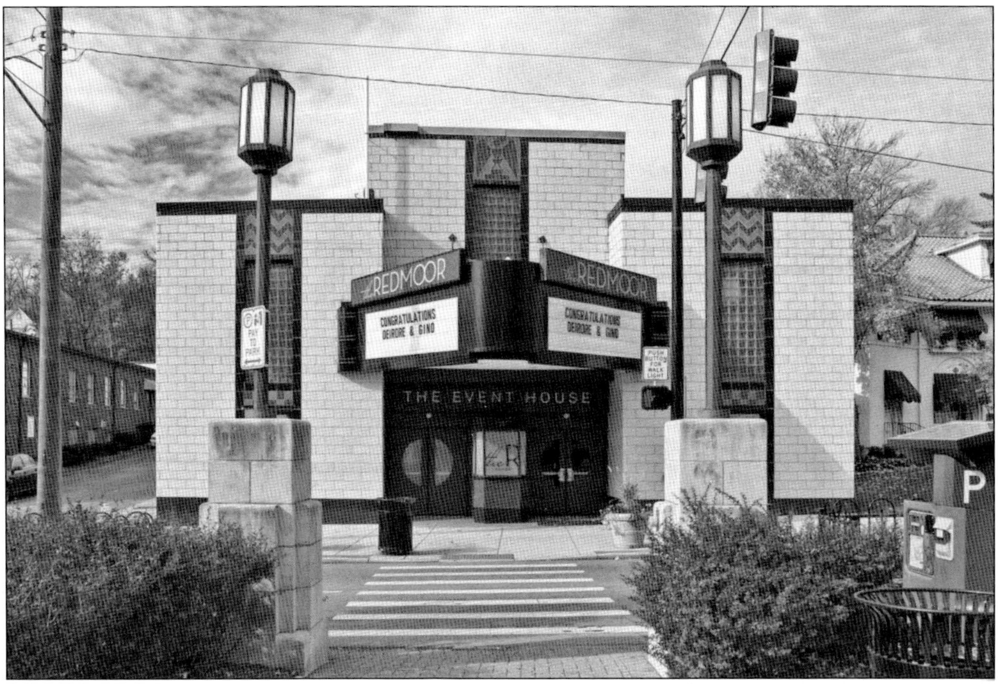

Lovers of Art Deco will want to slow down when driving through Mount Lookout Square and passing the Redmoor. This theater opened in 1928, a year after sound was introduced to film. Today, it hosts wedding receptions, meetings, and small concerts. (Photograph by Doug Weise.)

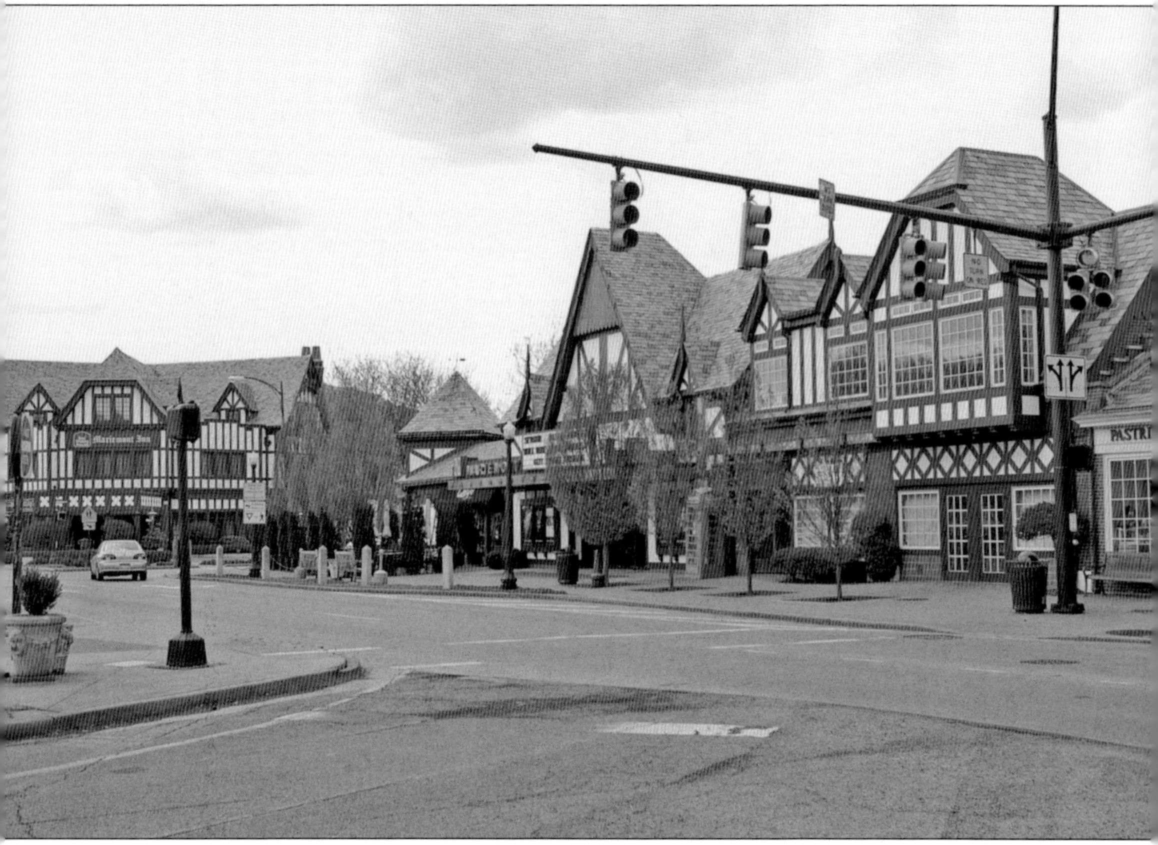

On the East Side, a surviving neighborhood movie house stands as a treasure from the past. With English Tudor–style architecture that reflects the nearby Mariemont Inn, the Mariemont Theater on the town square still holds to the tradition that once thrived in nearly every neighborhood. The area is a planned community named after its founder, Mary Emery, a name familiar to Cincinnati theater lovers. The theater originally shared a building with the Ohio Mechanics Institute. In 1906, the school decided that it needed a larger building. Emery, a philanthropist who had donated to a large number of artistic institutions in Cincinnati, took on the task of constructing the theater. Mariemont is unique, as it is one of the very few places in the nation that still features an elected town crier. Besides attending films at the theater, residents may also hear a weekly carillon concert in the park. (Photograph by Doug Weise.)

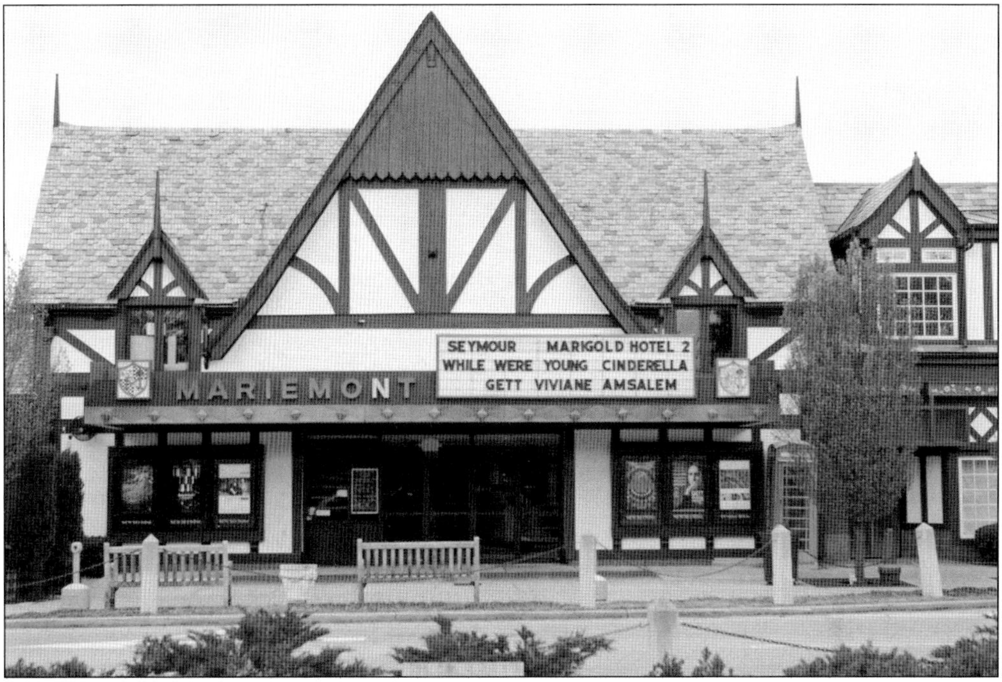

The picturesque Mariemont Theater opened its doors in 1939, 17 years after the community was built. The movie house closed briefly in the 1990s but soon reopened as an art-house theater. It was so successful that two more screens were later added. (Photograph by Doug Weise.)

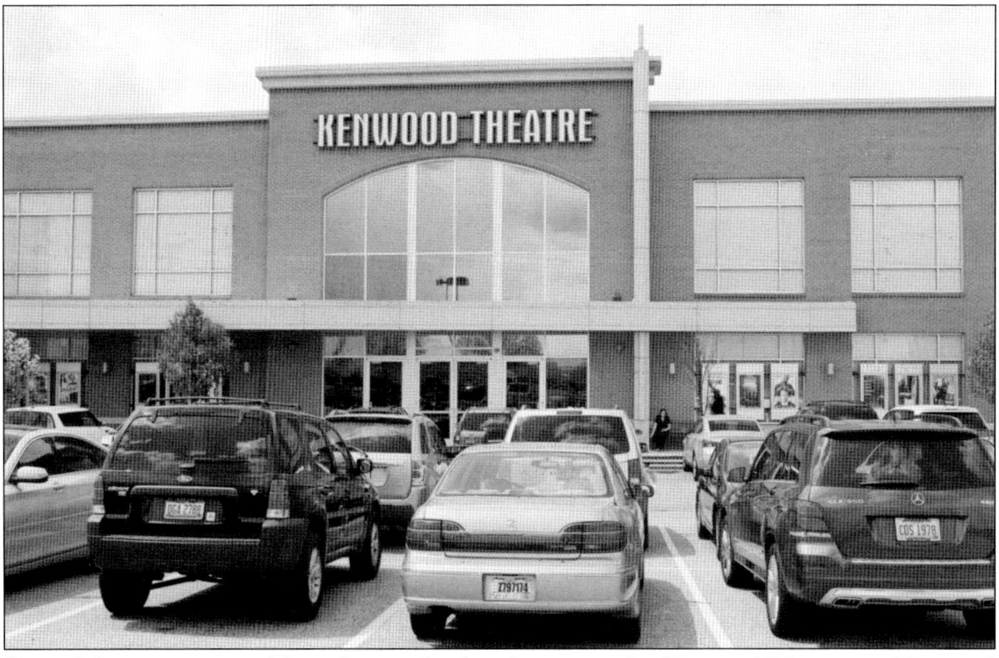

One of the most successful modern multiplex theaters is the Kenwood Theatre on Kenwood Road, near Galbraith Road. Located adjacent to the popular Kenwood Town Center shopping mall, this movie house was once a furniture store. It is now one of the most popular cinemas on the eastern side of Cincinnati. (Photograph by Doug Weise.)

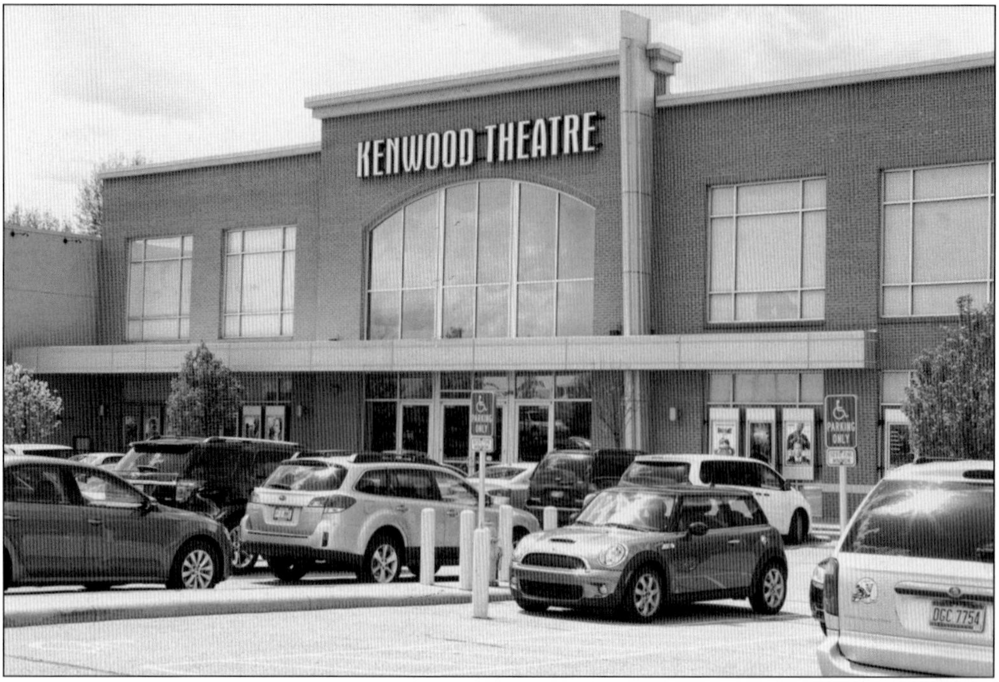

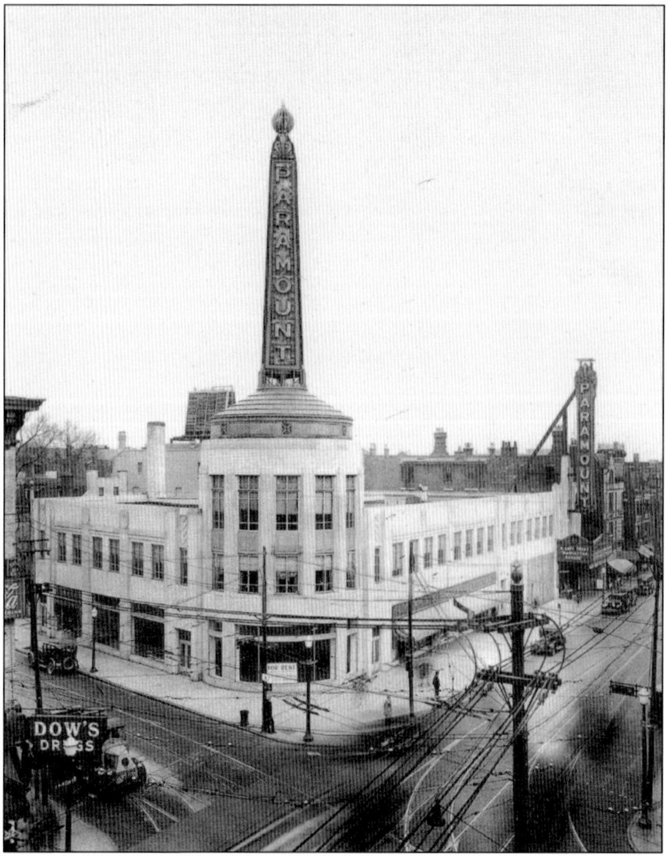

While the Kenwood Theatre is a modern, state-of-the-art multiplex cinema, founder Gary Goldman has a proud history of association with traditional Cincinnati movie houses. Besides running the Mariemont and the Esquire, he is also the grandson of the owner of the Regal on Linn Street, once known as the Casino. (Photograph by Doug Weise.)

This old photograph presents what was once a distinctive feature of the Paramount Theater at Peebles Corner. The high modernist steeple no longer towers above the building—it was removed, with much fanfare, during World War II so the metal could be contributed to the war effort. (Phil Lind.)

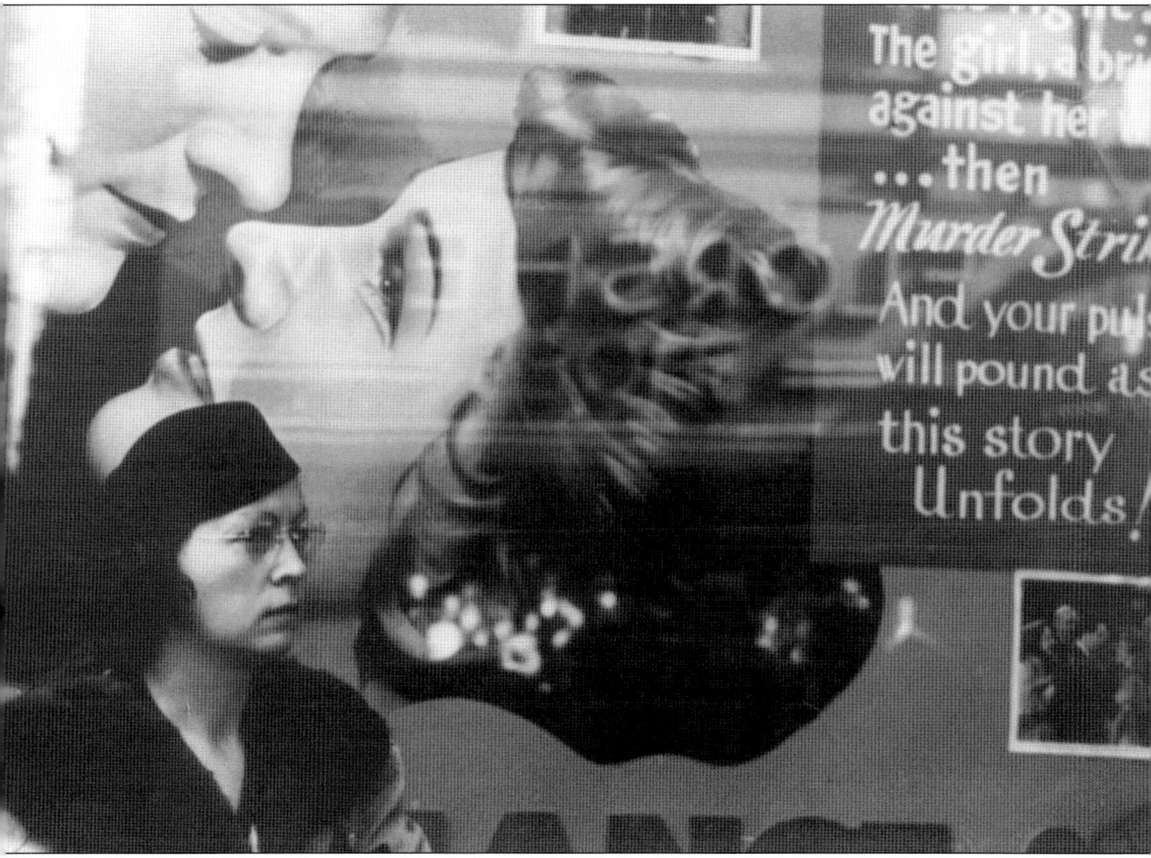

There are times when a photographer just happens to be in the right place at exactly the right time. This vintage photograph shows one of those moments. This ordinary woman is the epitome of reality, while directly behind her is the glamorous but fictional world of Hollywood motion pictures. (Library of Congress.)

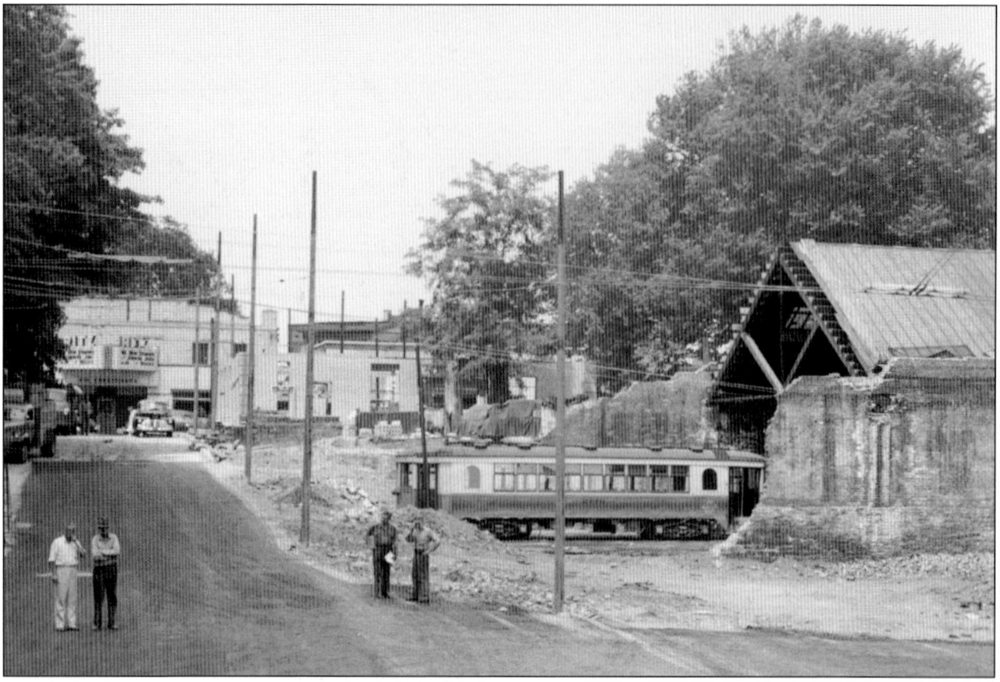

The Ritz Theater on Woodburn Avenue, located on the border of Walnut Hills and Evanston, opened in 1927, the same year that motion pictures were just beginning to include sound. The Cincinnati Transit Company opened one of its garages just across the street. This 1949 photograph shows one of the old buses with the theater in the background. (Phil Lind.)

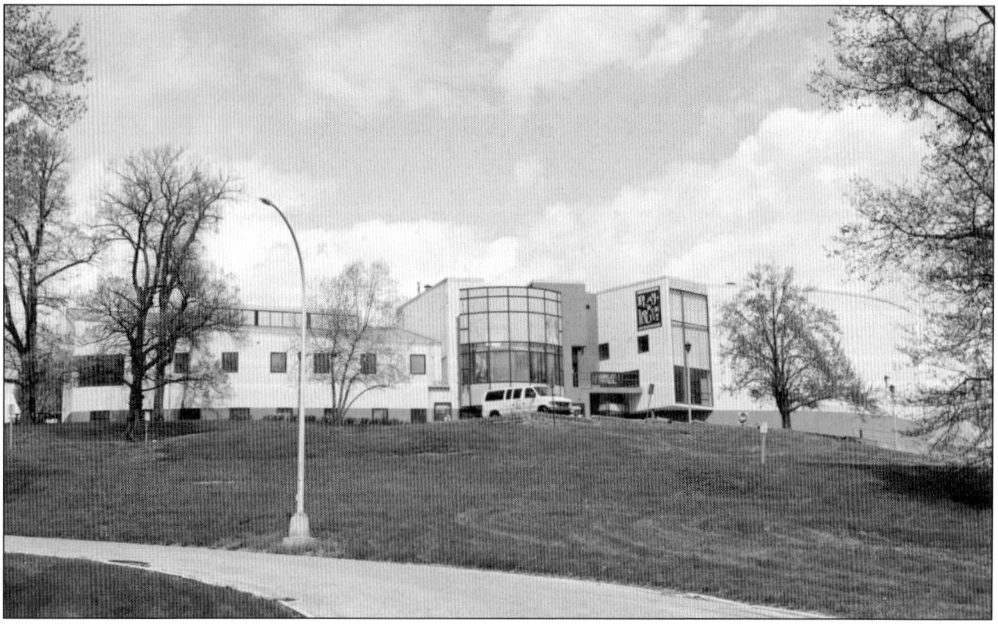

Playhouse in the Park, one of the finest attractions in the Queen City, is the home of live theater. Located in beautiful Eden Park, the Playhouse was originally founded in 1959 by a college student, Gerald Covell. It hosted its first production the following year and has been a Cincinnati favorite ever since. (Photograph by Doug Weise.)

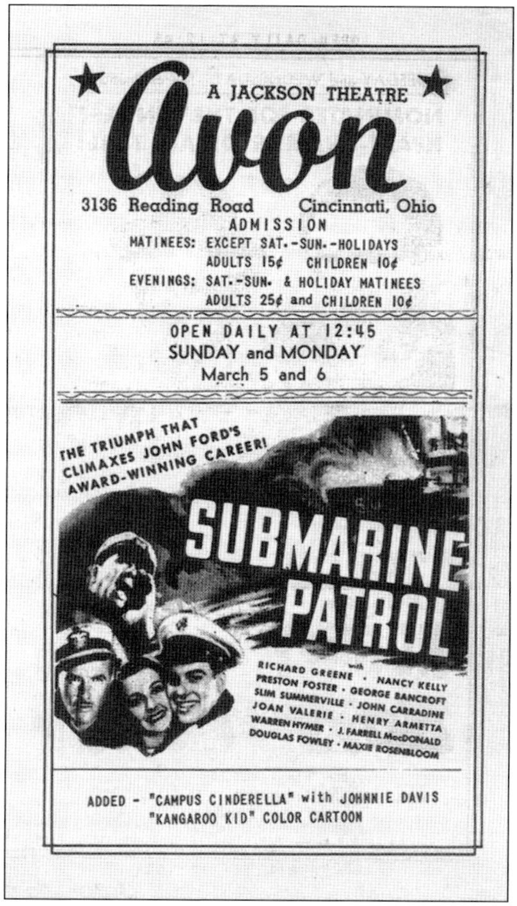

This 1938 advertisement for *Submarine Patrol* invites patrons to the Art Deco–style Avon Theater, located on Reading Road in southern Avondale, near the hospital district. The Avon was quite small, with seating for only 500 patrons, and by 1956, it had closed. (Phil Lind.)

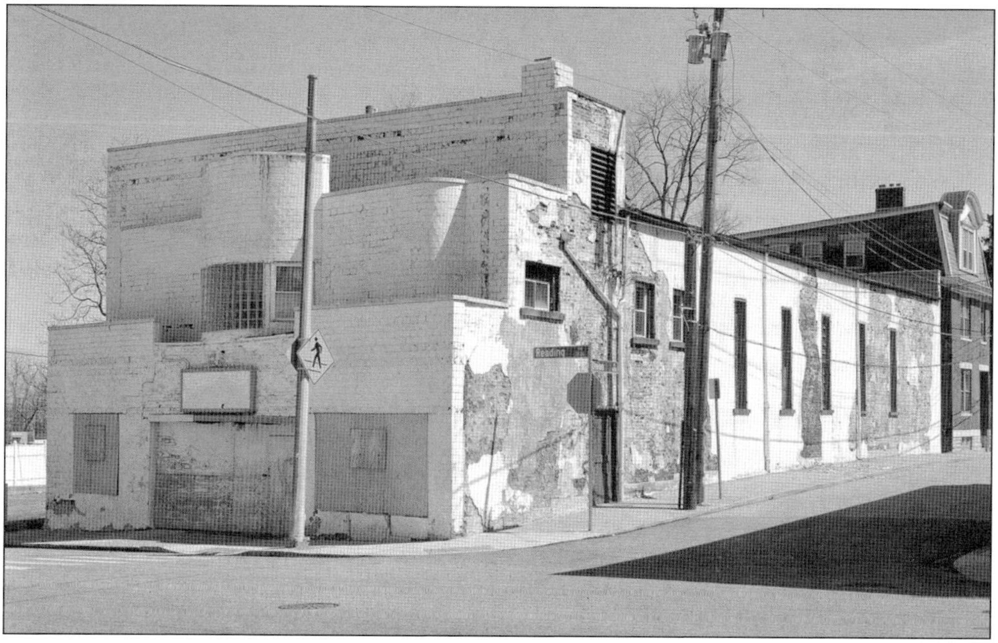

This timeworn building once housed the Avon Theater in southern Avondale. The modern ruins of this small movie house belie the sleek appearance of its original facade. Like many old neighborhood theaters, it was used as a church after being closed as a cinema. (Photograph by Doug Weise.)

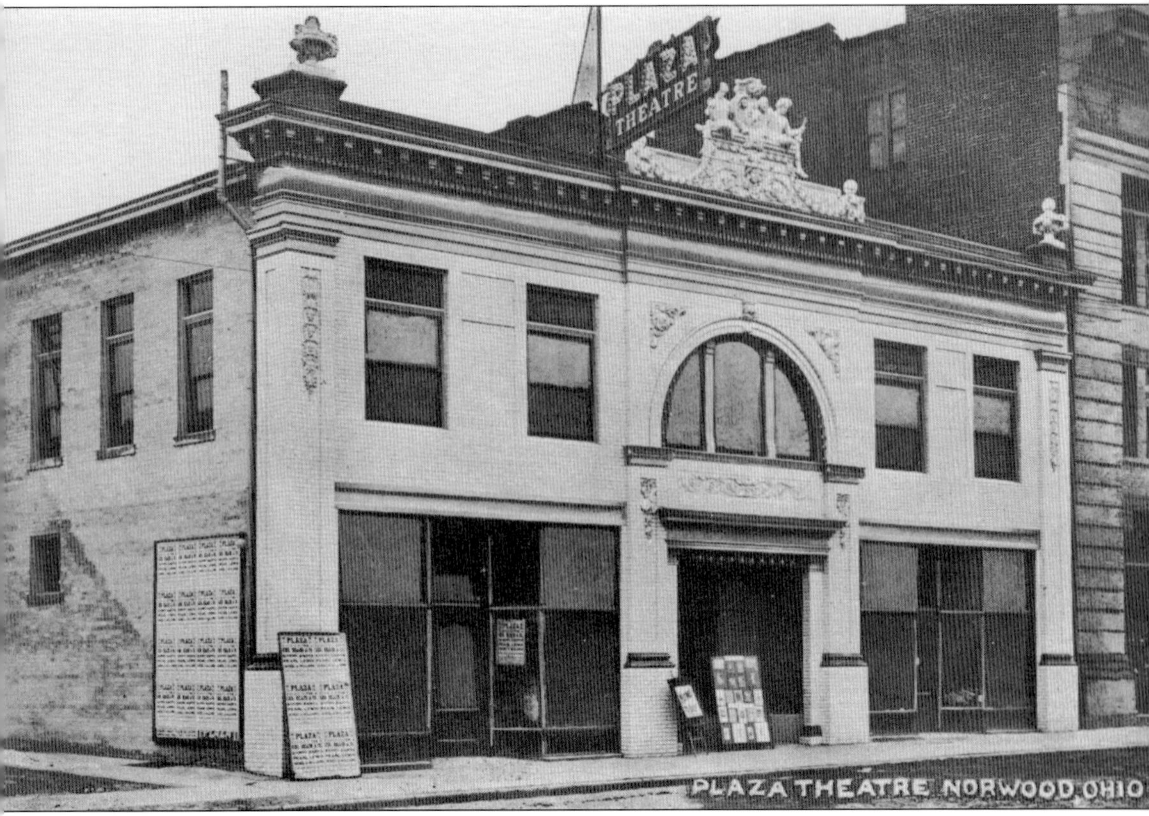

There is some debate as to which Norwood theater opened first. This movie house on Montgomery Road, the Plaza, is often said to be the first; in truth, it was the last. The Plaza opened in 1910, but both the Pike and the Minnette began their operations in 1909. By the late 1960s, the Plaza had become a venue for young people, featuring films such as Laurel and Hardy comedies and Tom and Jerry cartoons. The theater closed briefly in the mid-1960s but reopened for weekend business. This beautiful Victorian building fell to the wrecking ball in 1972, marking the demise of the last of the single-theater movie houses in the city of Norwood. A multiscreen theater that opened in the Central Parke shopping complex in 1992 did not survive; it had been converted into a fitness center by 2001. (Public Library of Cincinnati and Hamilton County.)

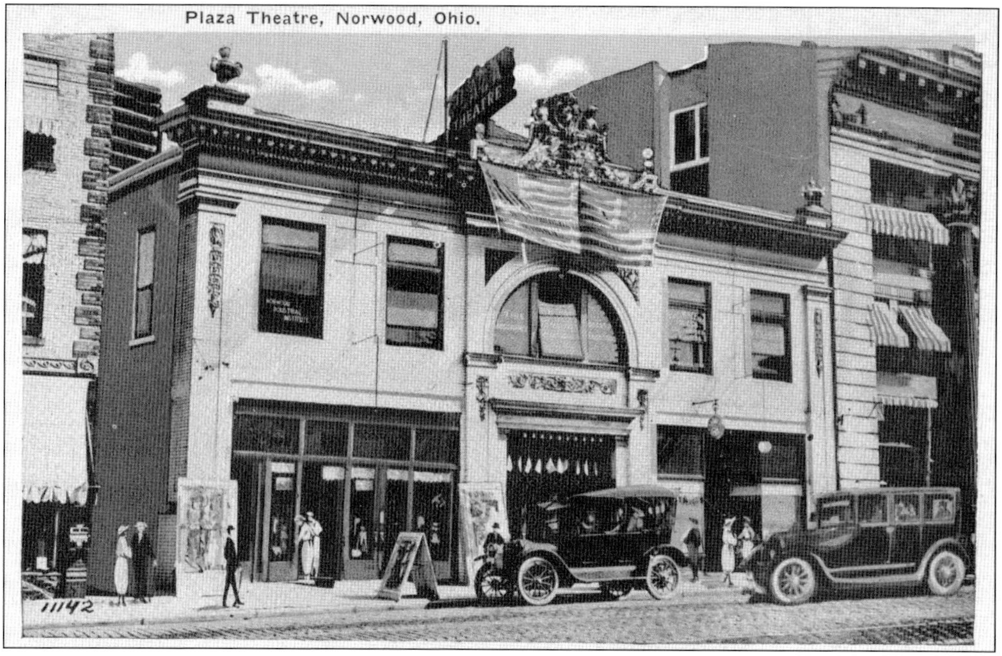

This vintage postcard shows Norwood's Plaza Theatre in its heyday. Note the ornamentation on the front of the building. Although they were physically separated from the great movie palaces of downtown, neighborhood theaters like the Plaza did everything possible to transport their customers into an escapist world of luxury. (Public Library of Cincinnati and Hamilton County.)

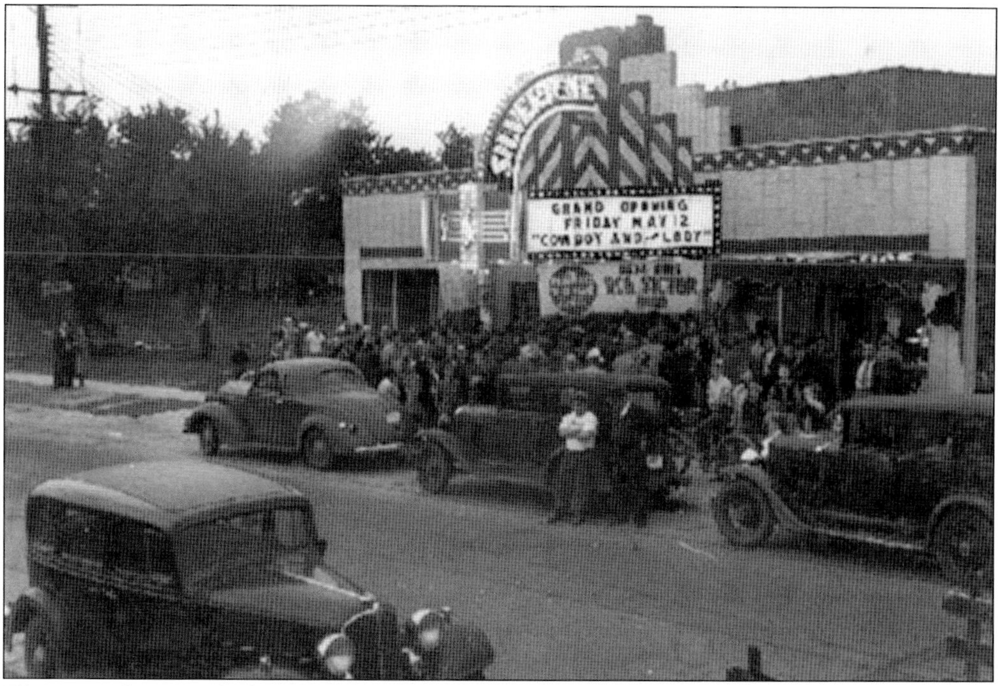

This 1938 photograph shows the grand opening of the Silvertone Theatre in the small northern city of Silverton. After starting off in a big way with a Gary Cooper western, the movie house survived the war years but did not make it beyond 1950. (Jim Repogle.)

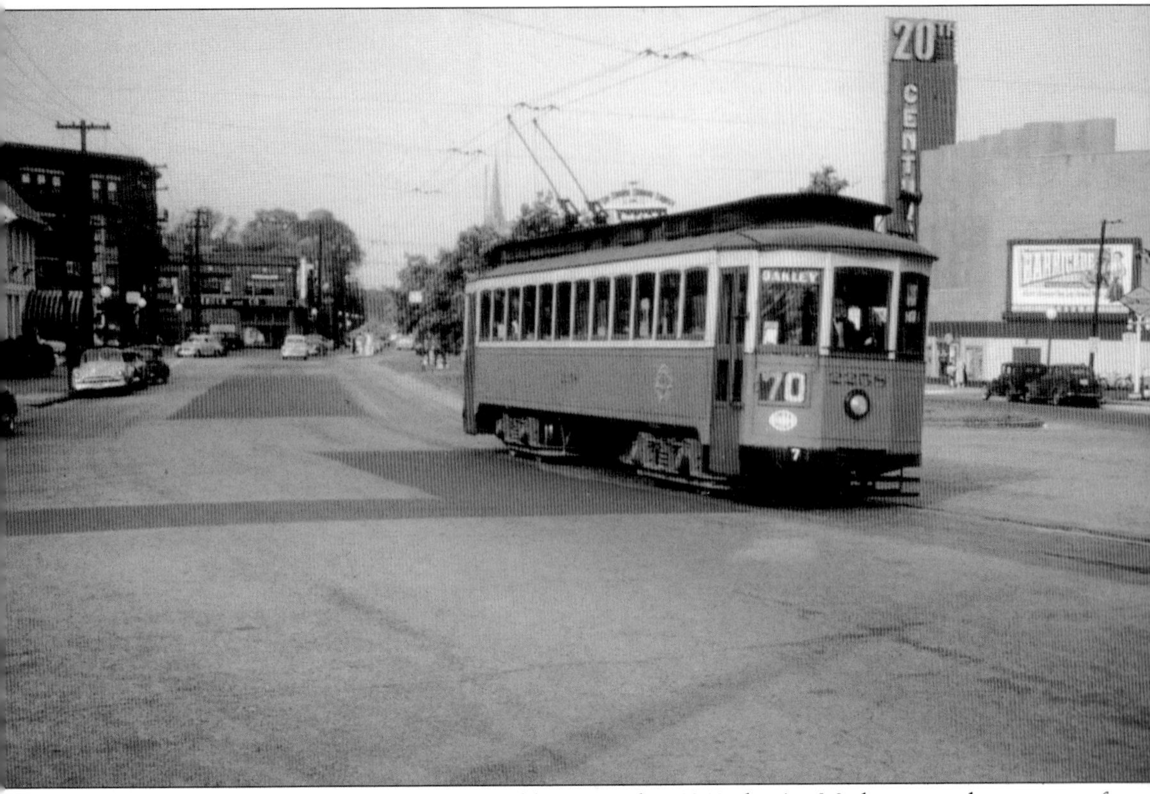

When the 20th Century Theater in Oakley opened in 1941, the Art Moderne wonder was one of the most opulent neighborhood theaters in the Cincinnati area. It featured a balcony and seating for 900 patrons. It closed as a movie theater in 1983. The neighborhood in which it is located is famous for being the home of celebrated sharpshooter Annie Oakley. Born Phoebe Ann Mosey in 1860, she defeated famed marksman Frank Butler in 1875 at the age of 15. She not only became a performer but also married the man she had beaten. She then took her stage name from the neighborhood she was living in at the time—Oakley. (Phil Lind.)

Oakley's 20th Century Theater on Madison Road was one of the few neighborhood movie houses to survive into the present day. Although it no longer shows films, it is now a popular venue for parties, wedding receptions, corporate events, meetings, and small concerts. (Photograph by Doug Weise.)

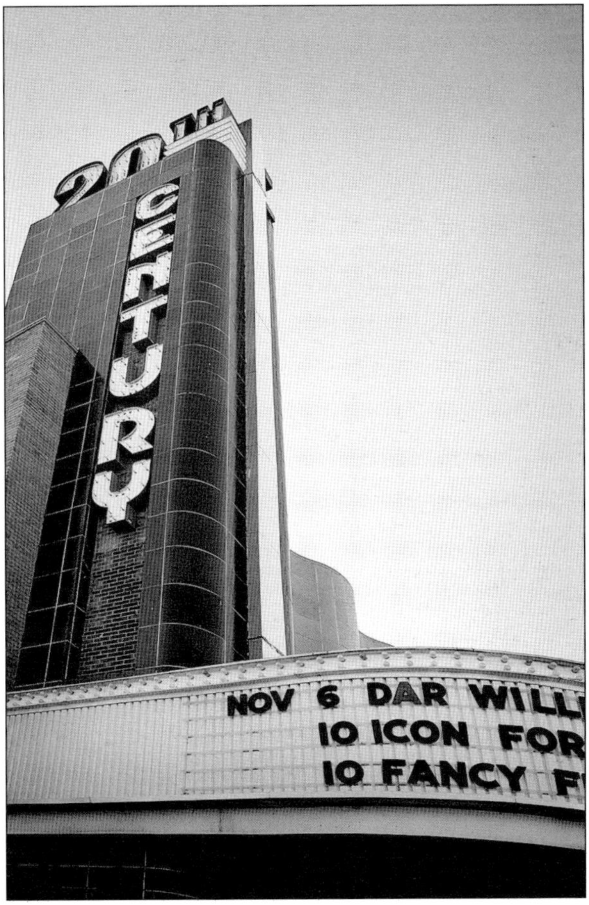

One feature that has endured in the 20th Century Theater is its architectural style. Rather than changing to adapt to the times, this neighborhood theater has remained a showplace of Art Deco and postwar modernism. This look at the lobby gives a hint of the beauty of the facility. (Photograph by Doug Weise.)

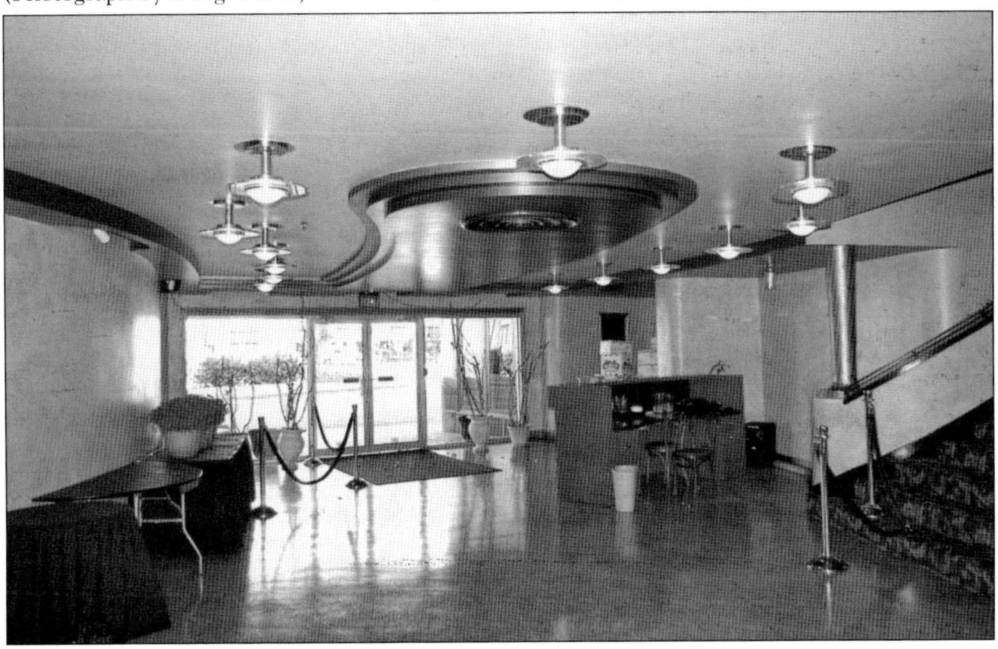

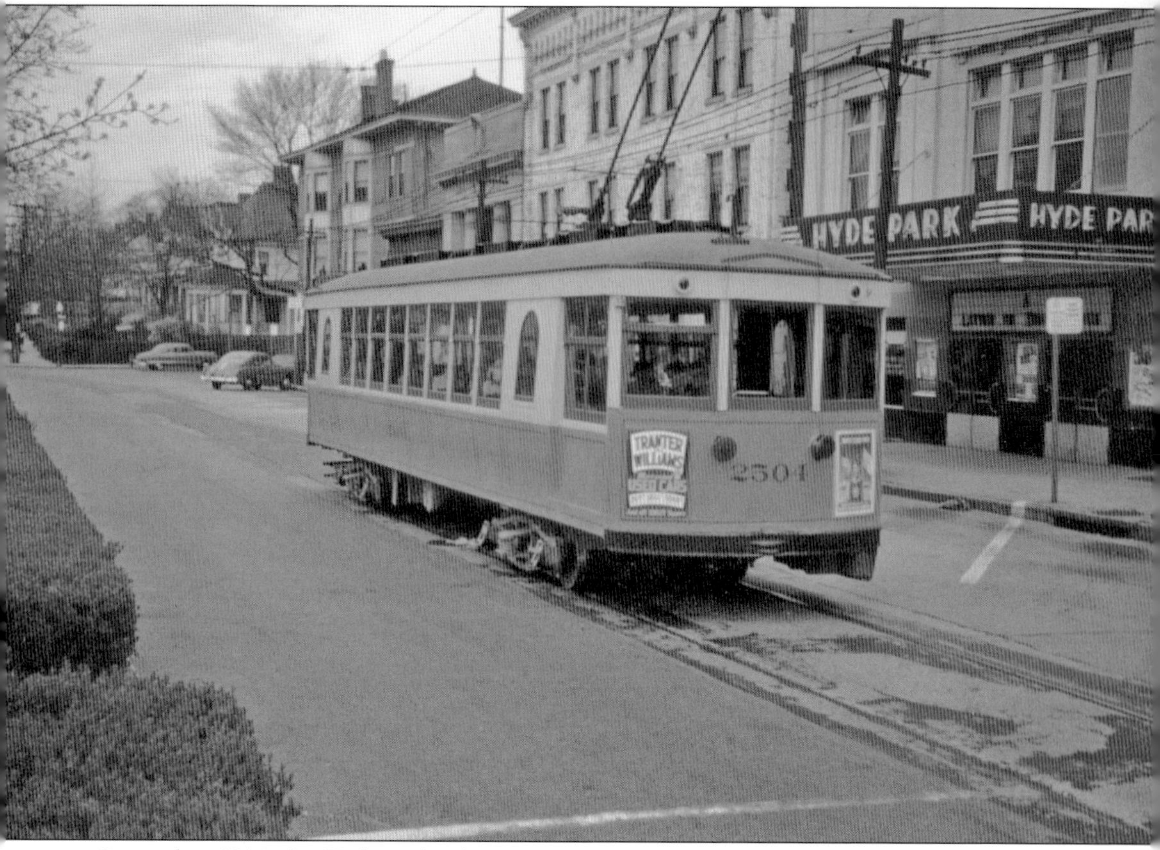

Opened in 1914, the Hyde Park Theatre on Erie Avenue at Hyde Park Square attempted an innovative—and ultimately unsuccessful—marketing ploy. The owners wanted to cater to patrons who might wish to purchase refreshments but did not want to leave the theater and miss part of the film. To remedy this, they moved the candy counter directly into the auditorium. However, the young workers, who had already seen the film several times, simply could not stop talking to each other. This forced management to return to the more traditional idea of lobby concessions. (Phil Lind.)

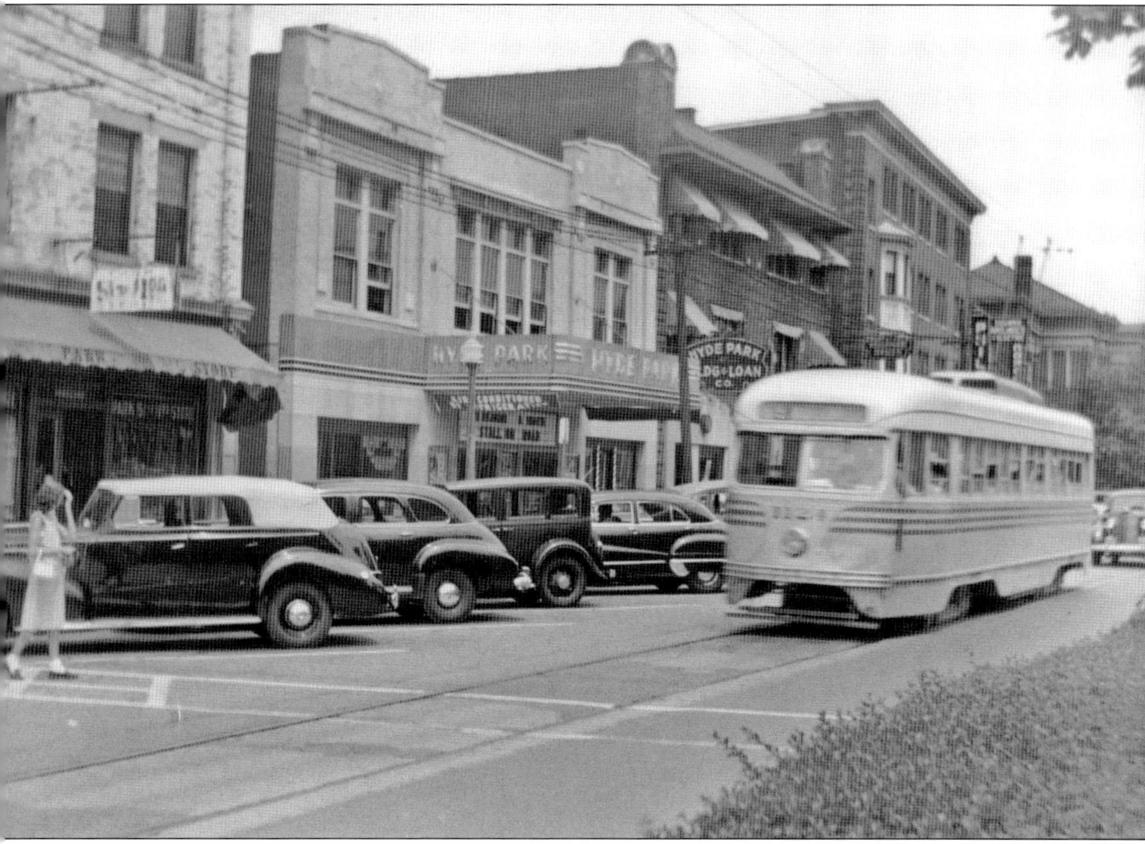

To attract casual customers, neighborhood movie houses were often constructed with eye-catching architecture. One of the most popular designs was the Art Deco style popularized in the decades immediately following the First World War. In this well-timed photograph, a modernistic streetcar passes the equally modernistic Hyde Park Theatre. Note how the motif of stacked parallel lines on the facade of the movie house matches the streamlined design along the side of the streetcar. (Photograph by Phil Adams.)

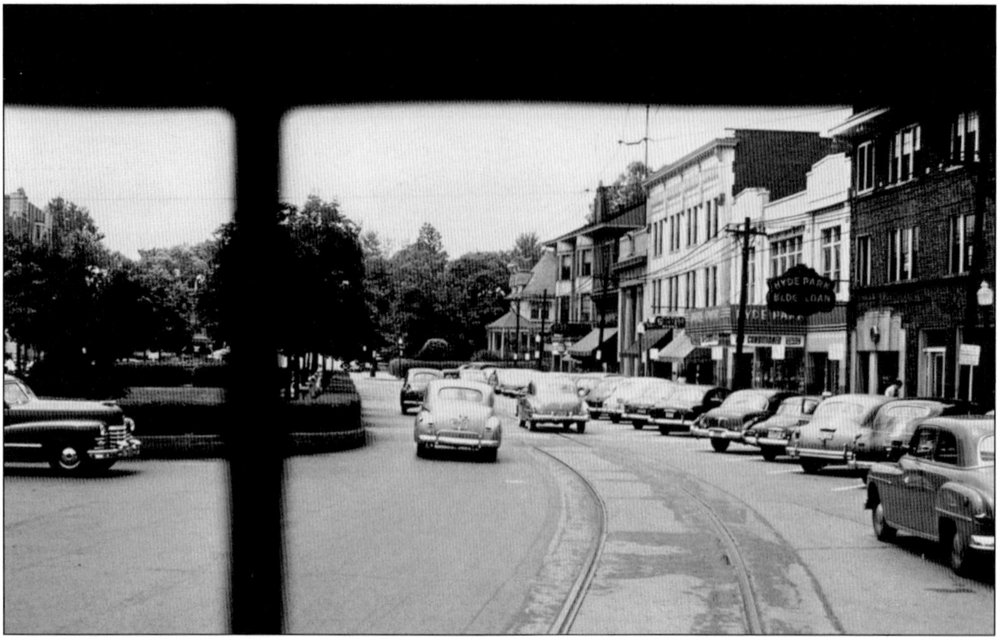

During World War II, one of the most popular forms of mental escape was via Hollywood films. Of course, due to wartime shortages, people would often catch public transportation to visit the theater, as shown in this photograph taken from inside a streetcar approaching the Hyde Park Theatre. (Phil Lind.)

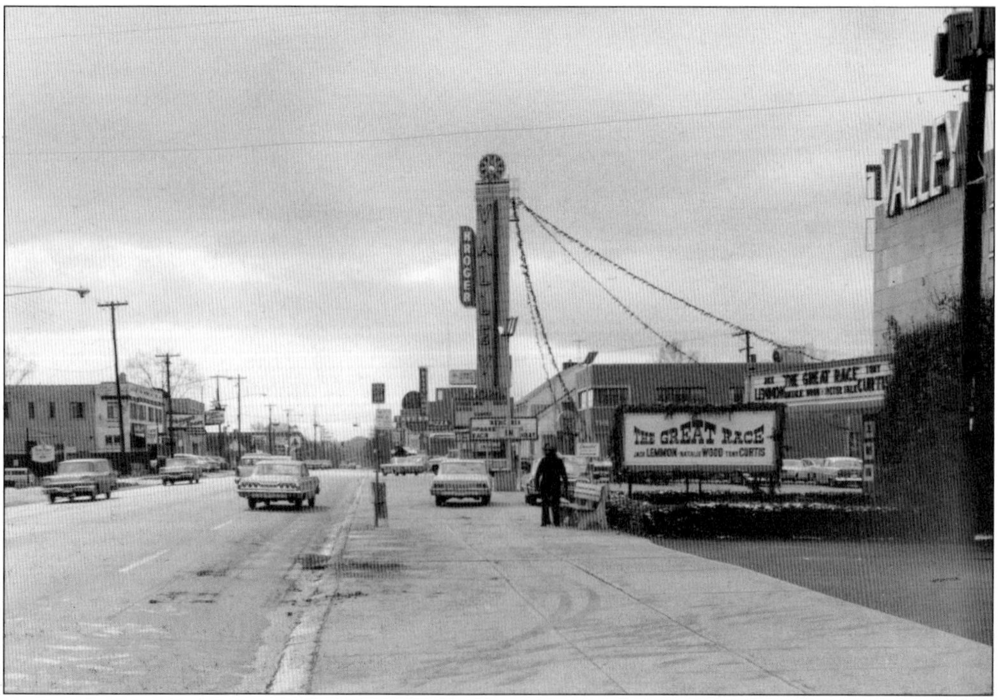

At the top of this 71-foot-tall sign advertising the Valley Theater (along with a Kroger grocery store) is a depiction of a reel of film. The Valley Theater, located in the northern suburb of Reading, was one of the largest and most luxurious venues outside the downtown area. (Phil Lind.)

This 1937 poster advertises films being shown at the Emery Theatre, located in the small town of Reading north of the city. During the catastrophic Ohio River flood in January 1937, electricity was rationed. Some neighborhood theaters tried to avoid the ban by staying open, only to be raided by the police. (Reading Historical Society.)

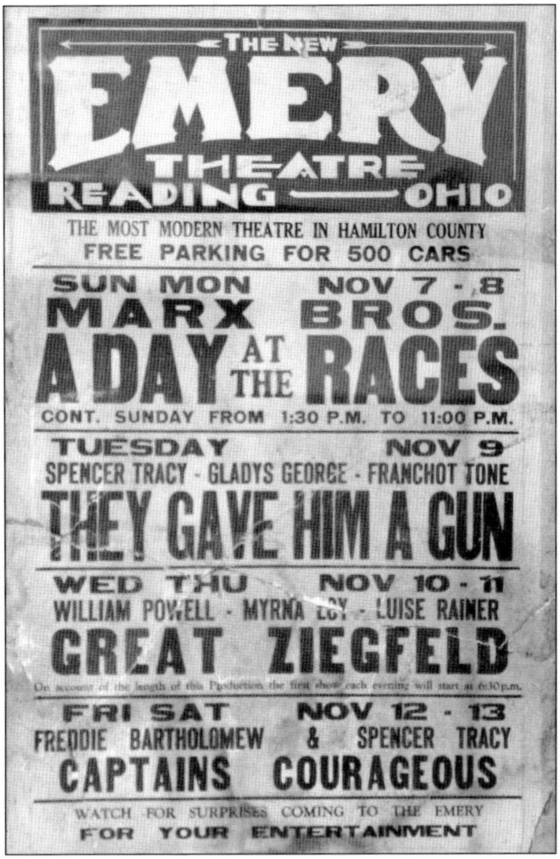

The Ritz Theater, located on Woodburn Avenue in Walnut Hills, began operation in 1927, the same year that talkie pictures began. Although it survived the Depression and World War II, the theater closed by the end of the 1950s. Like many other neighborhood movie houses, it became a church. Below is a modern view of the space's interior. (Phil Lind.)

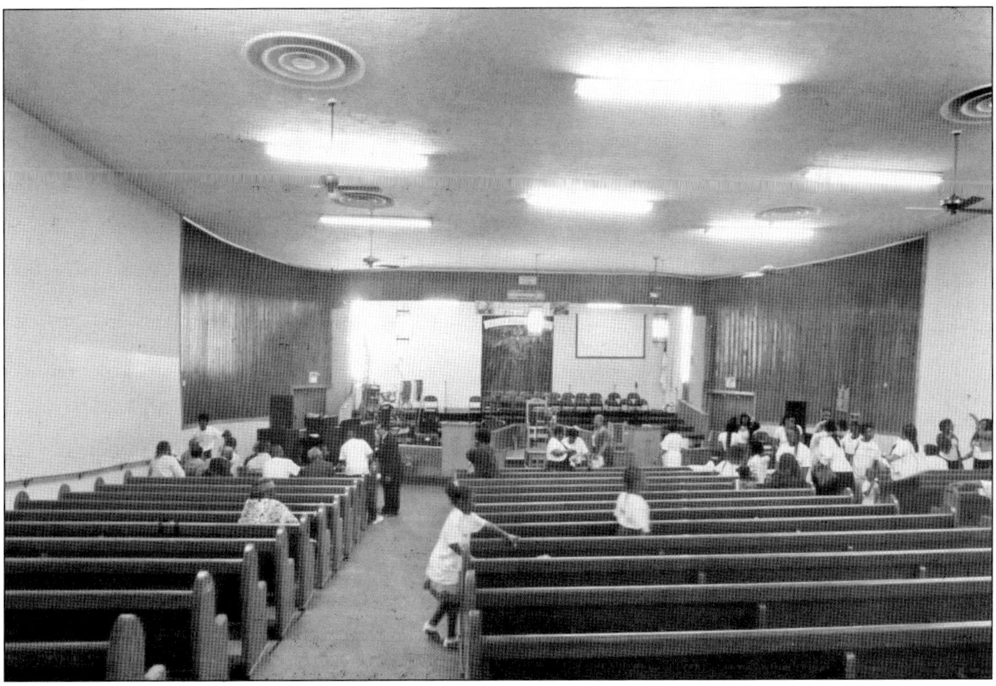

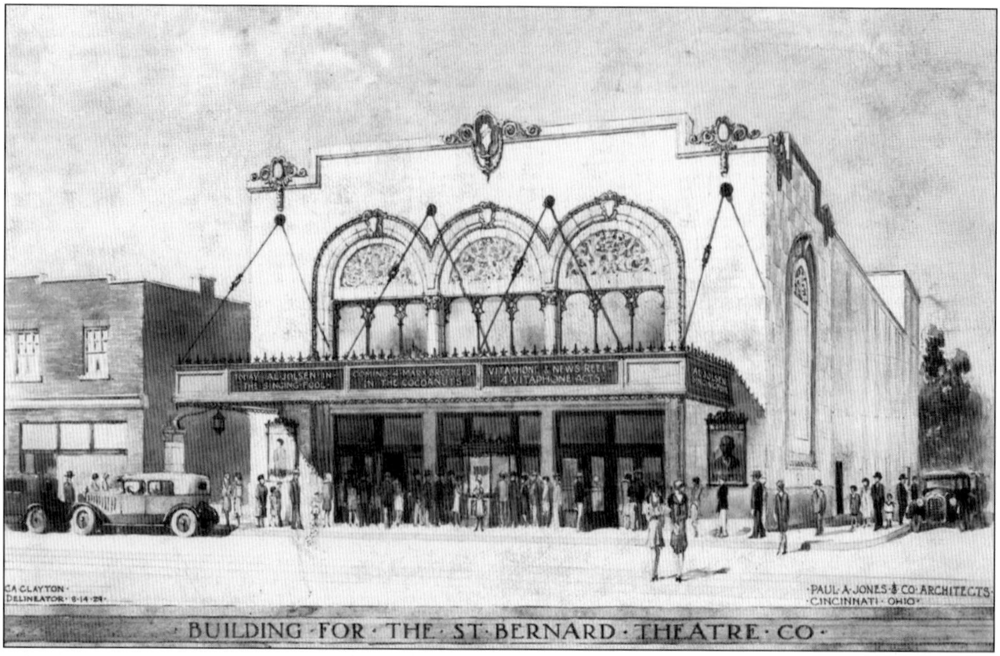

The dichotomy of the photographs on this page presents an interesting comparison: the rather grandiose vision of a theater in the mind of an architect, followed by a period image of the final product. Above is a 1929 rendering of the proposed St. Bernard Theatre Company. Note the advertisement on the marquee for the Vitaphone talkie feature. Two years after the above drawing was made, the St. Bernard Andalus Theatre opened for business. Although it was not nearly as ornate as the architect had envisioned, it remained a neighborhood movie house for nearly three decades. It finally closed as a cinema in 1958. Like many closed theaters, it was then used as a church for a short time. (Above, Sharon McCullough; below, Phil Lind.)

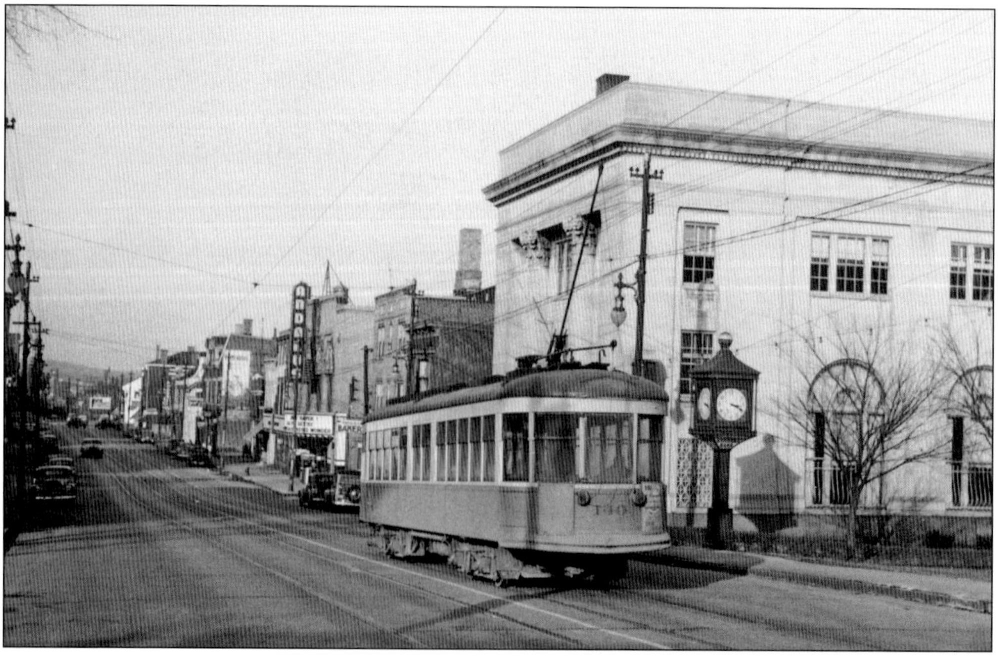

This schedule was from the St. Bernard Andalus Theatre, located on Vine Street in the small industrial city of St. Bernard. Like many neighborhood theaters, it eventually made the transition from cinema to church. However, an expansion of the local library led to the demolition of the building in 1999. Note that the theater was closed on Good Friday. (Sharon McCullough.)

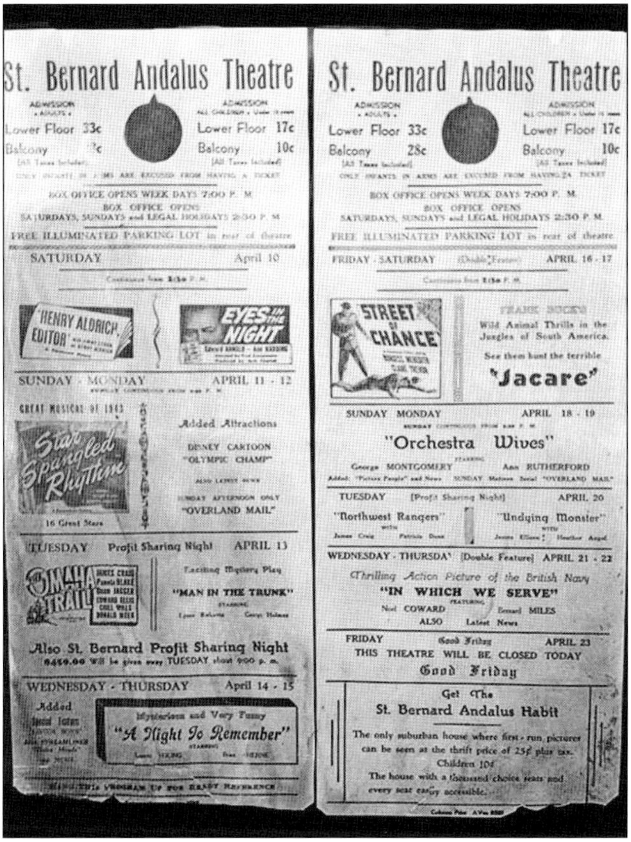

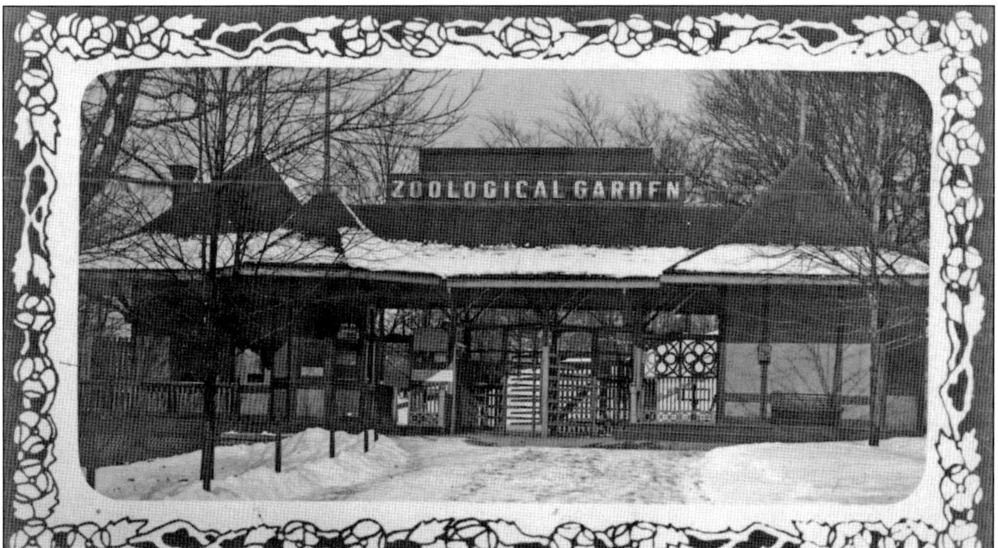

It is hard to believe that this was the entrance not only to the Cincinnati Zoological and Botanical Garden but also to one of the Queen City's most renowned theaters, the Cincinnati Zoo Pavilion. In 1920, the offerings of this popular attraction expanded to include the Cincinnati Opera. (Public Library of Cincinnati and Hamilton County.)

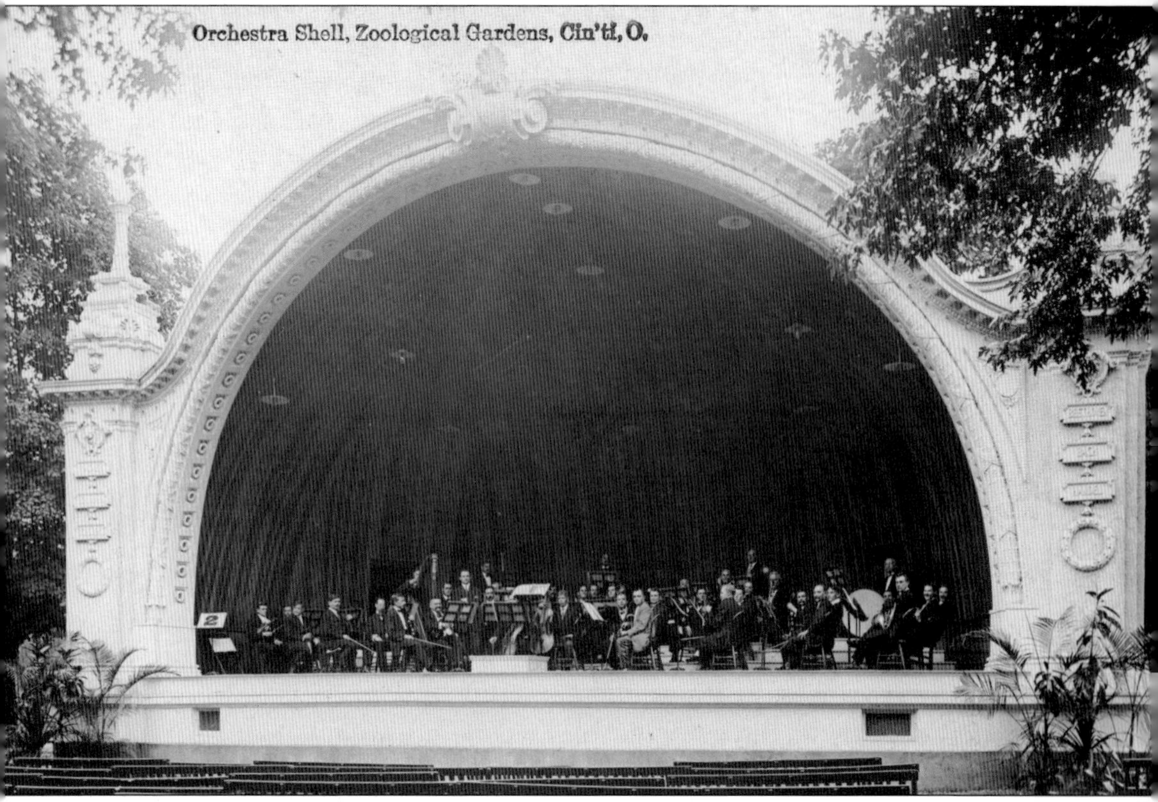

In June 1920, a sold-out audience gathered to watch *Martha*, the first opera performed at the Cincinnati Zoo. For decades, this unusual venue for operatic performances became a beloved tradition. Audience members would bring their children for a day of observing the animals, then expose the youngsters to the arts as they sat down for an evening of Wagner or Verdi. Over 50 years, a parade of opera greats—including Beverly Sills, Plácido Domingo, and James Morris—competed with the animals for the audience's applause. In 1972, the opera moved to Music Hall. (Public Library of Cincinnati and Hamilton County.)

Here, a small crowd takes a break from seeing the animals at the zoo by listening to a small concert. One of the reasons the Cincinnati Opera moved from the zoo to the Music Hall was the heat. The audience was likely anxious for the ice show at 3:00 in the afternoon. (Kenton County Public Library, Covington, Kentucky.)

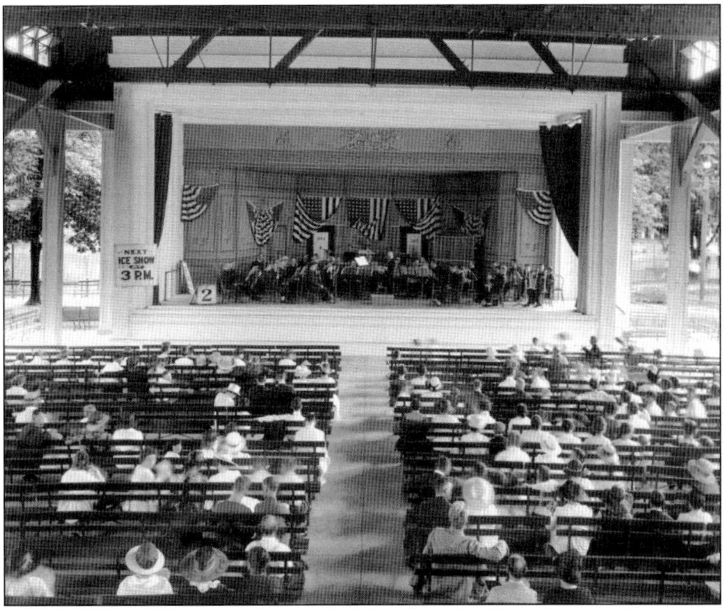

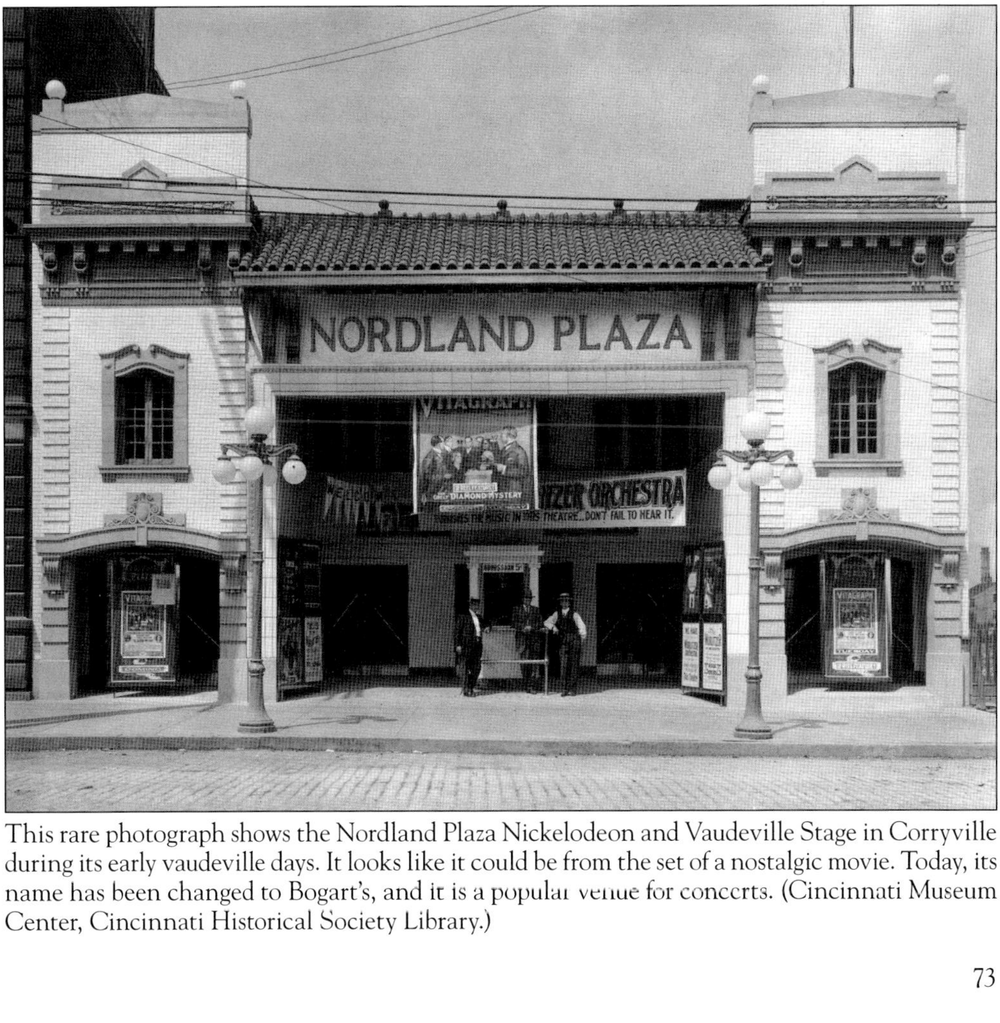

This rare photograph shows the Nordland Plaza Nickelodeon and Vaudeville Stage in Corryville during its early vaudeville days. It looks like it could be from the set of a nostalgic movie. Today, its name has been changed to Bogart's, and it is a popular venue for concerts. (Cincinnati Museum Center, Cincinnati Historical Society Library.)

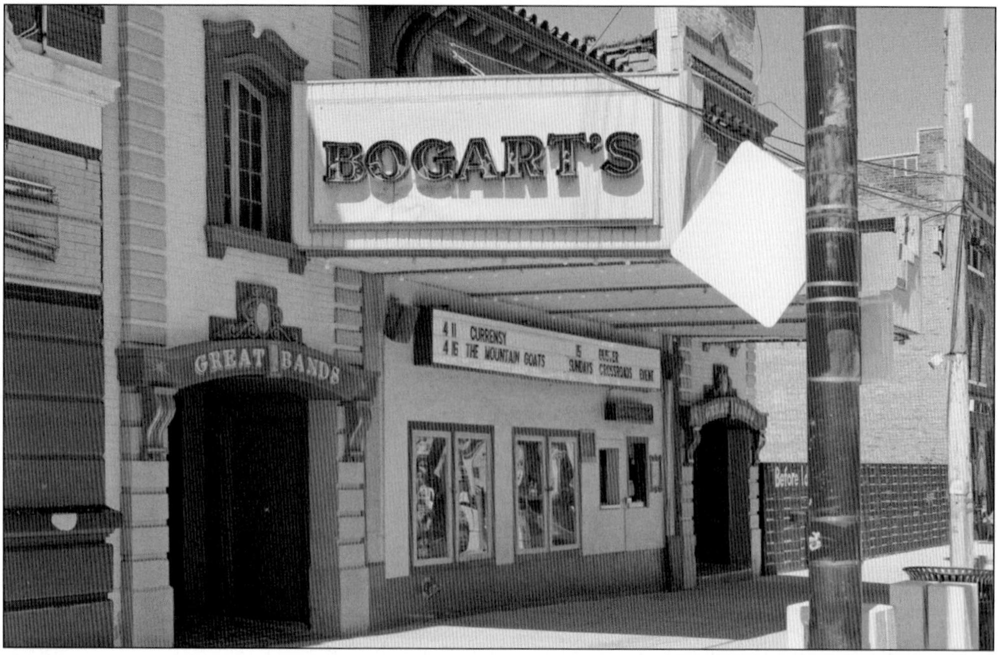

Bogart's is one of the most popular clubs in the University of Cincinnati area. Located on "short" Vine Street, the establishment opened in 1905 as the Nordland Plaza Nickelodeon, which served as a neighborhood theater for Corryville and the university until 1955. In 1960, it reopened, attempting a program of German art films, and later became a restaurant. In 1980, Bogart's was resurrected as a small concert venue. (Photograph by Doug Weise.)

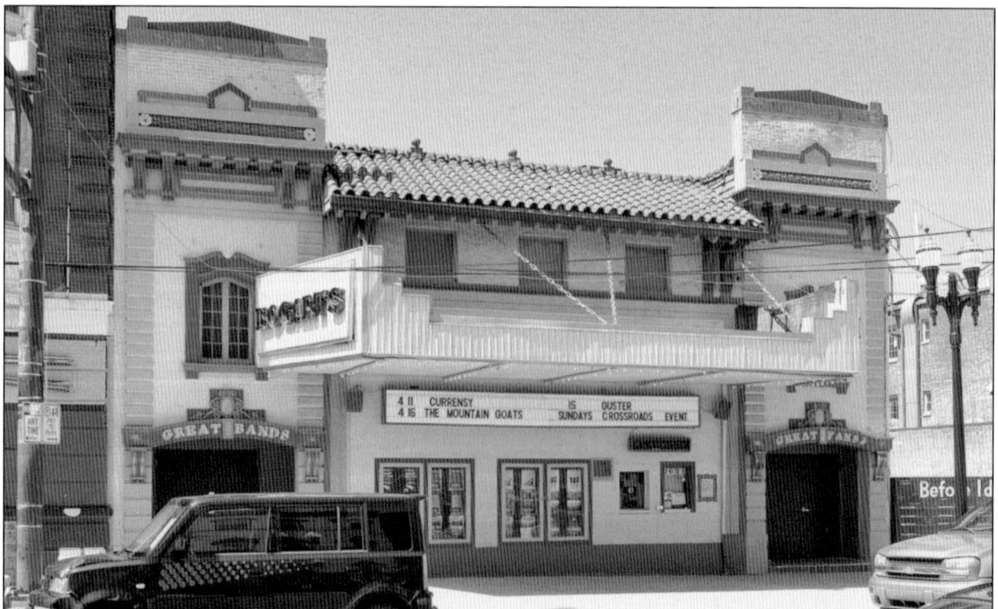

Bogart's is now a moderately sized club that features artists from across the spectrum. The list of famous entertainers who have graced the stage includes the Red Hot Chili Peppers, Billy Crystal, Slayer, Pearl Jam, The 69 Eyes, Cheech and Chong, and many others, including the Mountain Goats, who performed shortly after this picture was taken. (Photograph by Doug Weise.)

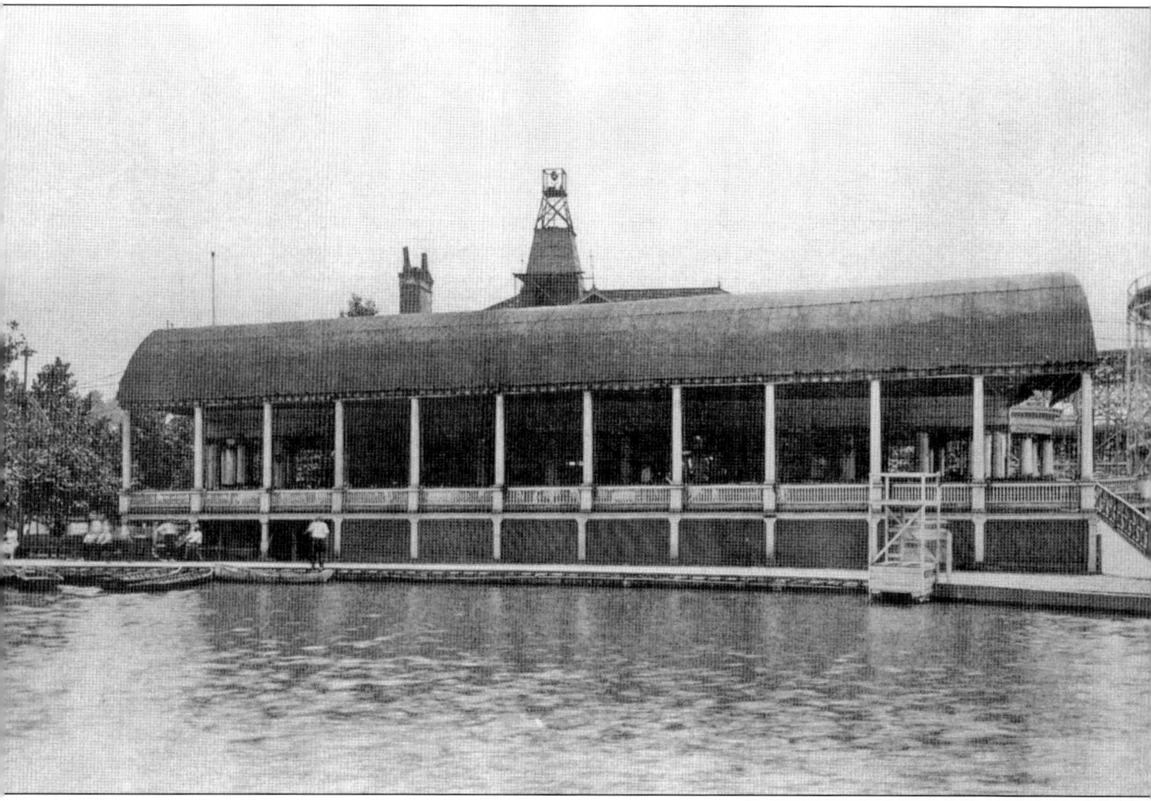

Amusement parks often included popular venues for dancing and listening to orchestras on a summer night. In more recent times, people would flock to Coney Island's Moonlight Gardens. This image, however, shows a venue from another favorite getaway spot—Chester Park near Northside. The land was originally a racetrack; in fact, the name "Chester" came not from a person but from the owner's racehorse. In 1911, this was the scene of a horrific fire. Although the flames did not destroy Chester Park, the park closed in 1932, a casualty of Prohibition and the Depression. (Kenton County Public Library, Covington, Kentucky.)

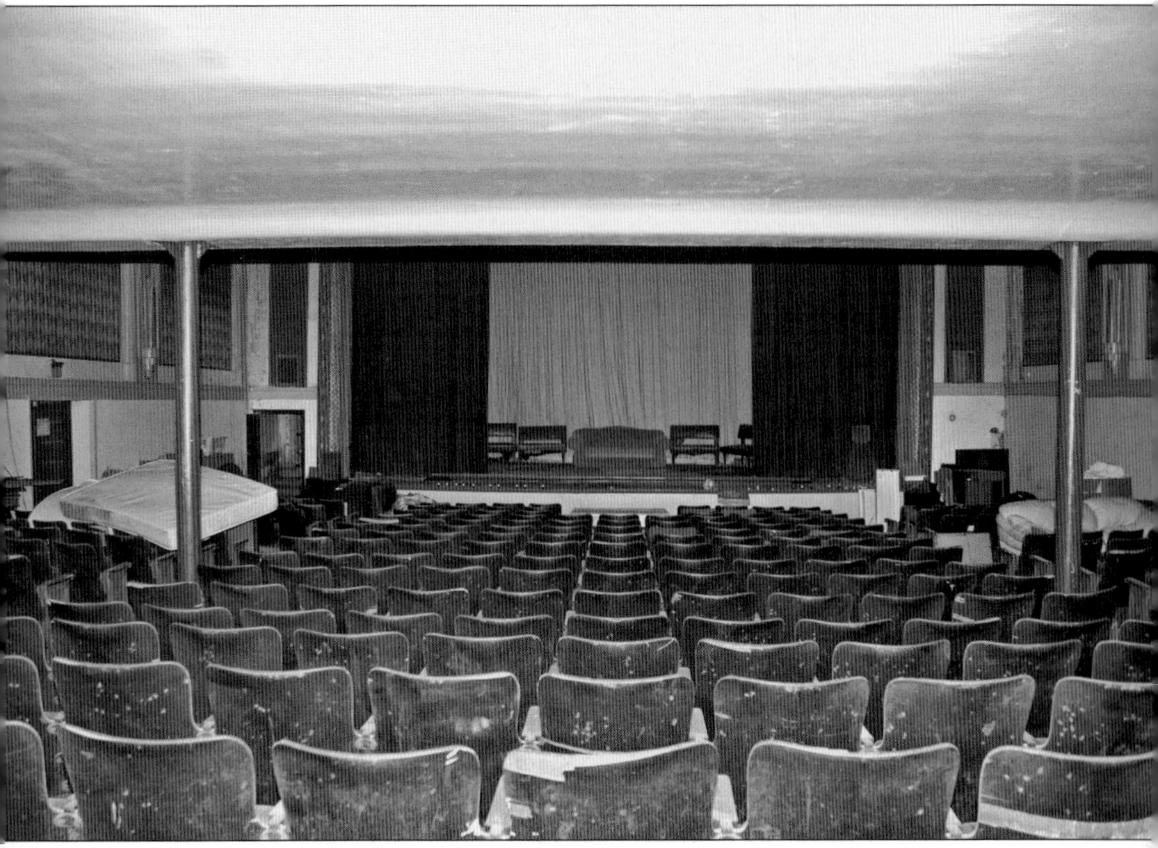

The old Imperial Theater still stands in the old Mohawk neighborhood. Over the years, it has been resurrected more often than Dracula. As the neighborhood and the movie business changed, families began heading to the new multiplexes in the suburbs. After many years as a true cinema, the Imperial went from being a movie house to a burlesque house, known as the Imperial Follies, in an effort to seek customers. When this transition did not work, the establishment became an adult theater. Since the theater closed, the space has been used as a mattress store. Here is a rare look inside the building. Note the mattresses on both sides of the photograph. (Photograph by Phil Lind.)

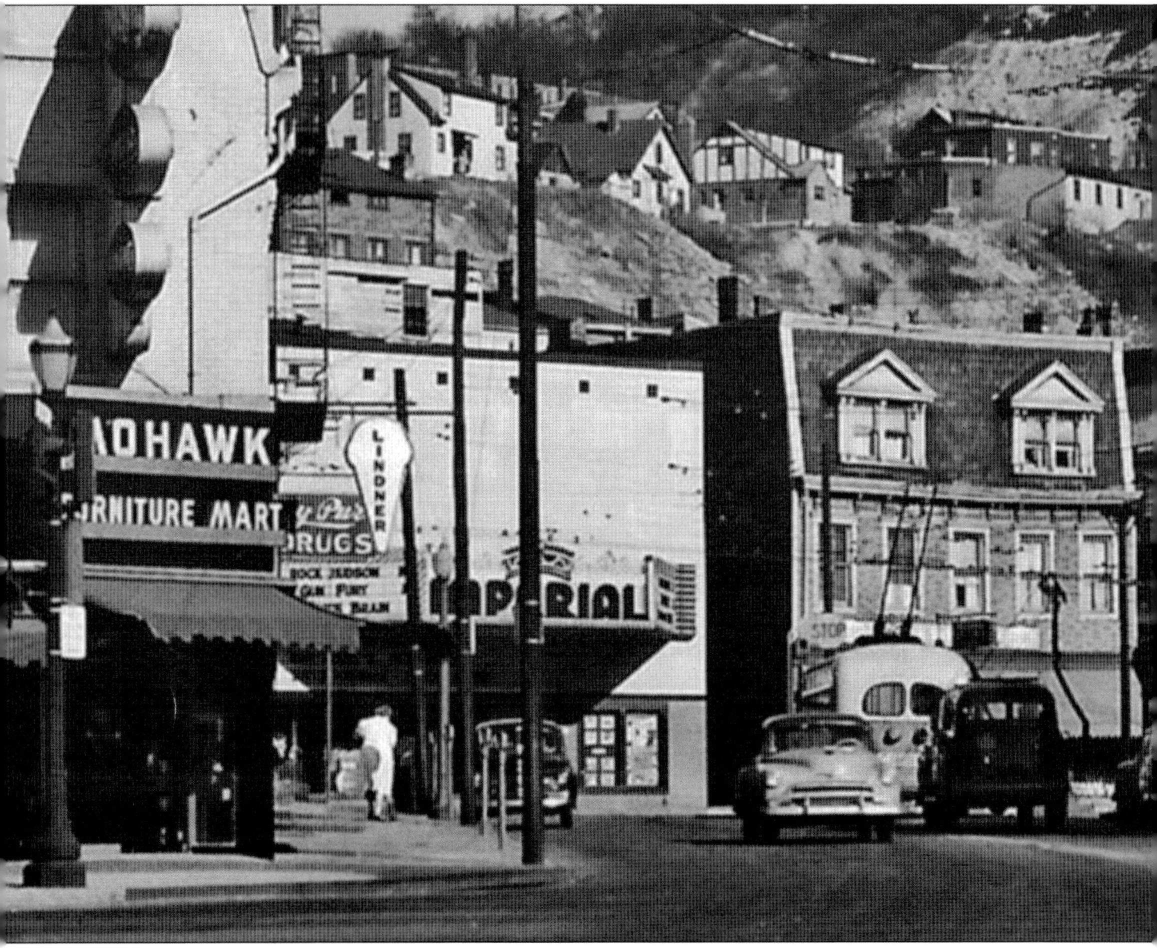

An important detail of this vintage photograph of the Imperial Theater in the Mohawk District is the Lindner ice cream sign just to the left of the marquee. This brand eventually grew into the convenience store giant, United Dairy Farmers. Born in Norwood in 1919, Carl Lindner Jr. rose from a small family dairy company to become one of the richest businessmen in the world. His holdings included part ownership of American Financial Group, United Brands (Chiquita Bananas), and even the Cincinnati Reds. Beloved by many for his philanthropy, Lindner passed away in 2011. (Phil Lind.)

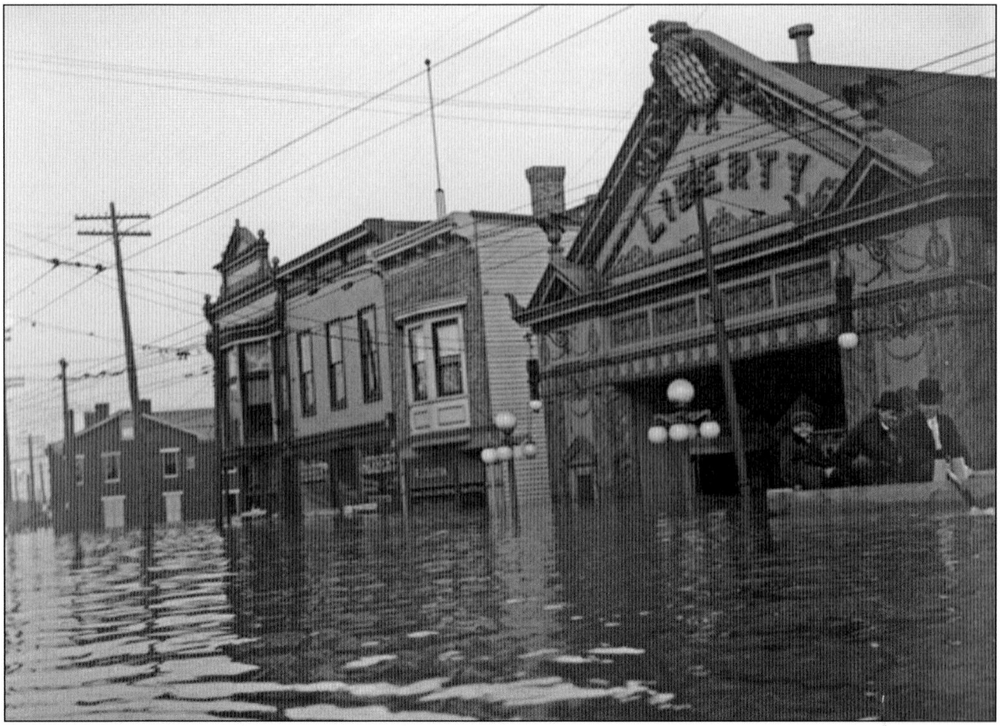

Everyone has heard of a drive-in movie, but how about a row-in? This photograph shows the Liberty Theater, near Knowlton's Corner, at a slight disadvantage during the January 1937 flood, the greatest natural disaster ever to strike Cincinnati. Part of the flood recovery efforts included the preservation of gasoline and electricity, thus shutting down all theaters in the area. (Phil Lind.)

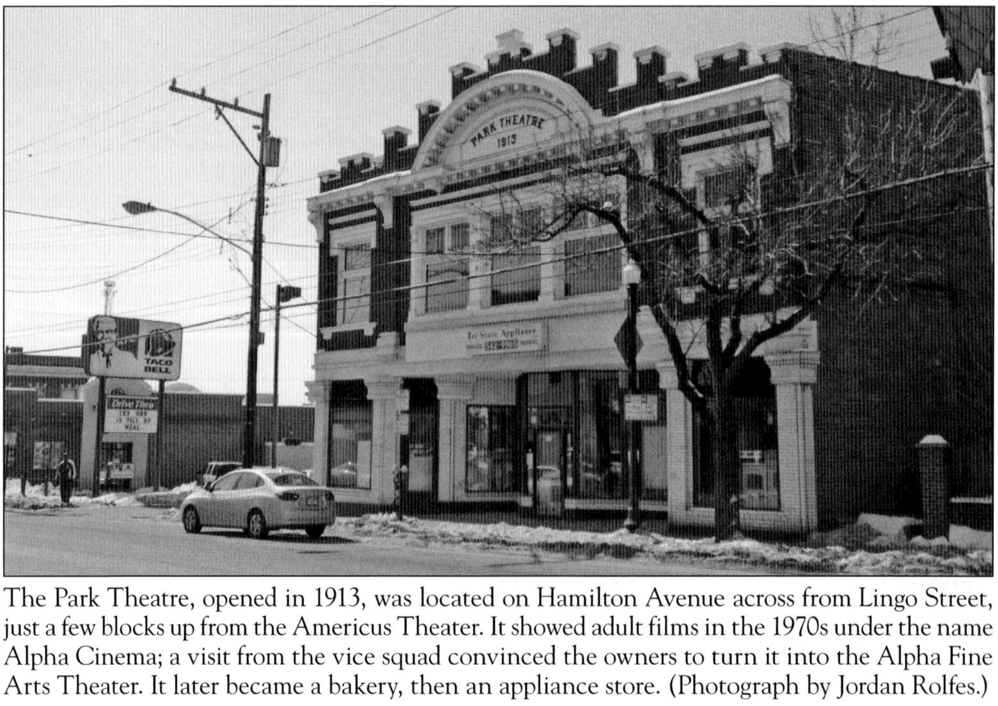

The Park Theatre, opened in 1913, was located on Hamilton Avenue across from Lingo Street, just a few blocks up from the Americus Theater. It showed adult films in the 1970s under the name Alpha Cinema; a visit from the vice squad convinced the owners to turn it into the Alpha Fine Arts Theater. It later became a bakery, then an appliance store. (Photograph by Jordan Rolfes.)

This stunning old movie house was once known as the Casino Theater, the original name inscribed on the building (above the circle in the archway). It opened in 1914, in sharp competition with the Metropolitan Theater located a few blocks away. It was renamed the Regal at the end of World War II. (Photograph by Doug Weise.)

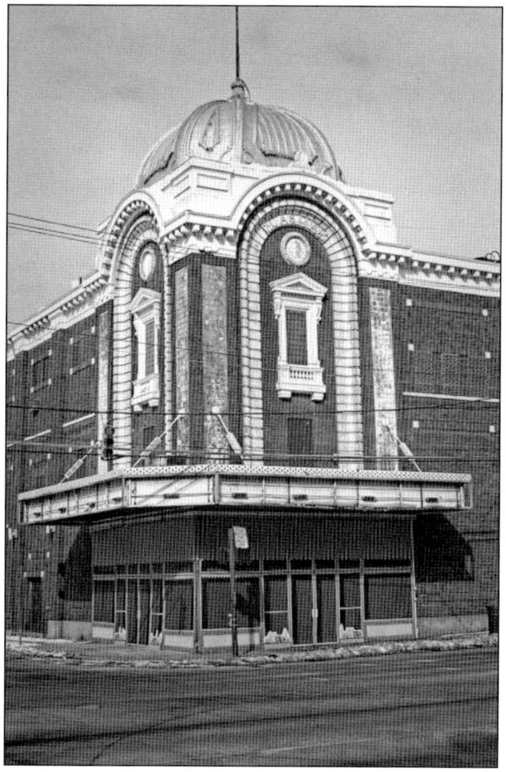

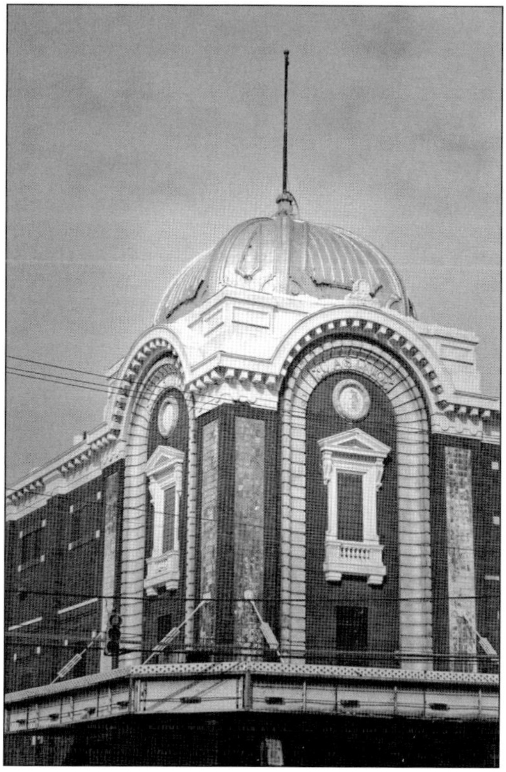

Long after most neighborhood theaters had closed their doors forever, the Regal, housed in this stately old building, managed to cling to life by offering a seemingly endless fare of formulaic kung fu movies. The Regal closed in 1996, but the building still stands. As parts of the West End are undergoing a transformation, it will be interesting to see what happens to this bit of history. Restoration work was underway as of late 2015. (Photograph by Doug Weise.)

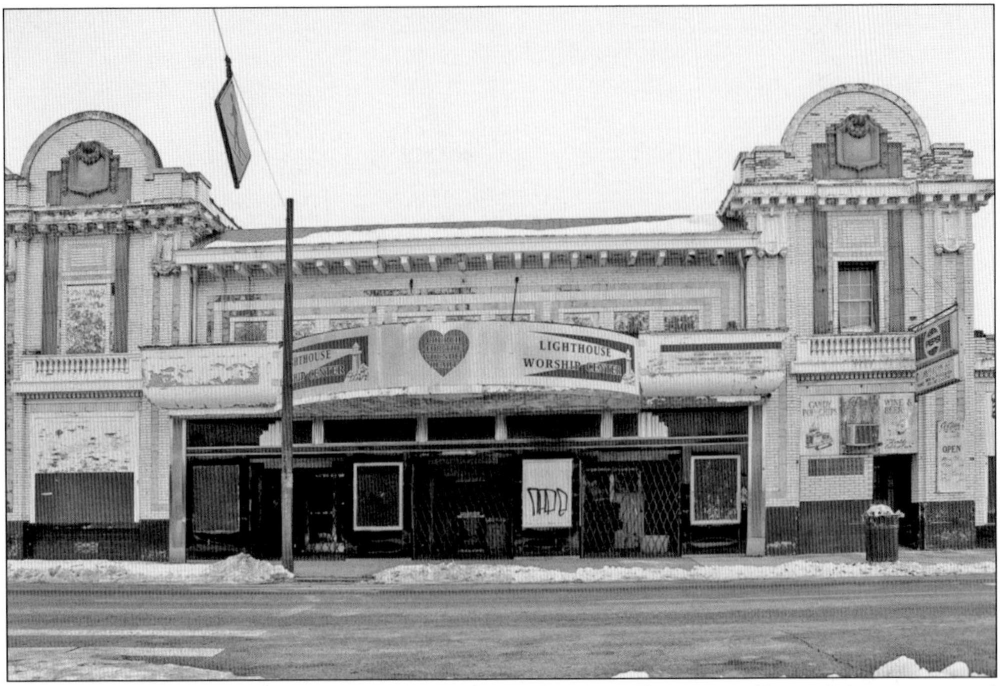

Located only a few blocks from the elegant Casino, the State Theater on Central Avenue opened in 1915 under the name "Metropolitan." It was a small vaudeville house and later showed silent films, surviving under various names until 1989. Today, like so many other former neighborhood movie houses, it houses a church. (Phil Lind.)

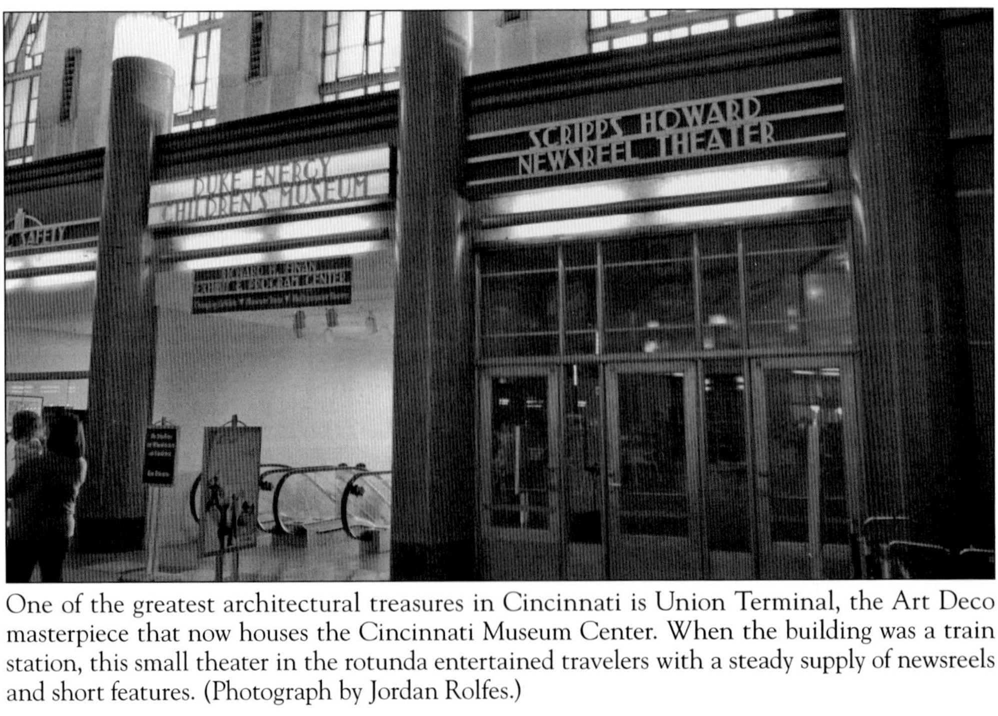

One of the greatest architectural treasures in Cincinnati is Union Terminal, the Art Deco masterpiece that now houses the Cincinnati Museum Center. When the building was a train station, this small theater in the rotunda entertained travelers with a steady supply of newsreels and short features. (Photograph by Jordan Rolfes.)

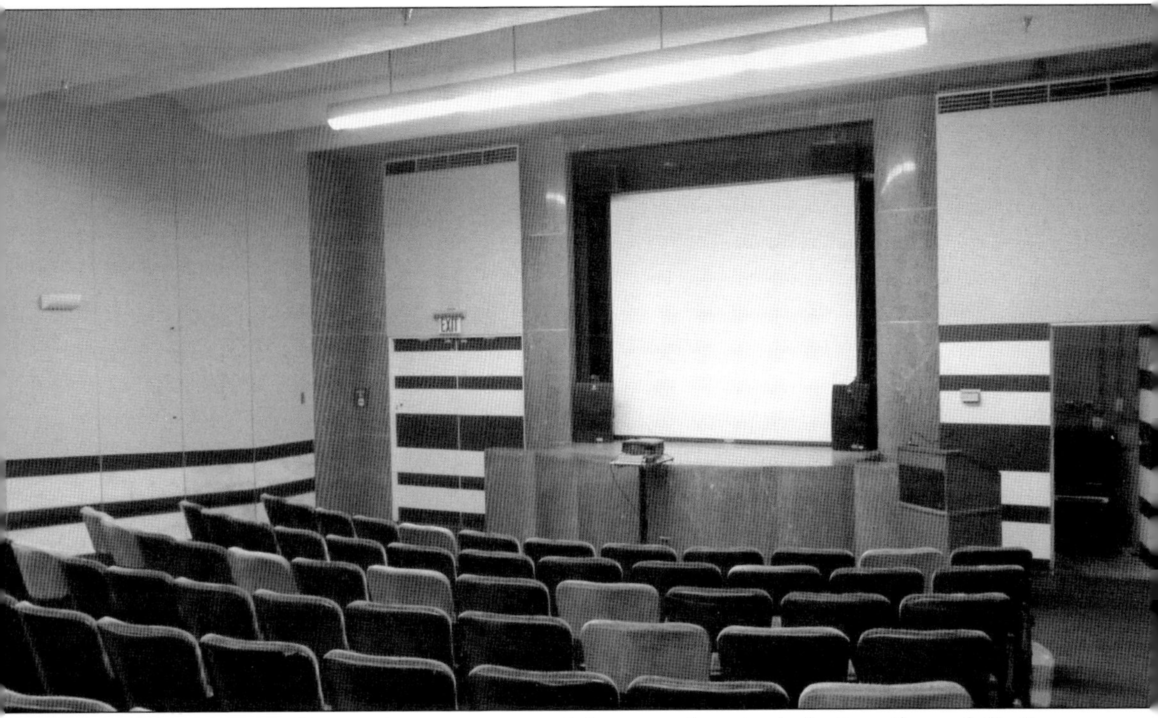

The stunning Union Terminal was once one of the nation's major hubs for rail travel. Earlier Cincinnati railroad stations were located near the Ohio River, causing them to be evacuated every few years because of flooding. It was finally decided that the four big railroads would combine their resources and construct a new depot that would be a source of pride for the Queen City. Construction on the building was completed in 1931, and the facility opened to rail travelers in 1933. Among its amenities was this theater. Found in the massive rotunda area, this small theater kept travelers up to date by showing newsreels. The facility is still used today for lectures and special events. (Photograph by Jordan Rolfes.)

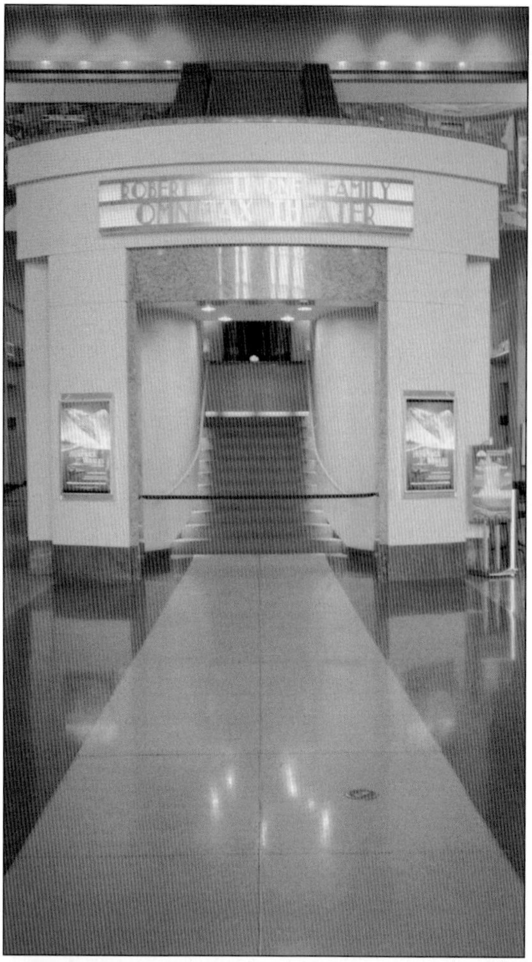

One of the most popular attractions in the Cincinnati Museum Center is the Robert D. Lindner Family Omnimax Theater. With an overwhelming sound system and a five-story dome screen, the audience does not merely watch a film—they experience it. (Photograph by Jordan Rolfes.)

This may look like a futuristic research facility, but it is actually the technical heart of the Robert D. Lindner Family Omnimax Theater. Patrons waiting in line can watch through glass walls as the projectionist runs the controls, preparing the system for the showing of a feature film. (Photograph by Jordan Rolfes.)

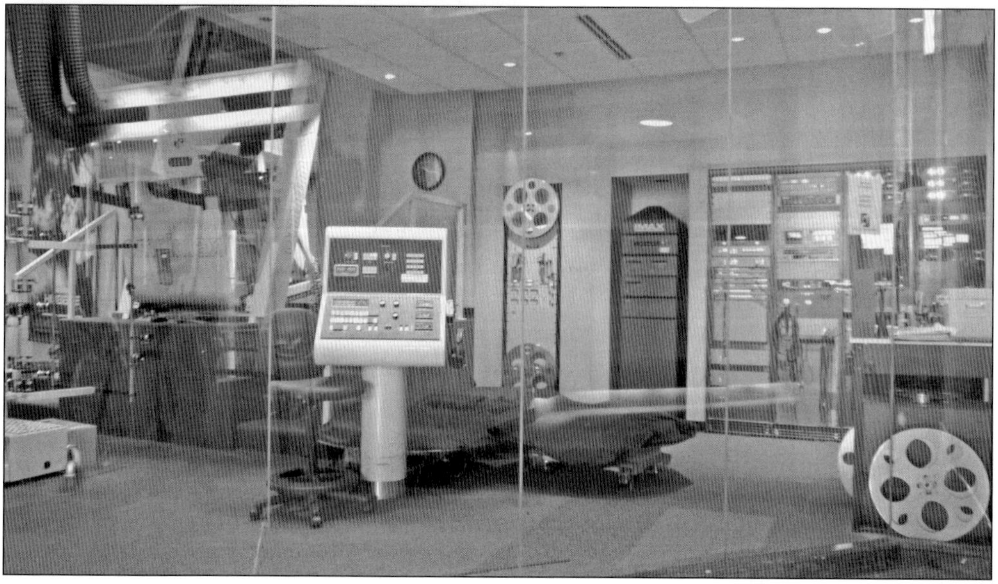

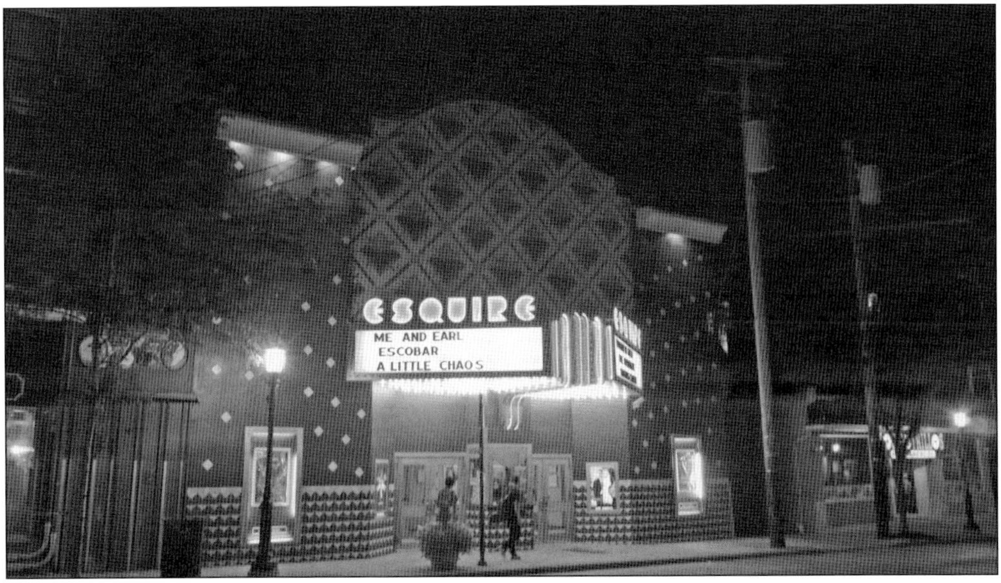

Many old theaters tried to survive the changing market by showing foreign, independent, and/or art films. Such attempts usually ended with the movie house becoming a church venue. One success, however, is the old Esquire Theater in the Gaslight district of Clifton. It is close to the University of Cincinnati, and it has thrived in this difficult corner of the market. (Photograph by Jordan Rolfes.)

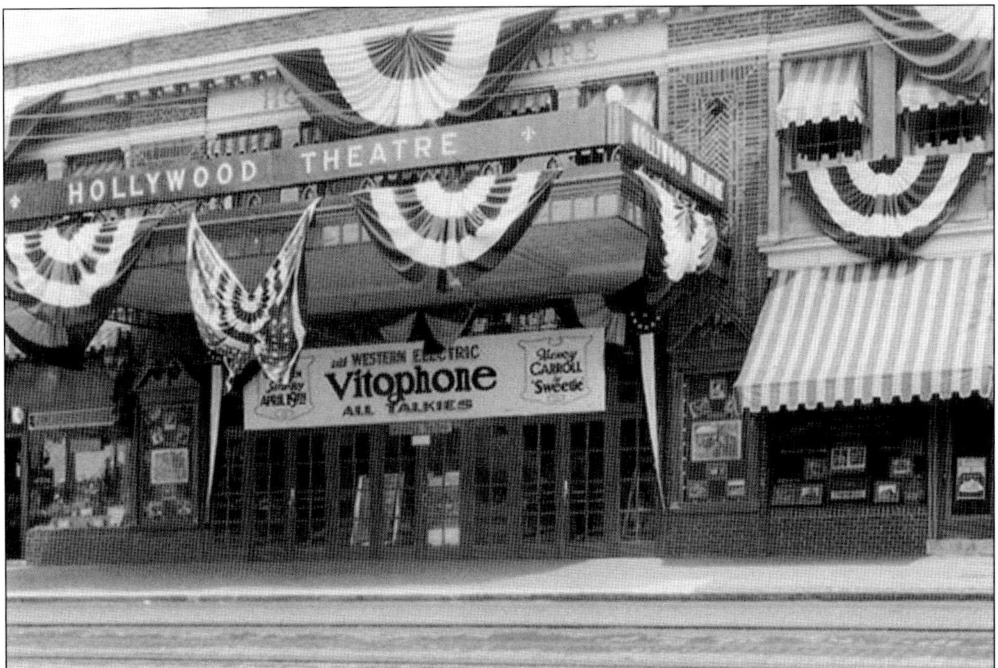

This 1929 image of College Hill's Hollywood Theatre illustrates the storm then raging within the film industry. Some proprietors of silent-movie houses held the opinion that talkies were a fad and did not spend the money to purchase the new equipment. By the time this photograph was taken, some of those houses had already closed. (College Hill Historical Society.)

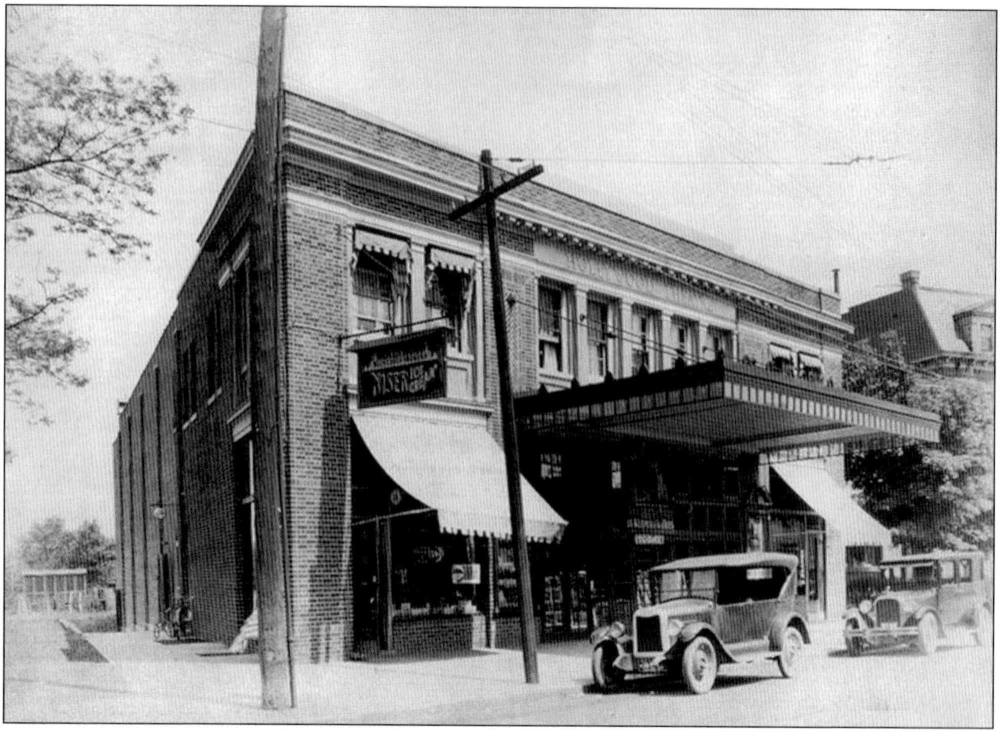

Hamilton Avenue once housed a number of theaters from Northside to Mount Healthy. One of these, the Hollywood, was located in the northern suburb of College Hill. The cinema opened in the 1920s, then underwent extensive remodeling in 1948. By the 1990s, it had closed, although the building remains and now serves as a church. (College Hill Historical Society.)

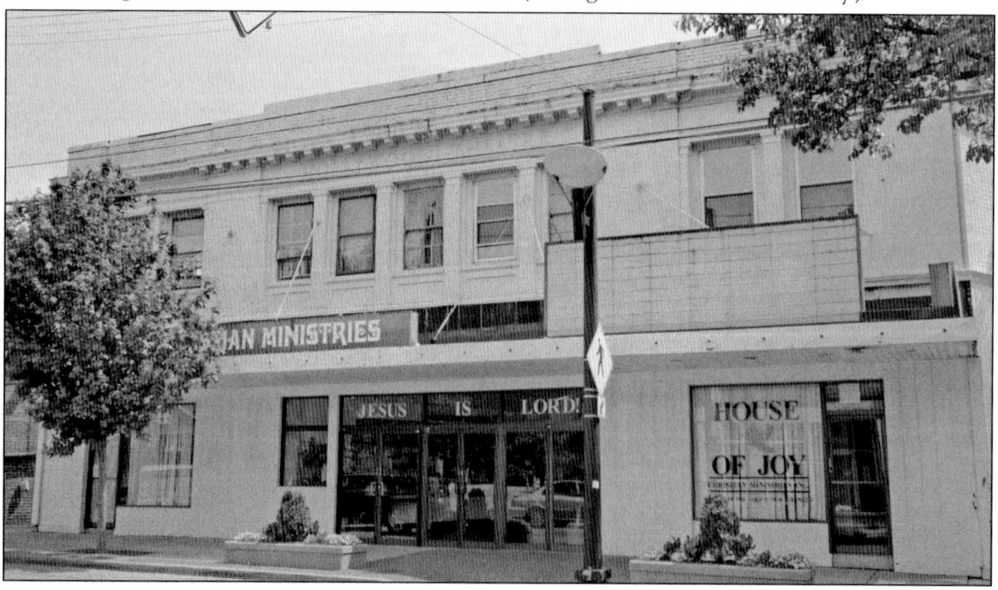

Hollywood Theatre, located on the corner of Cedar and Hamilton Avenues in College Hill, escaped the wrecking ball by being converted into a church in the 1990s. The blank marquee remains, along with the "Hollywood Theatre" inscription above the second-story windows. (Photograph by Jordan Rolfes.)

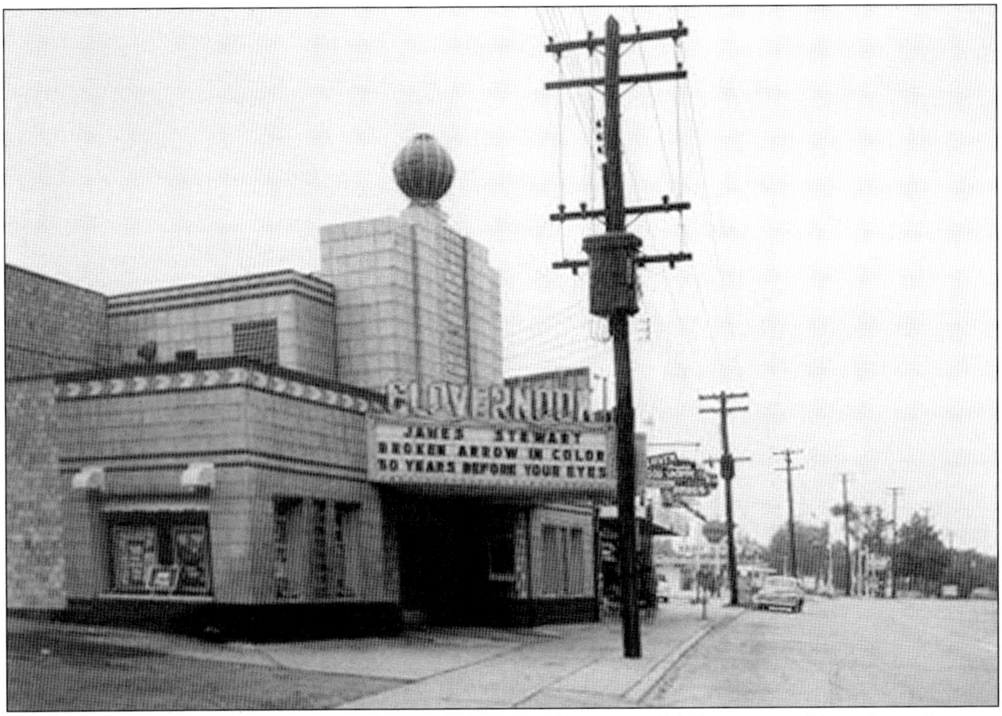

This is one of very few images of the little-known Clovernook Theater on Hamilton Avenue in the small city of North College Hill. The theater, built in an impressive Art Deco style, was erected in the 1940s but closed before the end of the 1950s. (Phil Lind.)

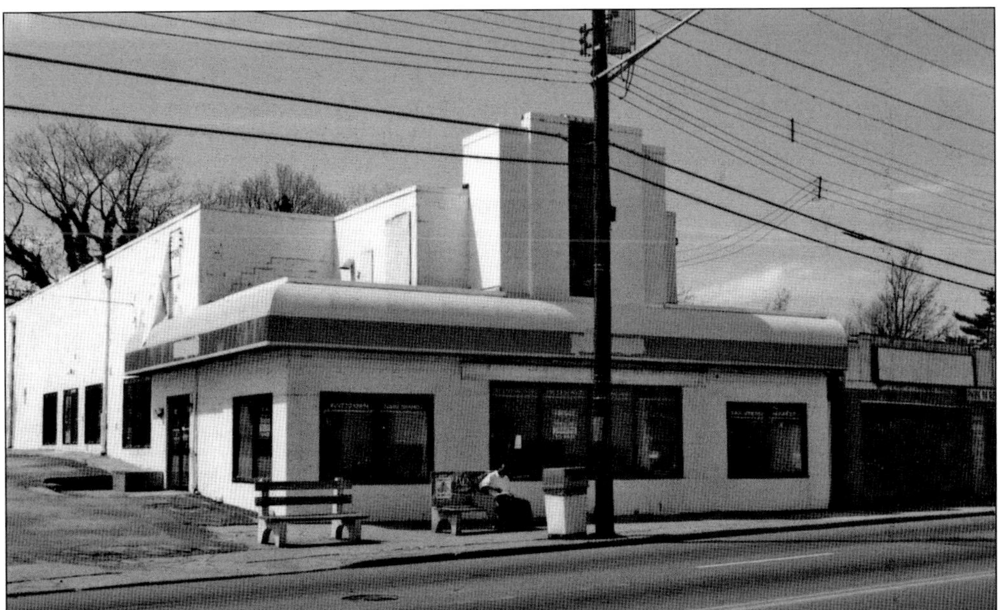

Although the Clovernook Theater closed, the beautiful building remained for a number of years, housing different businesses. For many years, it was a gymnasium. Later, it was converted into a pizza parlor. Sadly, the building was demolished in 2010, and the site is now merely an open field. (North College Hill Historical Society.)

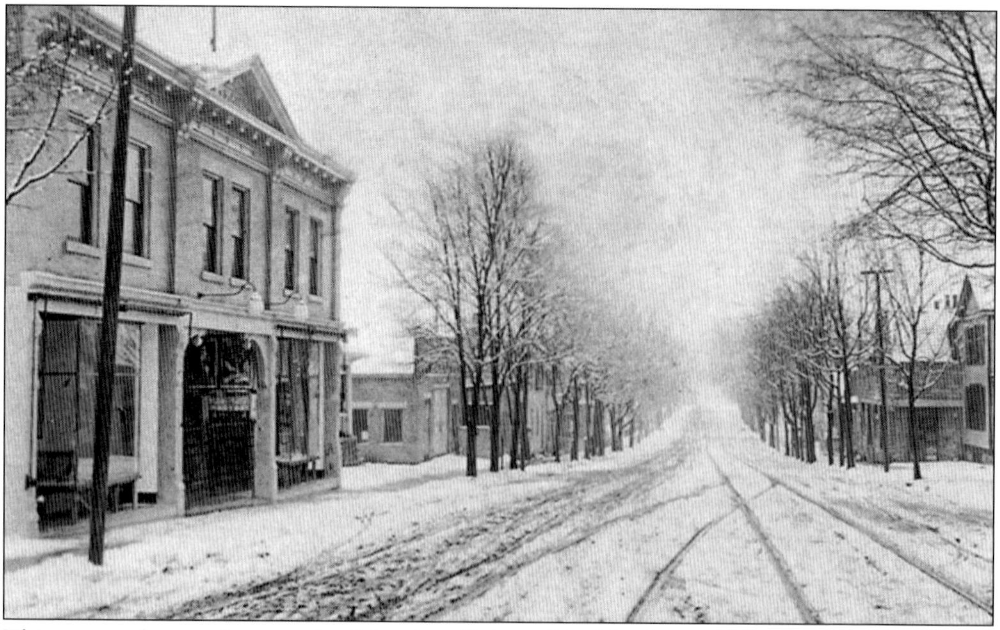

This extremely rare photograph of the city of Mount Healthy during the time of the First World War shows a snowy Hamilton Avenue. At left is the Main Theatre, a mainstay in the small community until it closed in the early 1970s. For a time, the Main Theatre was transformed into an auction house. (Mount Healthy Historical Society.)

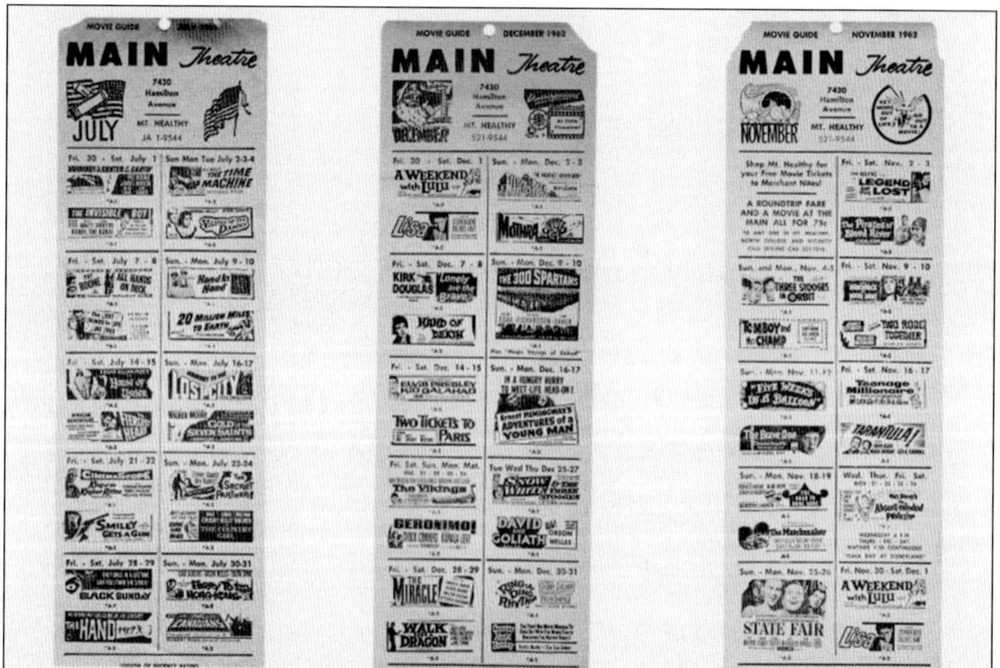

Mount Healthy's Main Theatre was the place for young people to go on a Saturday afternoon. Admission was only 25¢, and a lucky patron would occasionally receive a coupon at the bottom of the popcorn bag for a free admission. Upcoming films were advertised on flyers given to patrons at the beginning of each month. (Mount Healthy Historical Society.)

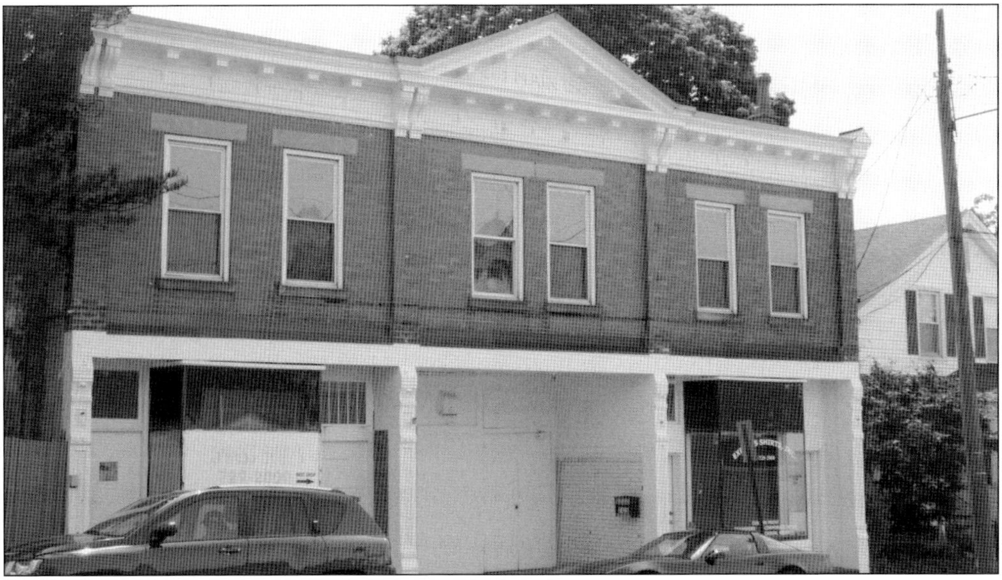

Today, there is almost no trace of the old Main Theatre in Mount Healthy. The only reminder of this building's cinematic past is at its very top, where a sharp eye can still spot the painted-over "Main." (Photograph by Jordan Rolfes.)

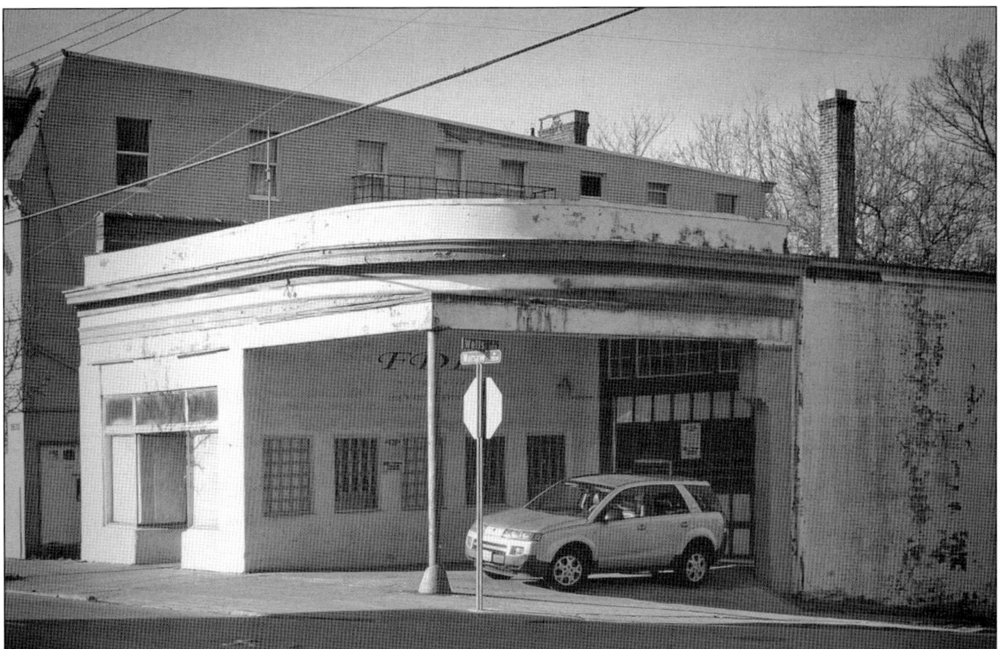

Looking at this modernist building, it may be difficult to believe that it was once the Warsaw Theater, one of four neighborhood theaters that served the Price Hill and Western Hills area. The Warsaw Theater, located at Warsaw Avenue and Wells Street, opened in 1911, showing silent films. (Photograph by Doug Weise.)

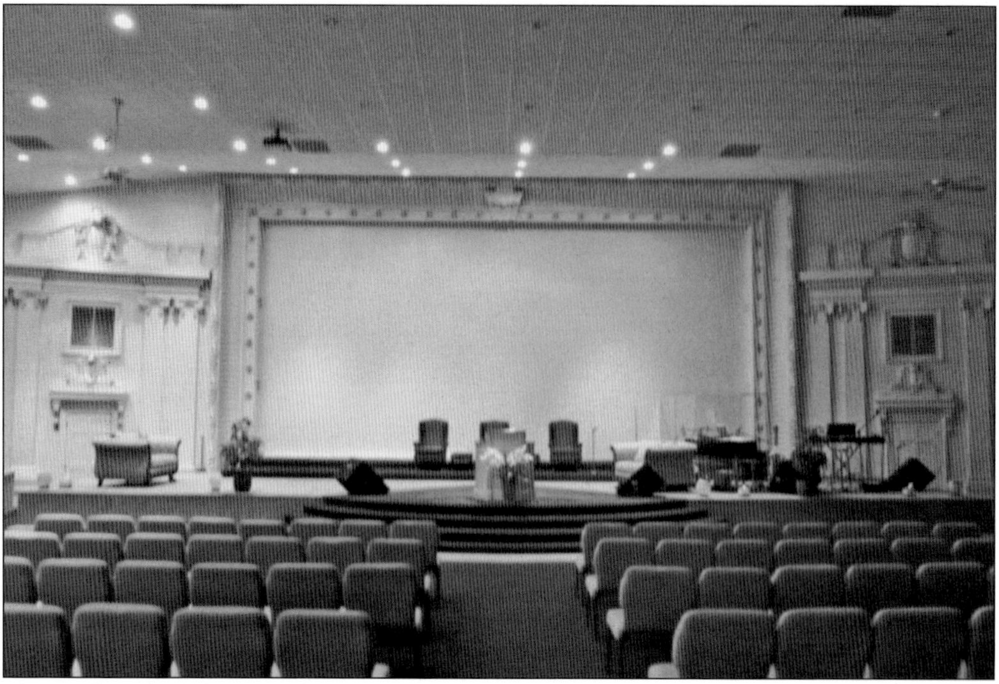

The inside of the old State Theater (originally the Metropolitan) has been converted to a church. It is apparent from this photograph that the stage, which is 20 feet deep, was once used for vaudeville. In 1944, it became the State Theater and showed only films. (Photograph by Phil Lind.)

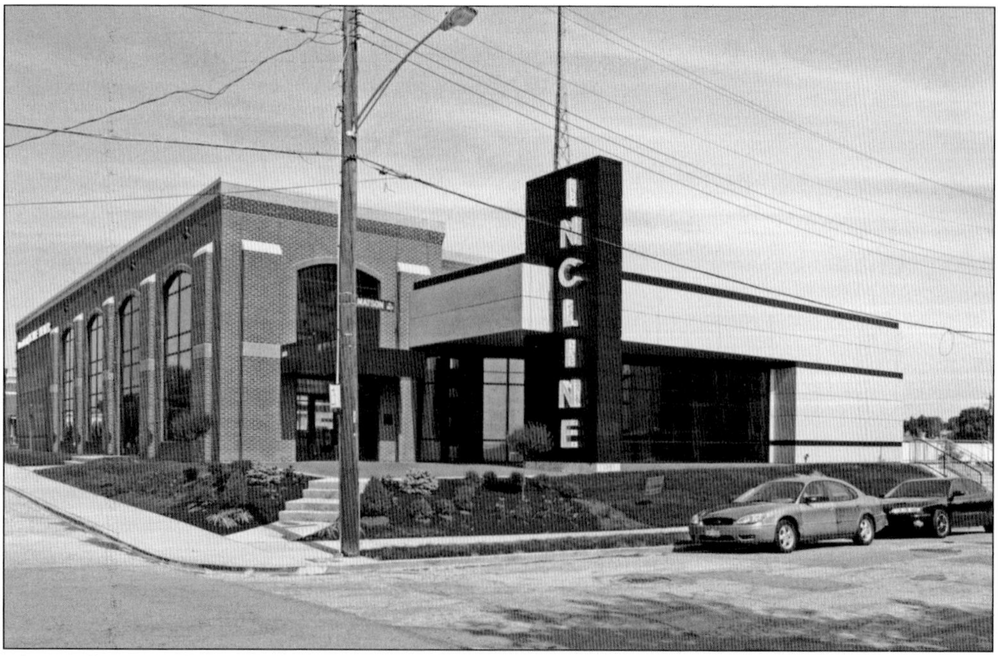

The tradition of the neighborhood theater is not entirely gone. The Incline Theater, located in upper Price Hill, is a new addition to the Cincinnati scene. Located near two popular eateries, this location reflects the 19th-century era, when a small picnic area and restaurant were located at the top of the Price Hill Incline. (Photograph by Doug Weise.)

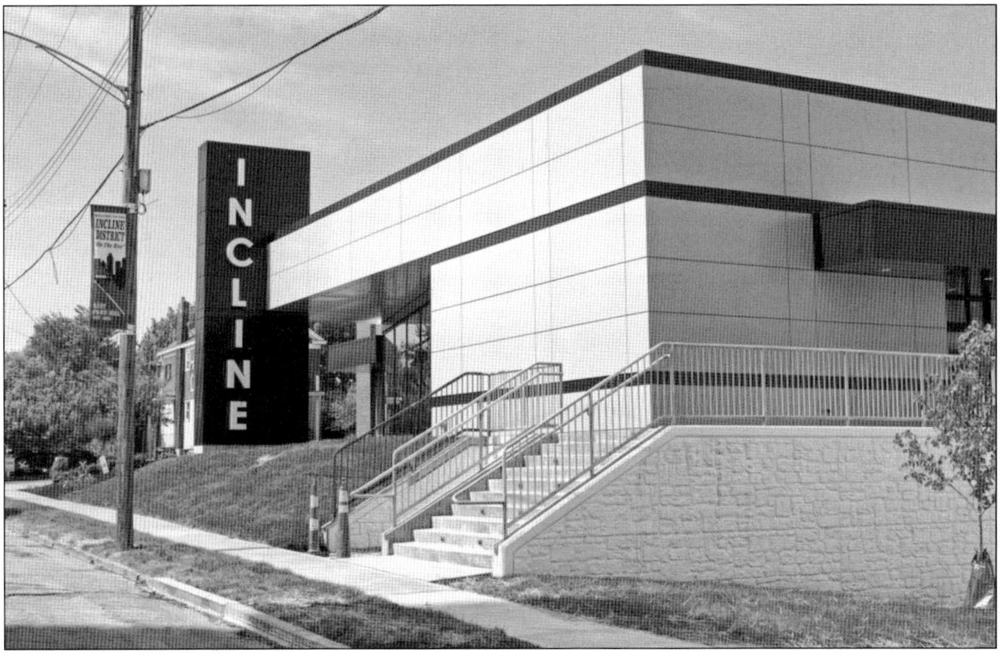

The banner on the telephone pole identifies this area as the Incline District. In the late decades of the 19th century, William Price provided food and entertainment for those who rode his Price Hill Incline to escape the congestion and foul air of the city below. However, he adamantly refused to sell alcohol, which led to his amusement complex, Price Hill House, being nicknamed "Buttermilk Mountain." (Photograph by Doug Weise.)

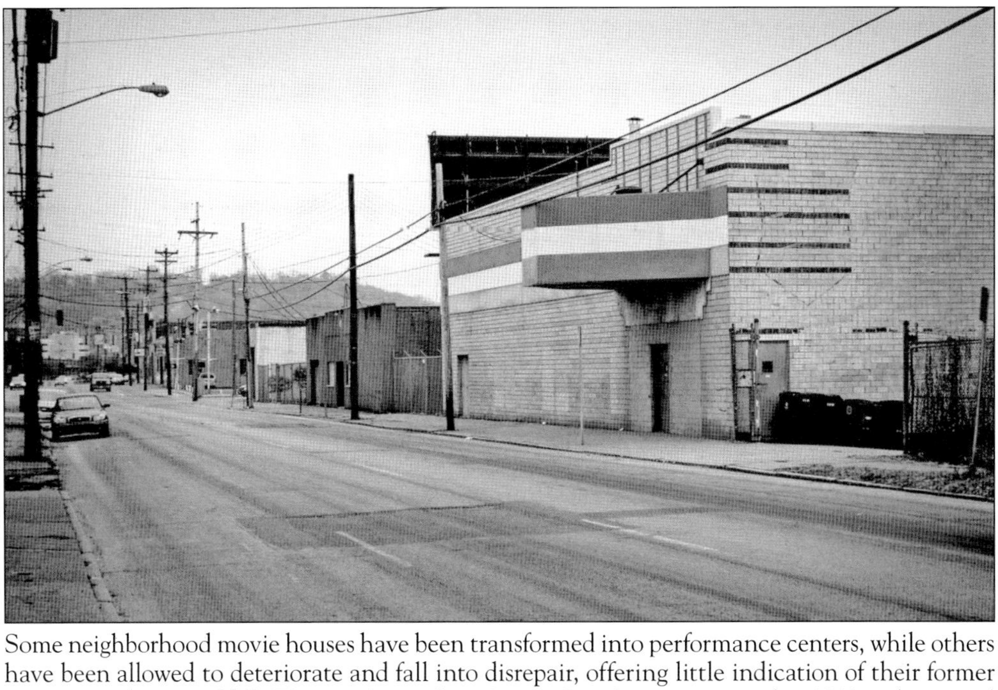

Some neighborhood movie houses have been transformed into performance centers, while others have been allowed to deteriorate and fall into disrepair, offering little indication of their former greatness. The West Hills Theater, located on Queen City Avenue, opened in 1942 and survived for two decades. It now houses a moving and storage firm. (Photograph by Doug Weise.)

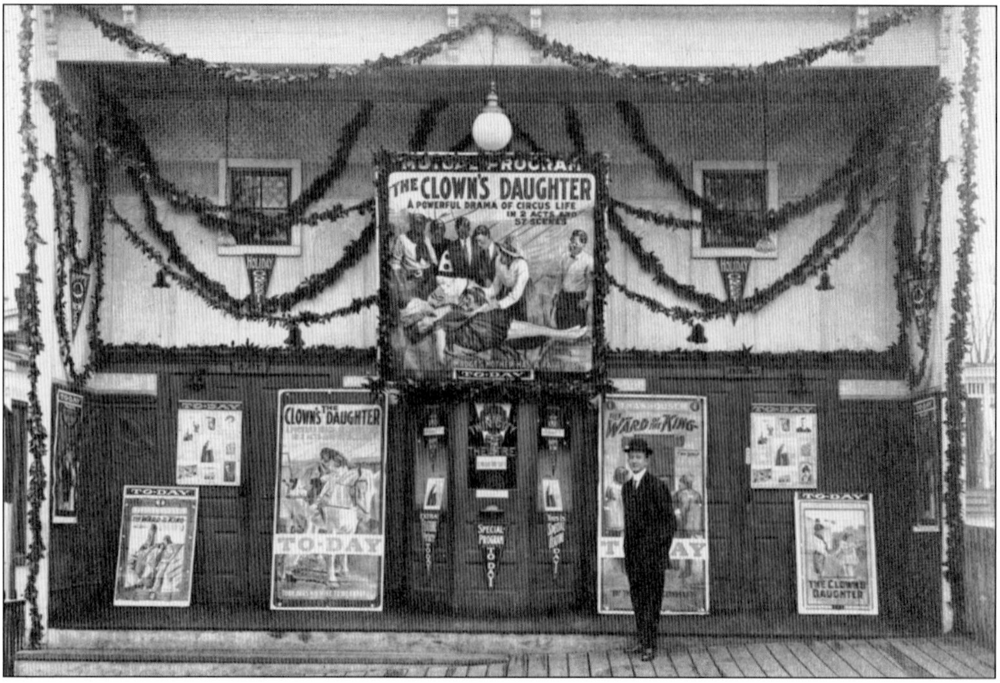

Twin City Theatre was located next to the popular Orr's Saloon on Harrison Avenue in the West Side. Admission was one nickel when this photograph was taken. Today, the spot is home to a fast-food restaurant. (Westwood Historical Society and Catherine Huebner.)

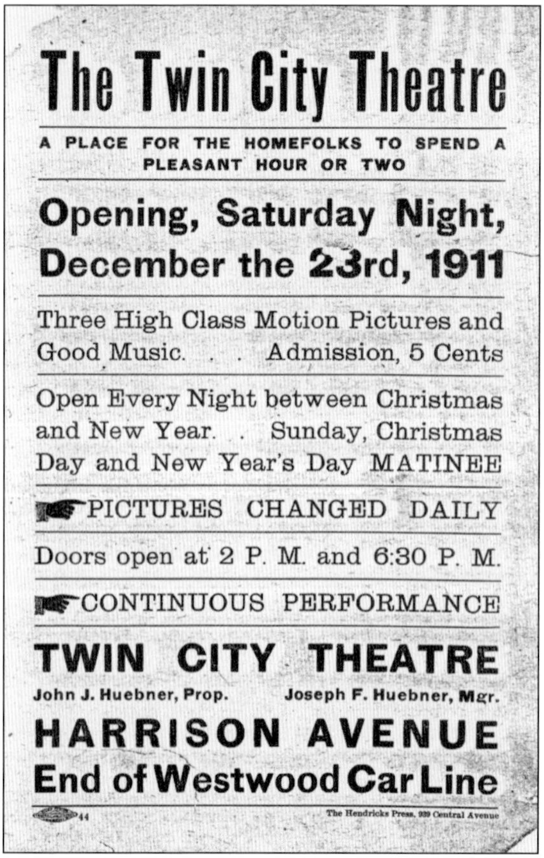

The Twin City Theatre

A PLACE FOR THE HOMEFOLKS TO SPEND A PLEASANT HOUR OR TWO

Opening, Saturday Night, December the 23rd, 1911

Three High Class Motion Pictures and Good Music. . . Admission, 5 Cents

Open Every Night between Christmas and New Year. . Sunday, Christmas Day and New Year's Day MATINEE

PICTURES CHANGED DAILY

Doors open at 2 P. M. and 6:30 P. M.

CONTINUOUS PERFORMANCE

TWIN CITY THEATRE

John J. Huebner, Prop. Joseph F. Huebner, Mgr.

HARRISON AVENUE

End of Westwood Car Line

44 The Hendricks Press, 939 Central Avenue

This poster from the newly opening 1911 Twin City Theatre promised patrons that they would view not one but three different silent films accompanied by "good music." In addition to listing the location, the advertisement provided details for arriving via streetcar. (Westwood Historical Society and Catherine Huebner.)

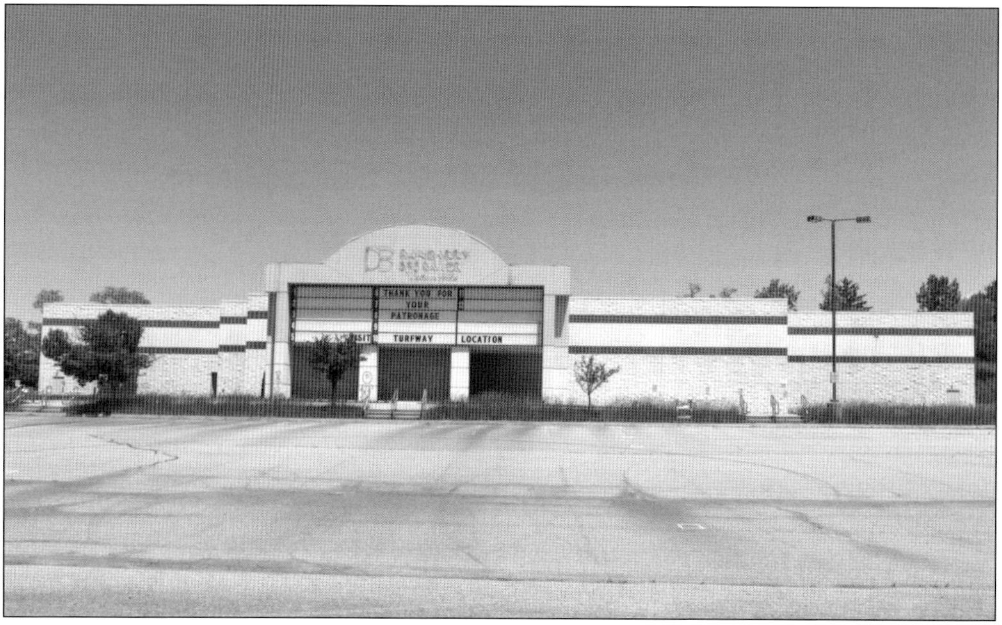

Far to the west, near the Glenway Crossing Shopping Plaza, was the Danbarry Theater. Located behind the shopping center, the small theater opened in 1997, showing second-run films for an admission price of only a few dollars. Although the Danbarry offered a bargain, the theater's audiences could not experience the excitement of a film's initial opening. The theater closed its doors in 2014. (Photograph by Phil Lind.)

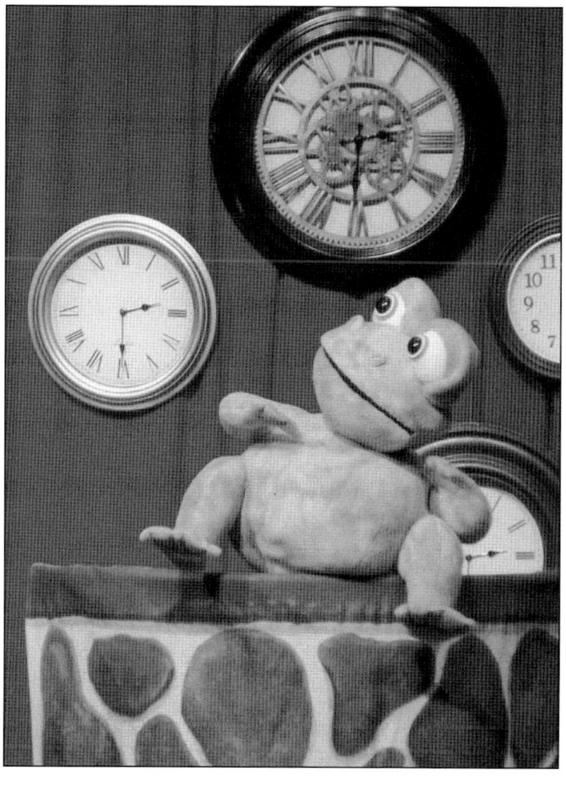

One of the most delightful theatrical institutions in the Cincinnati area is the Madcap Puppets, based on Glenmore Avenue in Western Hills. Madcap's displays of the ancient art of puppetry began when the theater was founded by Jerry Handorf and Beth Kattelman in 1981. Today, the production company is nationally recognized and performs not only children's stories but also more serious works, such as *Amahl and the Night Visitors*. (Madcap Productions, Inc.)

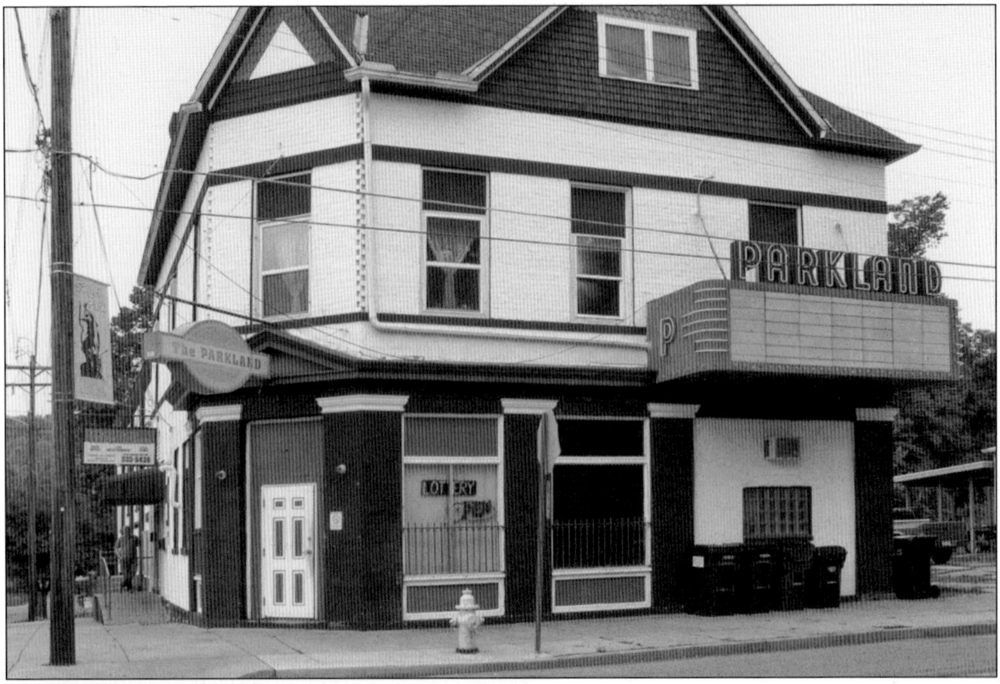

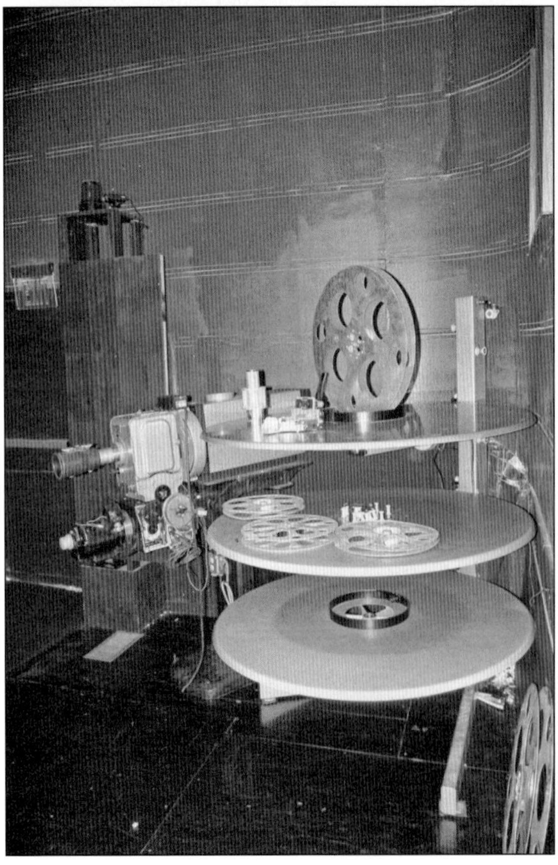

The Parkland Theatre, far to the west in Sayler Park, holds the record for being the oldest active theater in Cincinnati. According to the theater's website (parklandtheatre.com), it was built as a vaudeville theater in 1881 and converted to a silent-movie house in the 1920s. The only older standing theater building is the Casino Theater, located in the West End, which has been closed since 1996. (Photograph by Isabelle Weise.)

The historic Parkland Theatre holds a bit of a surprise for nostalgia buffs. In the front of the theater, near the screen, is a small "museum" displaying some of the technical equipment that old theaters used in years past. (Photograph by Doug Weise.)

Four

My Old Kentucky Movie House

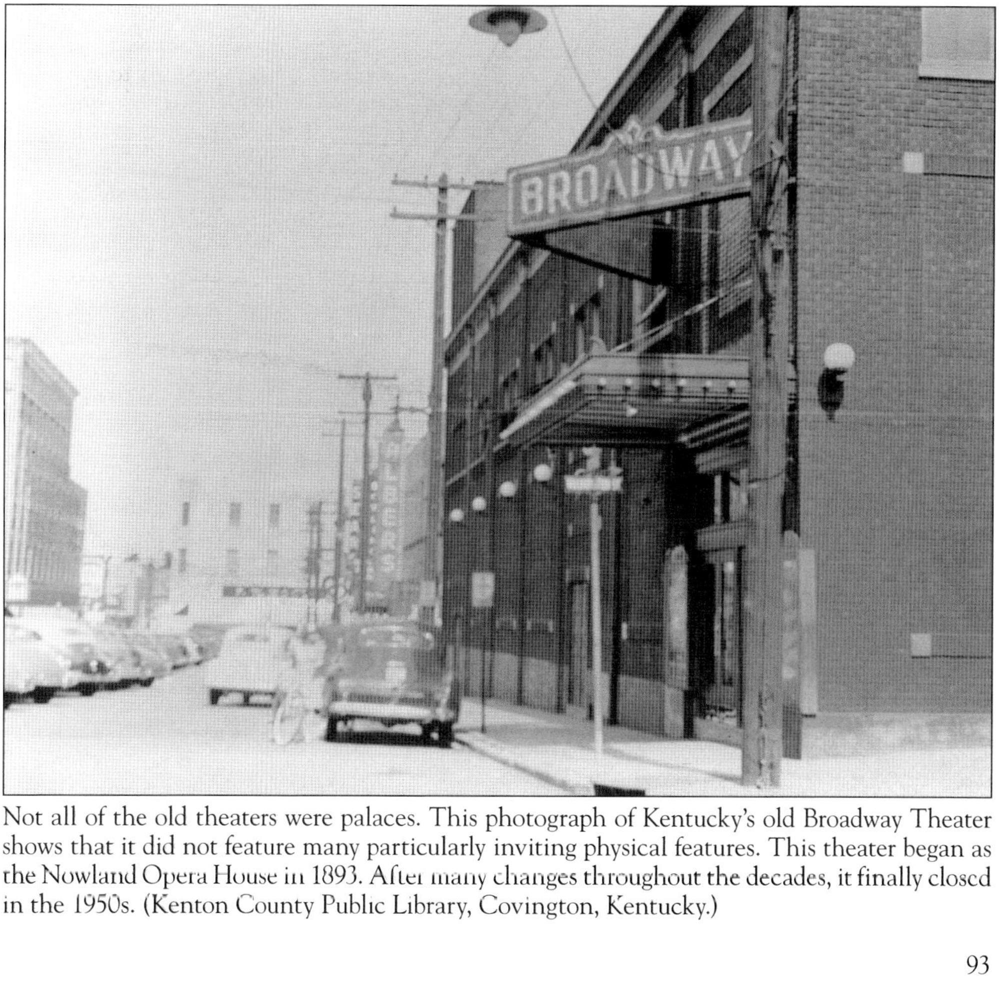

Not all of the old theaters were palaces. This photograph of Kentucky's old Broadway Theater shows that it did not feature many particularly inviting physical features. This theater began as the Nowland Opera House in 1893. After many changes throughout the decades, it finally closed in the 1950s. (Kenton County Public Library, Covington, Kentucky.)

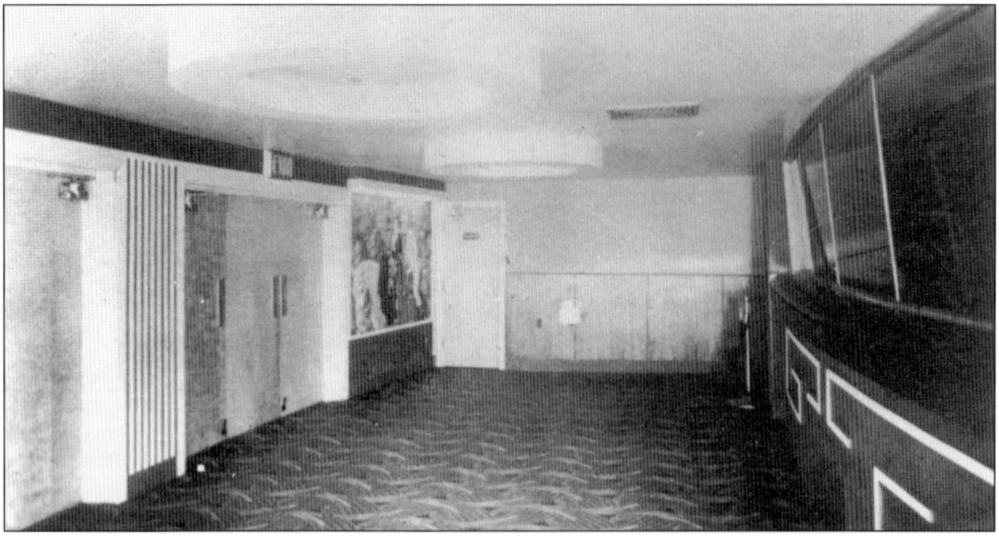

The Art Deco elegance of the exterior of the Madison Theater, located in Covington, Kentucky, continued inside its lobby. Note the stylish pattern on the carpeting and the artwork on the wall. (Kenton County Public Library, Covington, Kentucky.)

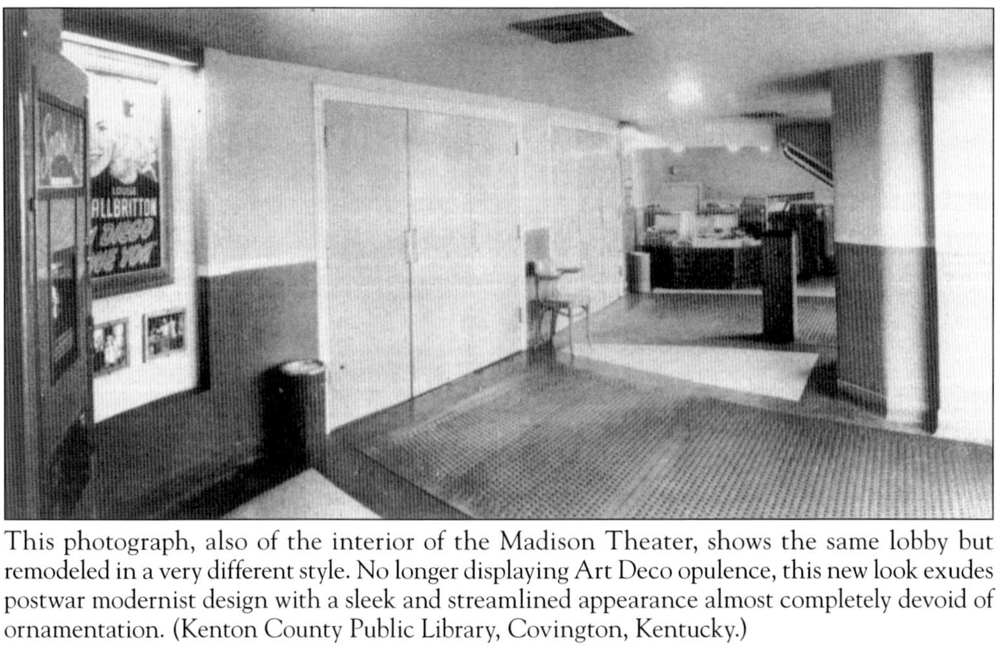

This photograph, also of the interior of the Madison Theater, shows the same lobby but remodeled in a very different style. No longer displaying Art Deco opulence, this new look exudes postwar modernist design with a sleek and streamlined appearance almost completely devoid of ornamentation. (Kenton County Public Library, Covington, Kentucky.)

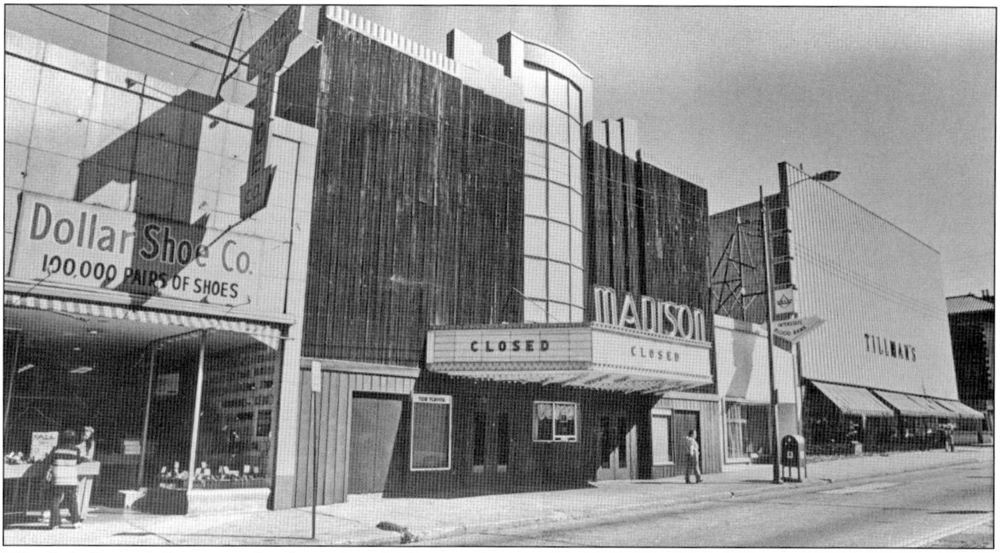

The Madison Theater, which is situated in Covington's Renaissance District, is like the mythical phoenix. It opened in 1912 as the Lyric Theatre. It suffered a devastating fire in 1944, but two years later, it was up and running again. It could not survive as a film house but now thrives as a venue for live performances and events. (Kenton County Public Library, Covington, Kentucky.)

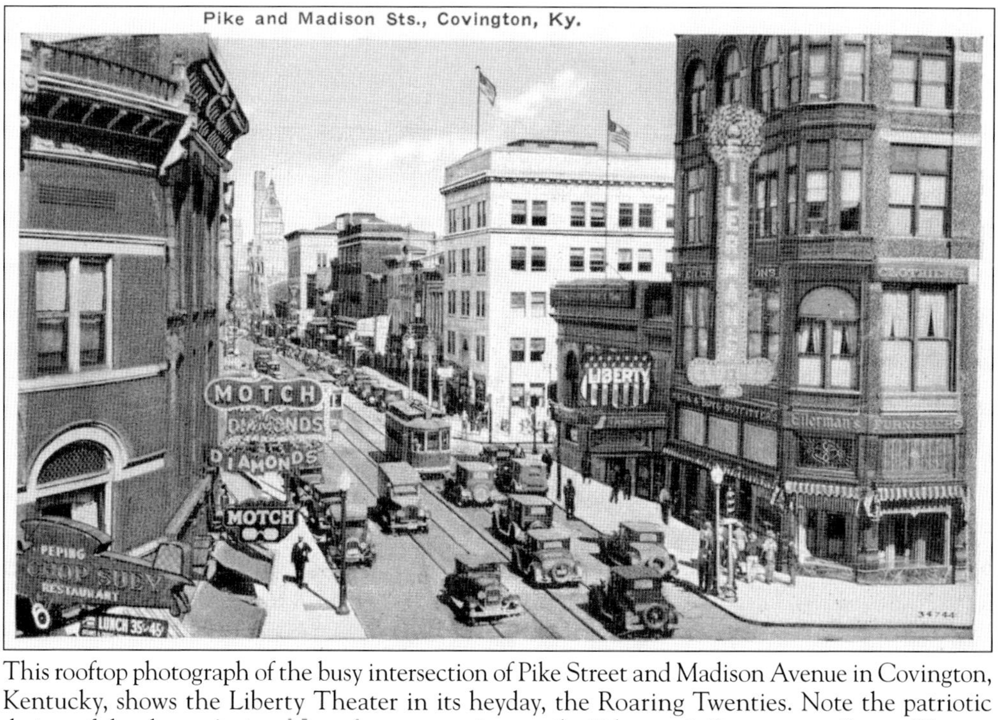

This rooftop photograph of the busy intersection of Pike Street and Madison Avenue in Covington, Kentucky, shows the Liberty Theater in its heyday, the Roaring Twenties. Note the patriotic design of the theater's sign. Next door was major retailer Eilerman's Department Store. (Kenton County Public Library, Covington, Kentucky.)

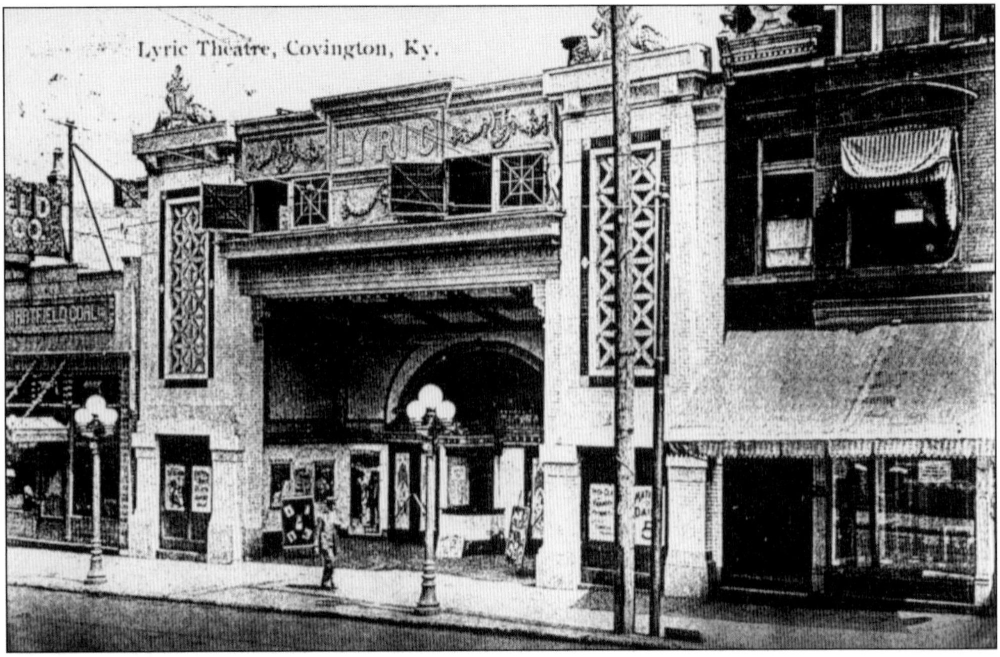

Not only was there a Lyric Theatre in Cincinnati, there was also one across the river in Covington. This 1930s photograph shows both the popular Lyric Theatre and the Hatfield Coal Company next door. The Lyric was later transformed into the Madison Theater. (Kenton County Public Library, Covington, Kentucky.)

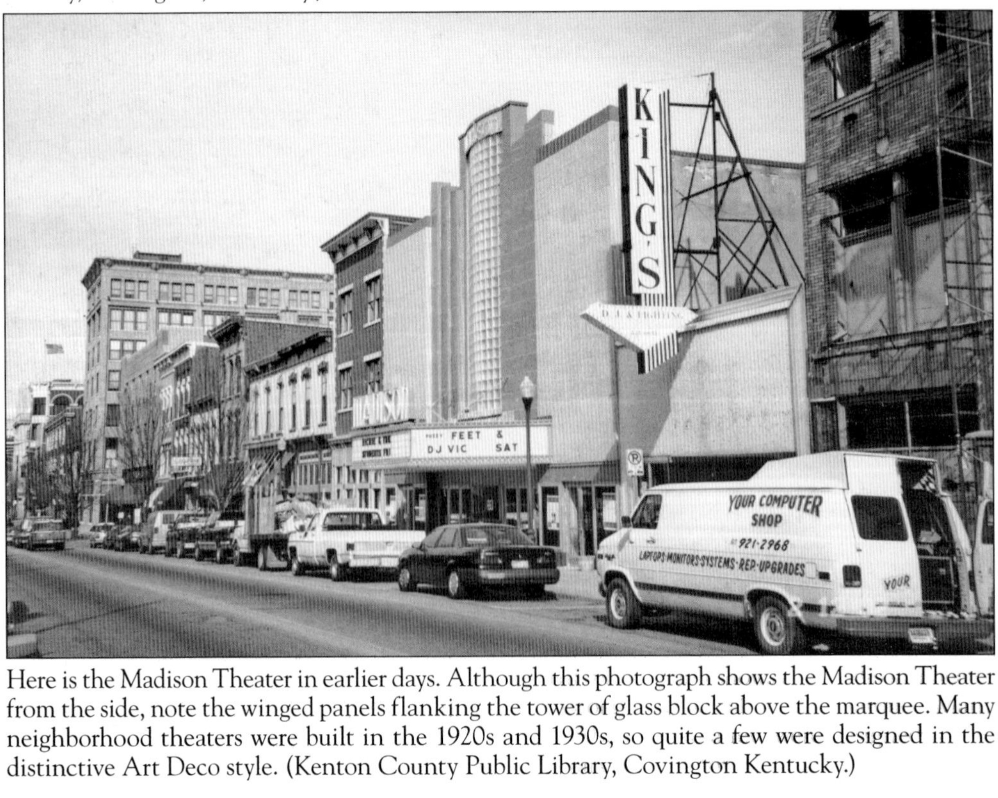

Here is the Madison Theater in earlier days. Although this photograph shows the Madison Theater from the side, note the winged panels flanking the tower of glass block above the marquee. Many neighborhood theaters were built in the 1920s and 1930s, so quite a few were designed in the distinctive Art Deco style. (Kenton County Public Library, Covington Kentucky.)

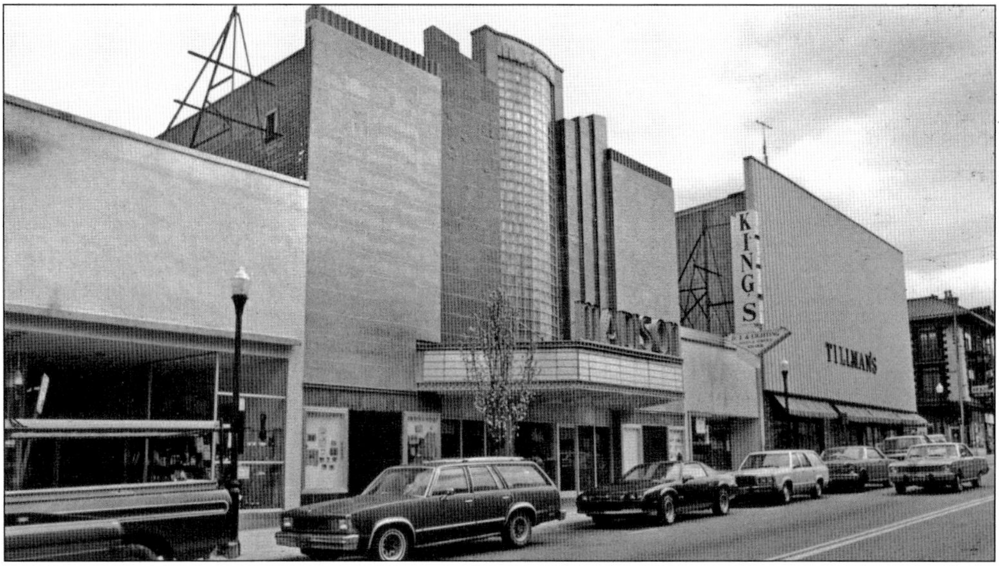

This image offers a closer look at the Art Deco exterior of the Madison Theater. When this establishment opened as the Lyric Theatre in September 1912, it featured live vaudeville performances, and admission was only 5¢. Ticket prices for today's live performances are a bit more expensive. The reborn Madison is so popular that the owners recently opened another venue, Madison Live, next door. (Kenton County Public Library, Covington Kentucky.)

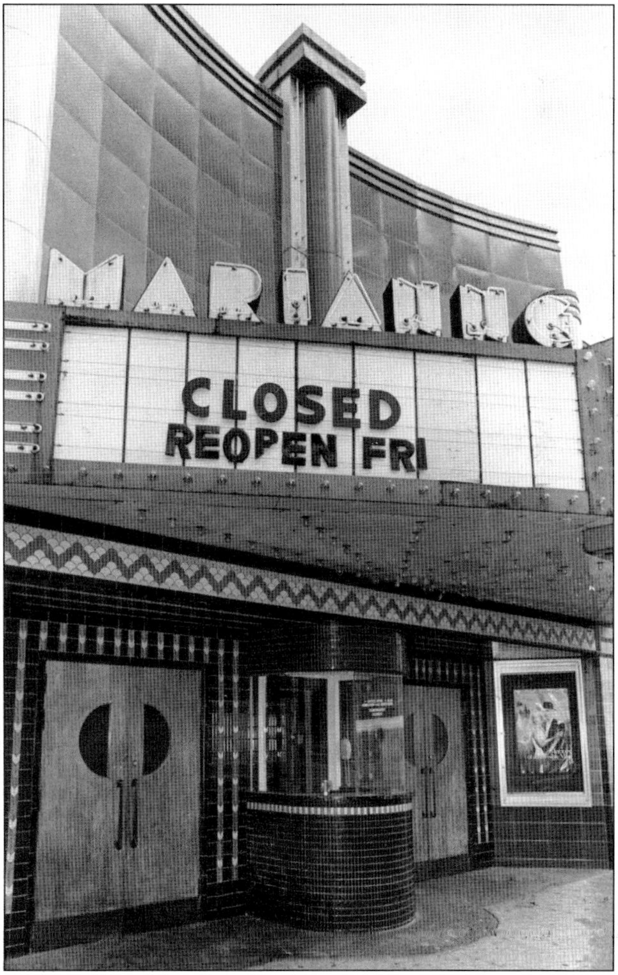

While Covington's Madison Theater may be the most successful Art Deco style theater in northern Kentucky, its beauty is rivaled by the that of the Marianne, located in nearby Bellevue. Opened in 1942, the theater features a curved, towerlike structure over the marquee and an exterior ticket booth. It closed in 1997. The city of Bellevue recently purchased the building and has secured its place in the National Register of Historic Places. (Kenton County Public Library, Covington Kentucky.)

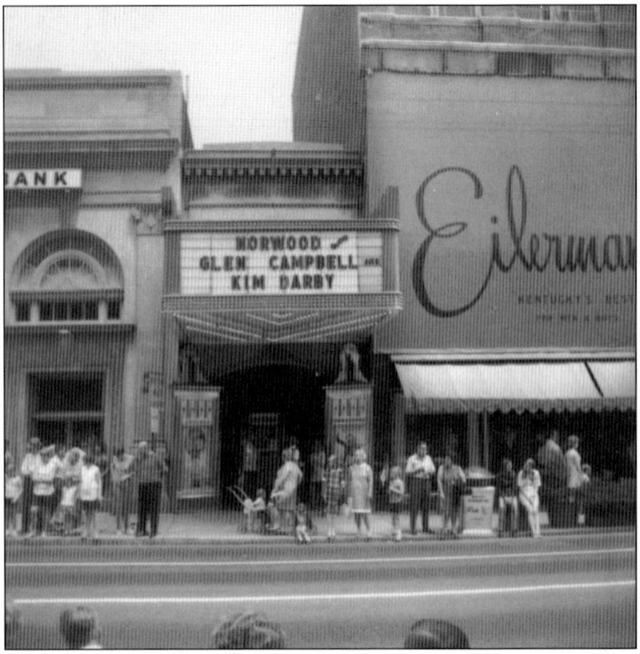

The Liberty Theater in Covington, Kentucky, was once a small movie palace. When it opened on July 21, 1923, the Liberty featured plush leather seats, a massive pipe organ, and a wonderful mural of the New York Harbor. It closed in the 1970s and was later demolished. (Kenton County Public Library, Covington, Kentucky.)

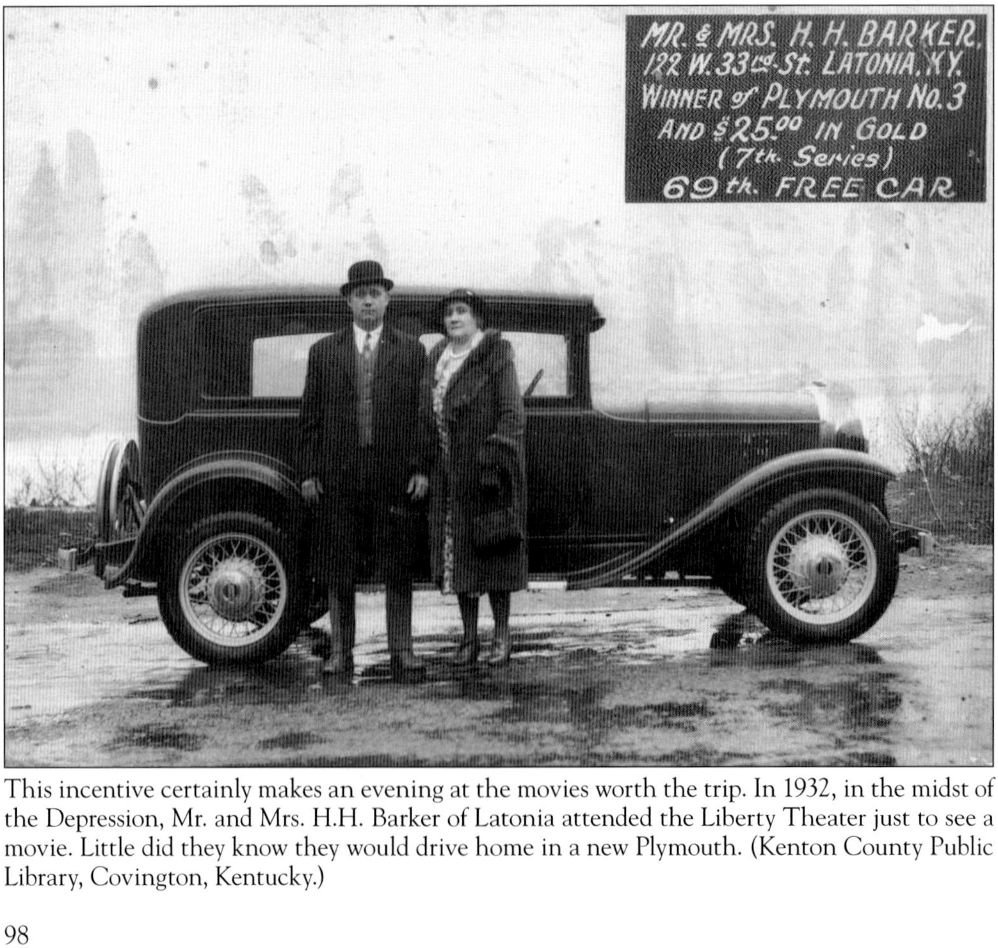

This incentive certainly makes an evening at the movies worth the trip. In 1932, in the midst of the Depression, Mr. and Mrs. H.H. Barker of Latonia attended the Liberty Theater just to see a movie. Little did they know they would drive home in a new Plymouth. (Kenton County Public Library, Covington, Kentucky.)

These women are taking a close look at a detailed replica of the Statue of Liberty in the elegant Italian marble lobby of the Liberty Theater on Madison Avenue in Covington. The theater opened on July 21, 1923, and closed in the 1970s; it was replaced with an office building. (Kenton County Public Library, Covington, Kentucky.)

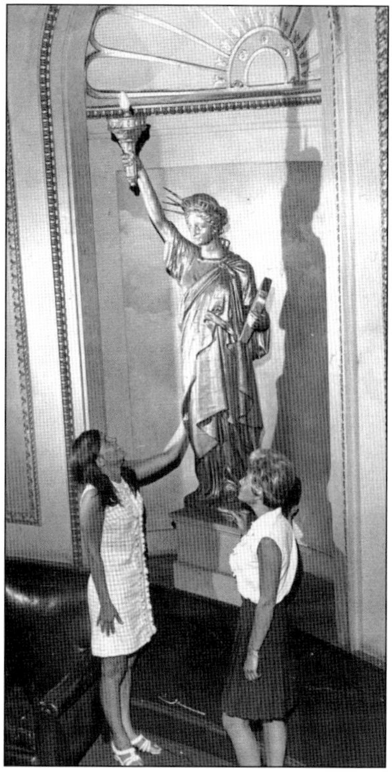

This image from 1943 shows the Liberty Theater devoid of its patriotic sign. During World War II, many decorative pieces of prominent local buildings—including a pyramid roof on the top of the temple-like structure on Cincinnati's Union Central (now PNC) Building—were taken away to be used as scrap metal for the war effort. (Kenton County Public Library, Covington, Kentucky.)

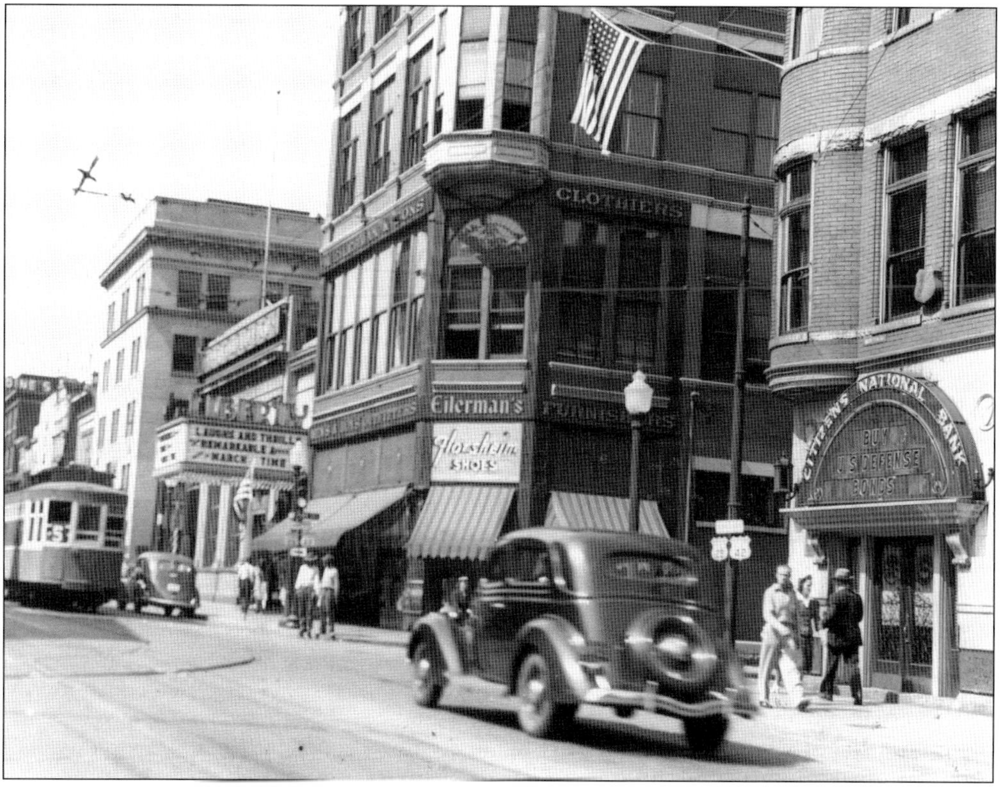

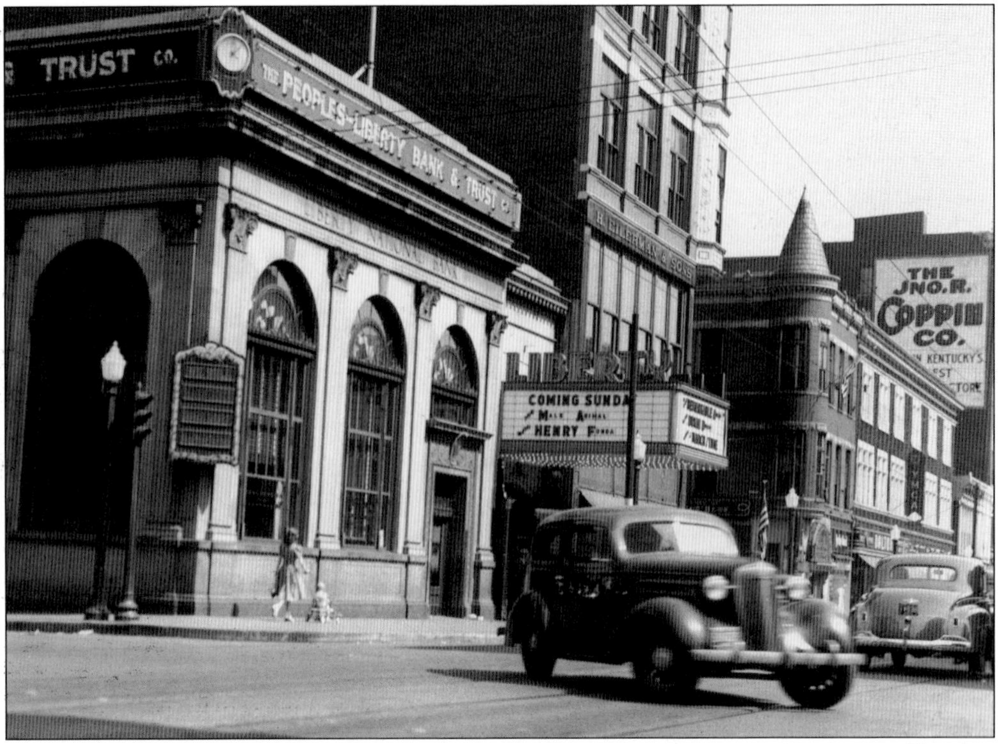

In this image, the Liberty Theater on Madison Avenue in Covington is advertising a film that reflects its name. The 1942 wartime offering *The Male Animal* stars Henry Fonda as a professor battling against tyrannical college trustees by reading a controversial poem to his students. (Kenton County Public Library, Covington, Kentucky.)

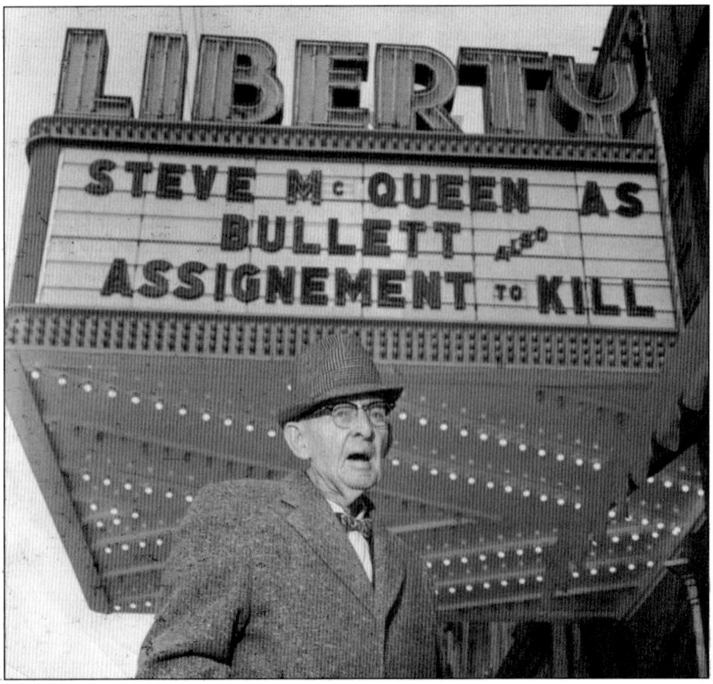

Much of the appeal of the old neighborhood theaters came from seeing familiar faces in the establishments. One of these was the long-serving ticket taker at the Liberty Theater, the charming Henry Hahn. (Kenton County Public Library, Covington, Kentucky.)

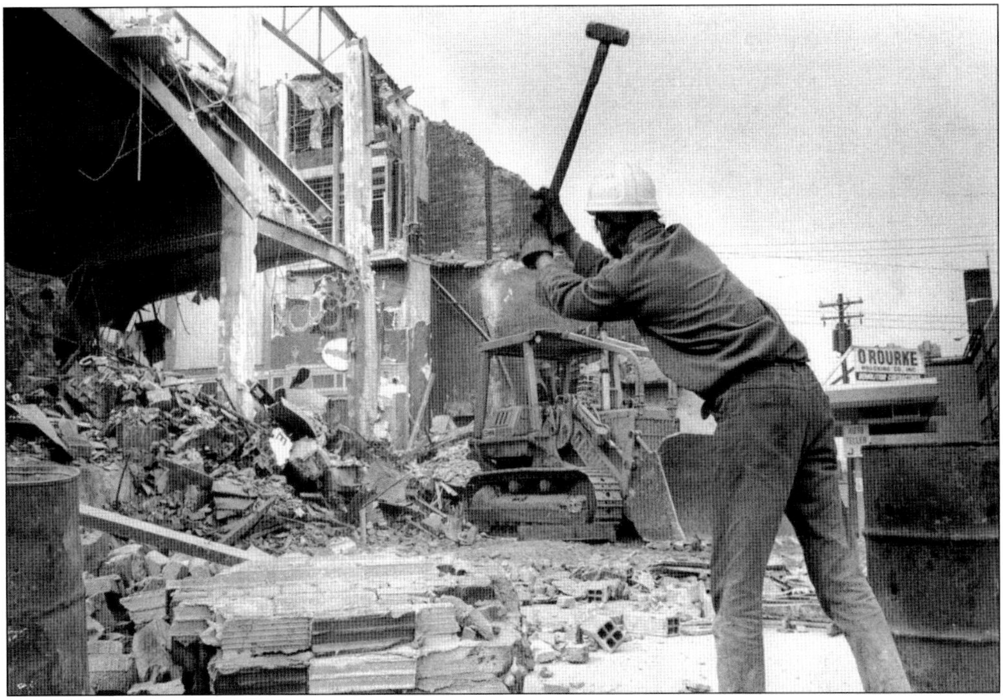

This image of demolition worker Dan Krabacher swinging his mallet recalls the following line from Shakespeare's *Cymbeline*, Act IV, Scene II: "Thou thy worldly task hast done, Home art gone, and ta'en thy wages; Golden lads and girls all must, As chimney-sweepers, come to dust." The same end came to the Liberty Theater in 1970. (Kenton County Public Library, Covington, Kentucky.)

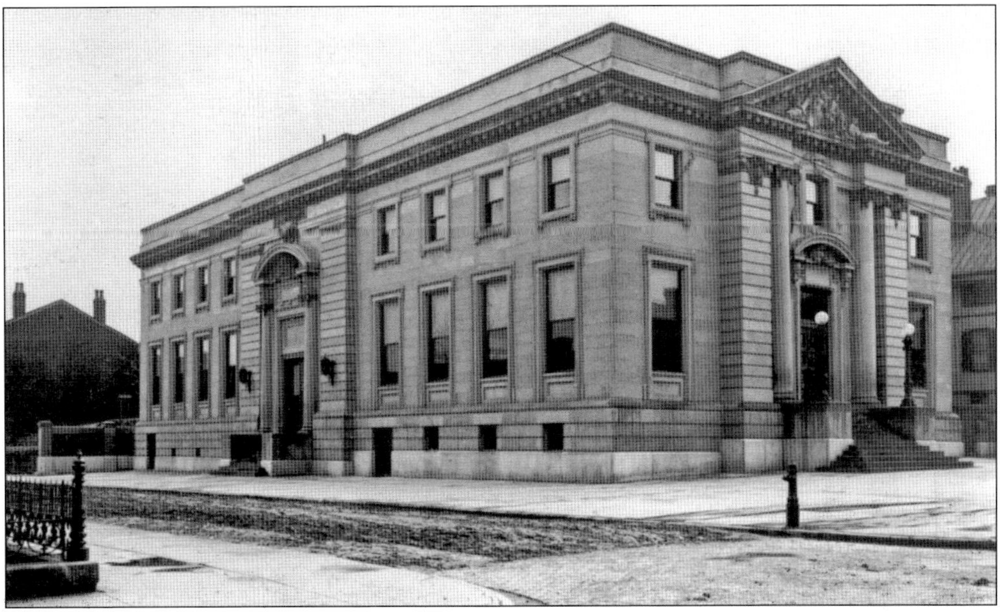

While Music Hall is undoubtedly the finest theater in Cincinnati proper, another marvelous showplace from the Gilded Age is right across the river in Covington, Kentucky. The Carnegie is one of very few Carnegie libraries that has a working theater connected to it. (Carnegie Library, Covington, Kentucky.)

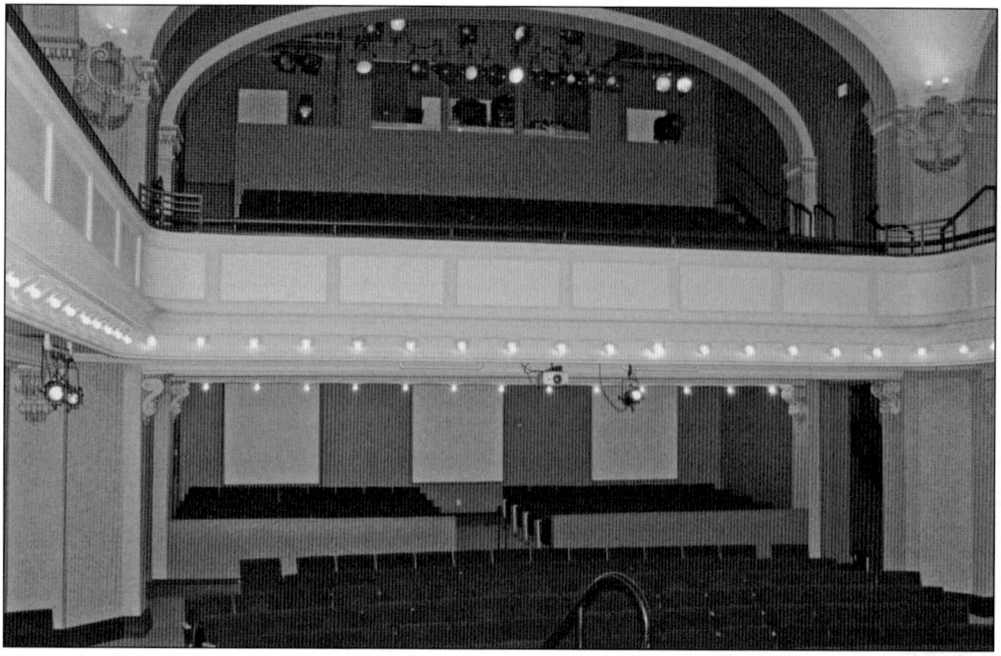

Industrialist and philanthropist Andrew Carnegie provided the funds for a first-rate library in Covington. Covington mayor Joseph Rhinock journeyed to New York to petition for a theater adjacent to the library. Carnegie agreed, sending a telegram simply stating, "Hearty congratulations. Go ahead." The theater opened in 1906. (Carnegie Library, Covington, Kentucky.)

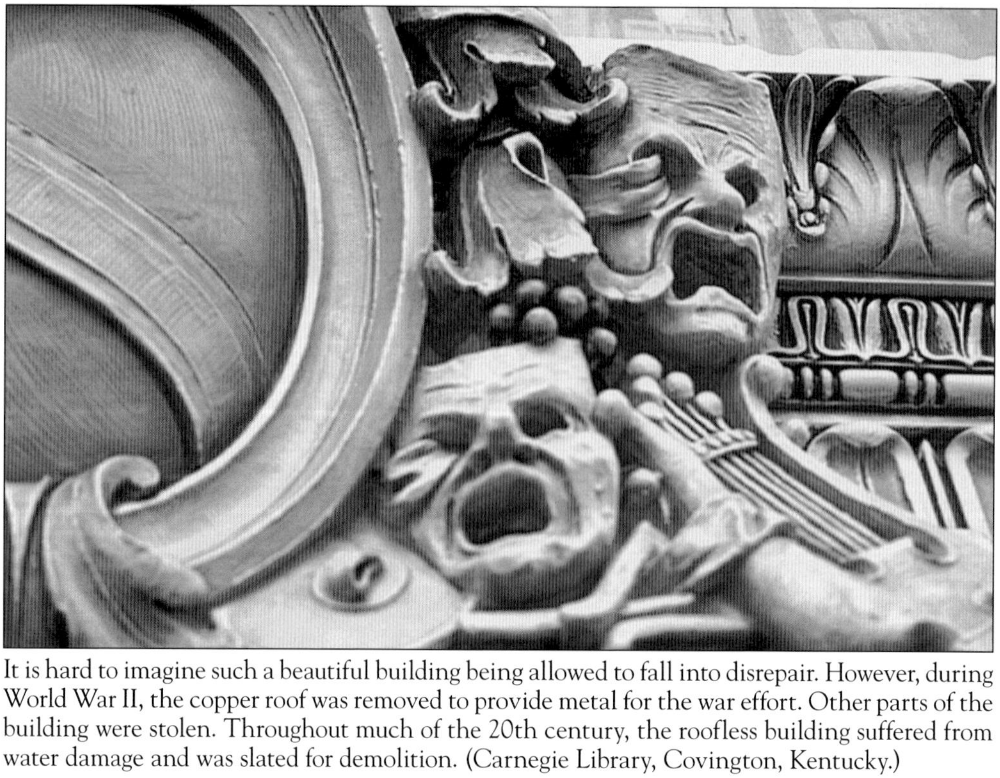

It is hard to imagine such a beautiful building being allowed to fall into disrepair. However, during World War II, the copper roof was removed to provide metal for the war effort. Other parts of the building were stolen. Throughout much of the 20th century, the roofless building suffered from water damage and was slated for demolition. (Carnegie Library, Covington, Kentucky.)

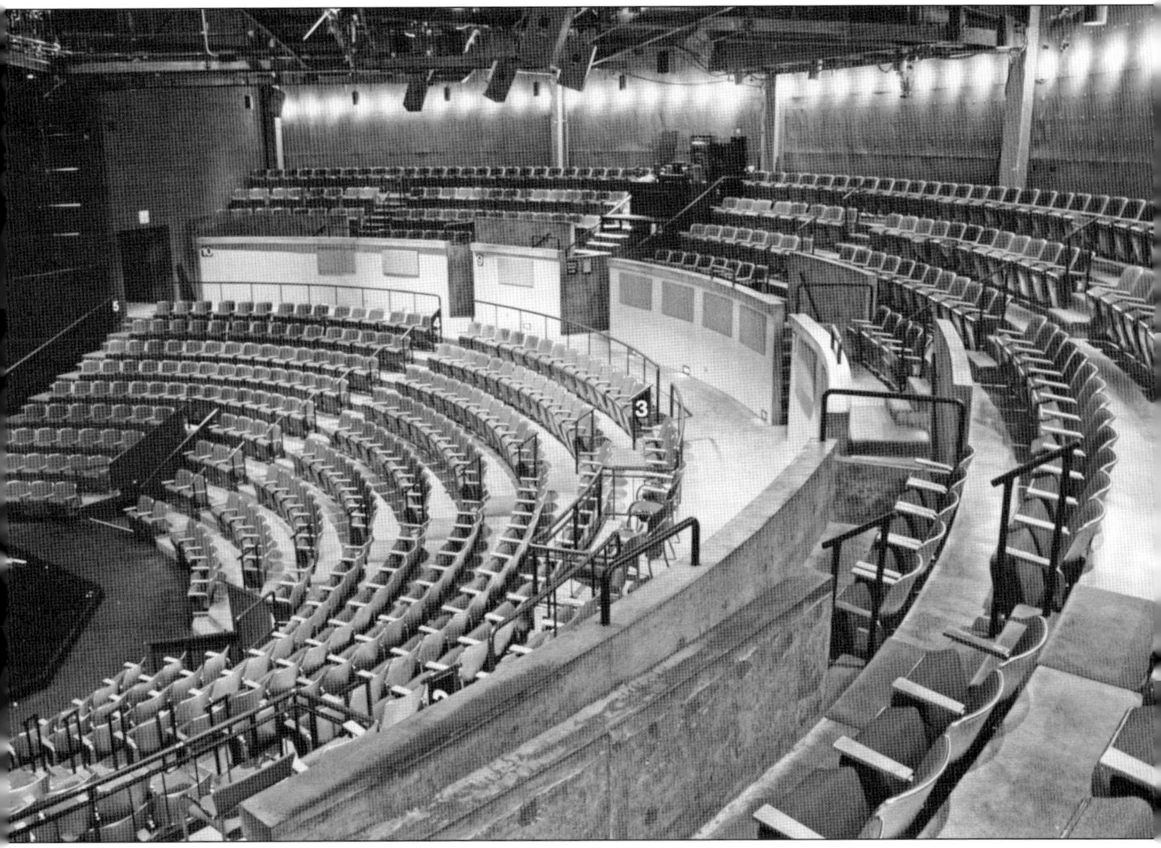

Despite having vines and even complete trees growing in what was once the theater, civic-minded people did not give up, instead gathering resources and contacting noted theatrical consultant Peter Wingate. Wingate examined the building and enthusiastically declared that the auditorium was acoustically perfect. It was now time to resurrect the glory of a past age. The Northern Kentucky Arts Council (now called The Carnegie Visual and Performing Arts Center) collected funds for necessary repairs. In 1979, an audience of 400 patrons sat in the theater on folding chairs and enjoyed a program featuring opera, Broadway tunes, and other musical selections. With hard work over many years, sufficient funds were raised, and thankfully, the Carnegie was restored. The Otto M. Budig Theatre at The Carnegie celebrated its grand reopening during the weekend of March 24–26, 2006. (Carnegie Library, Covington, Kentucky.)

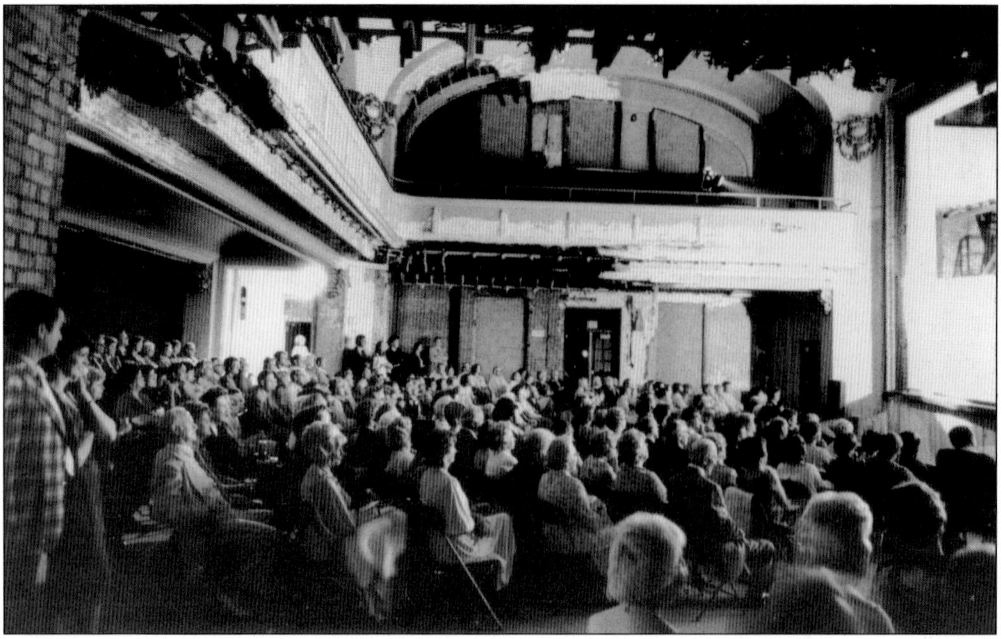

Another look at the building's interior reveals the repairs needed at The Carnegie prior to its restoration. As mentioned on the previous page, attendees at this 1979 fundraising event were seated in regular folding chairs rather than comfortable theater seats. (Kenton County Public Library, Covington, Kentucky.)

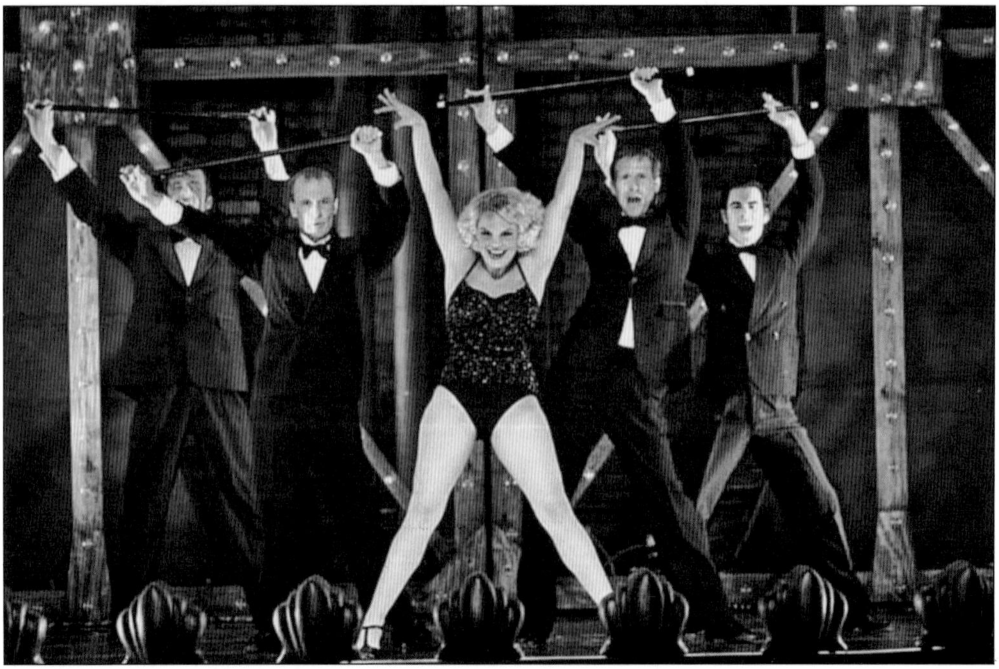

In 1909, the Carnegie hosted the rousing politician William Jennings Bryan. It is heartening to know that this historic venue has been saved. Today, people in the tristate area can still visit this wonderful institution to see first-rate productions, such as this 2013 performance of the musical *Chicago*. (Carnegie Library, Covington, Kentucky.)

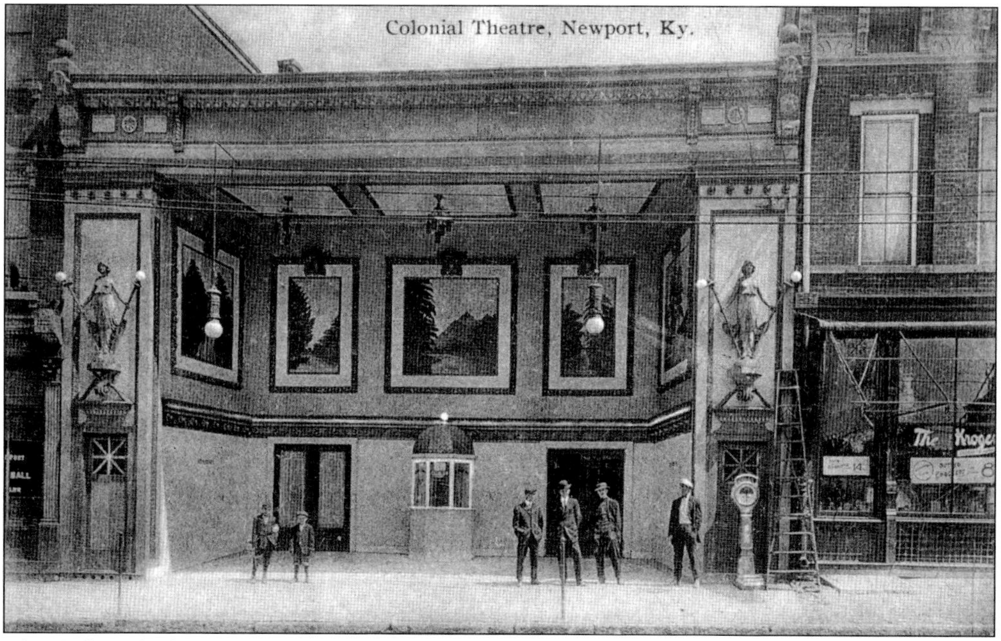

The Colonial Theatre was located in Newport, Kentucky, on the famous Monmouth Street, just south of Ninth Street. Built around 1911, it appeared to be one of the finest-looking small theaters in the area. However, looks can be deceiving, for the building was condemned and demolished in 1921. (Public Library of Cincinnati and Hamilton County.)

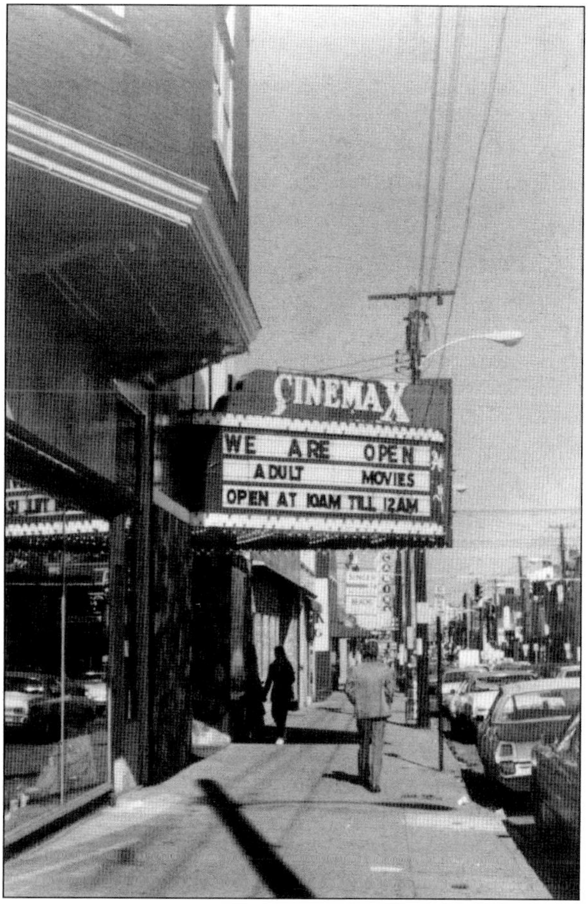

After the embarrassing George Ratterman scandal of the early 1960s, the gambling industry in Newport, Kentucky, closed shop and moved to Las Vegas. However, the city quickly degenerated into what had earlier been a sideline, the sex trade. On Monmouth Street, the old State Theater was converted into Cinema X. (Kenton County Public Library, Covington, Kentucky.)

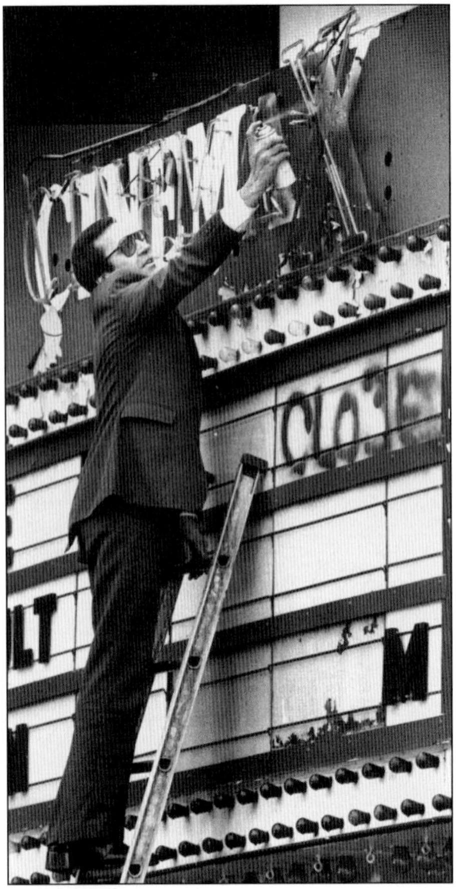

By the 1980s, the people of Newport were fed up with vice and corruption in their city. When Cinema X finally closed on March 11, 1982, Campbell County official Lloyd K. Rogers climbed a ladder and spray-painted over the offending sign. (Kenton County Public Library, Covington, Kentucky.)

By 1983, things were changing in Newport. The Cinema X was torn down, and its former location is now a parking lot. Today, Newport remains Cincinnati's playground, but now it is one that the entire family can visit. (Kenton County Public Library, Covington, Kentucky.)

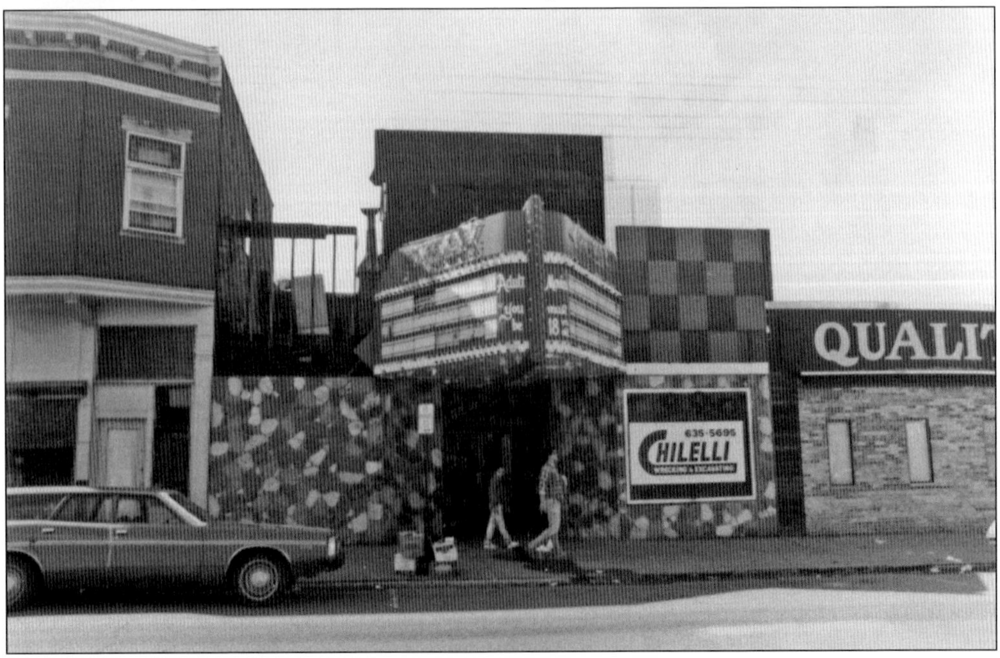

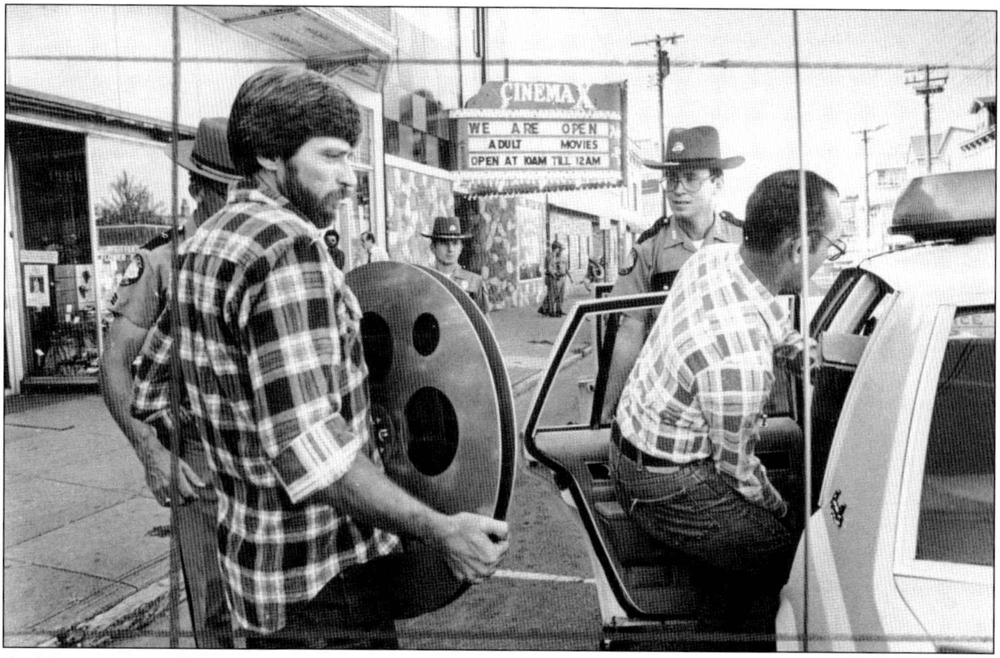

As Newport tried to clean up its image, one of the biggest targets was Cinema X, which showed hard-core pornography. Although the theater claims to be open, as shown on the marquee in the background, a police raid has removed a film from the premises. (Kenton County Public Library, Covington, Kentucky.)

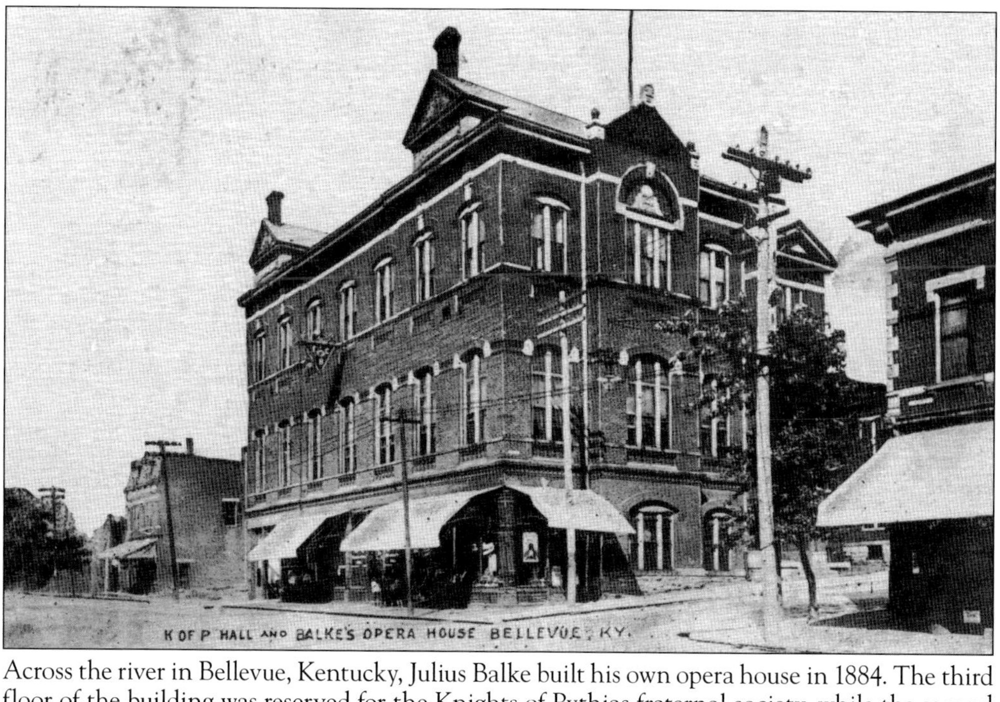

Across the river in Bellevue, Kentucky, Julius Balke built his own opera house in 1884. The third floor of the building was reserved for the Knights of Pythias fraternal society, while the second floor was an auditorium. Sadly, this beautiful old building was demolished in 1964. (Public Library of Cincinnati and Hamilton County.)

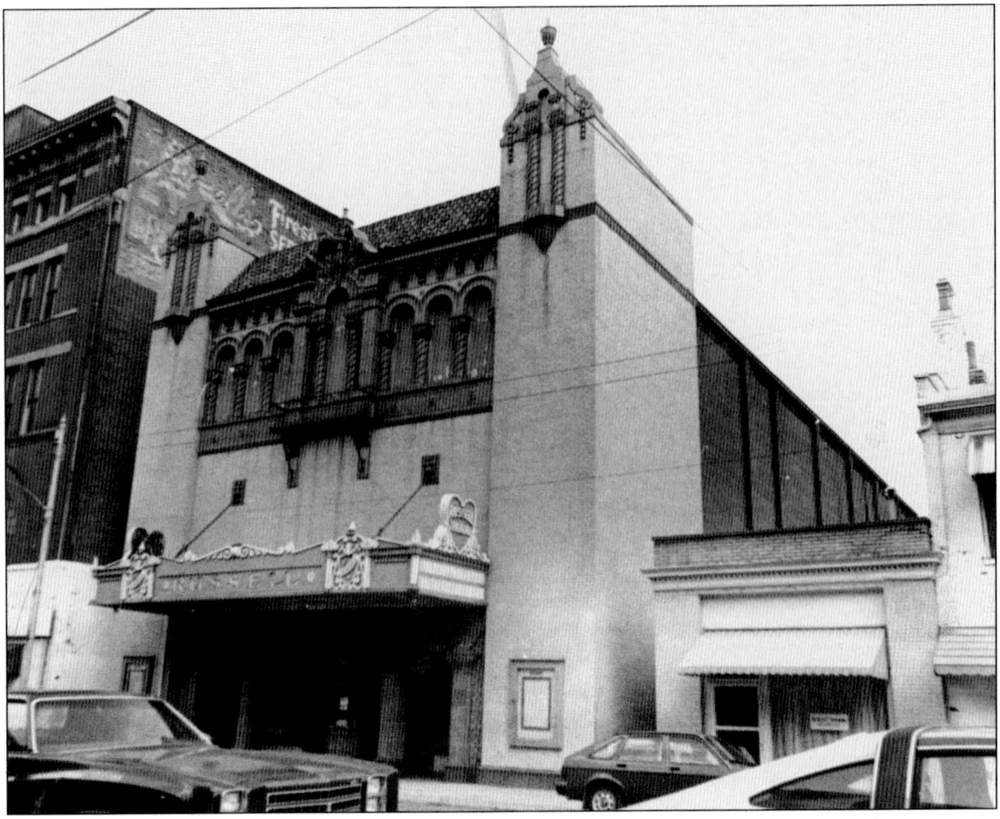

The Russell Theater in Maysville, Kentucky, opened in 1930. In 1953, it hosted the premiere of Rosemary Clooney's film *The Stars are Singing*. It closed in 1983. The building later housed a restaurant and a used clothing store before being abandoned. The roof was severely damaged in a storm, which allowed rain to ruin the building's interior plasterwork. (Kenton County Public Library, Covington, Kentucky.)

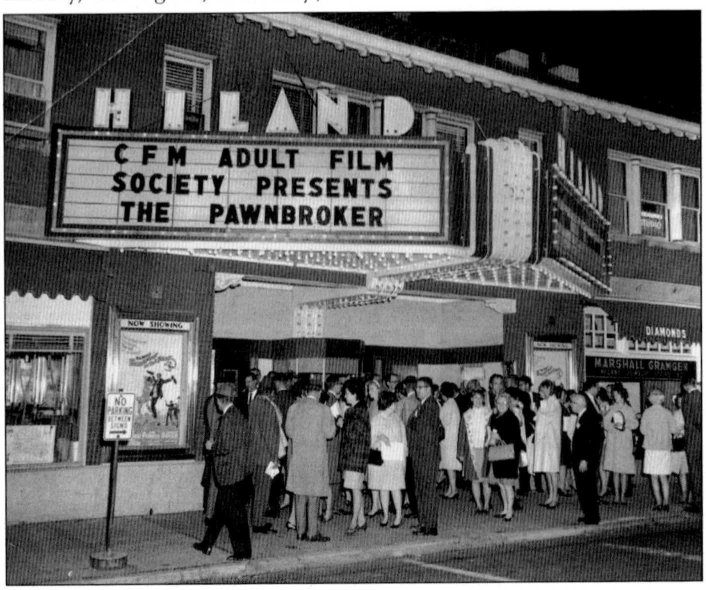

The Hiland Theater in Fort Thomas, Kentucky, was housed in one of the first buildings in the business district. During its long history, the building was also a tearoom and even a candy shop. The theater closed in the 1970s. (Kenton County Public Library, Covington, Kentucky.)

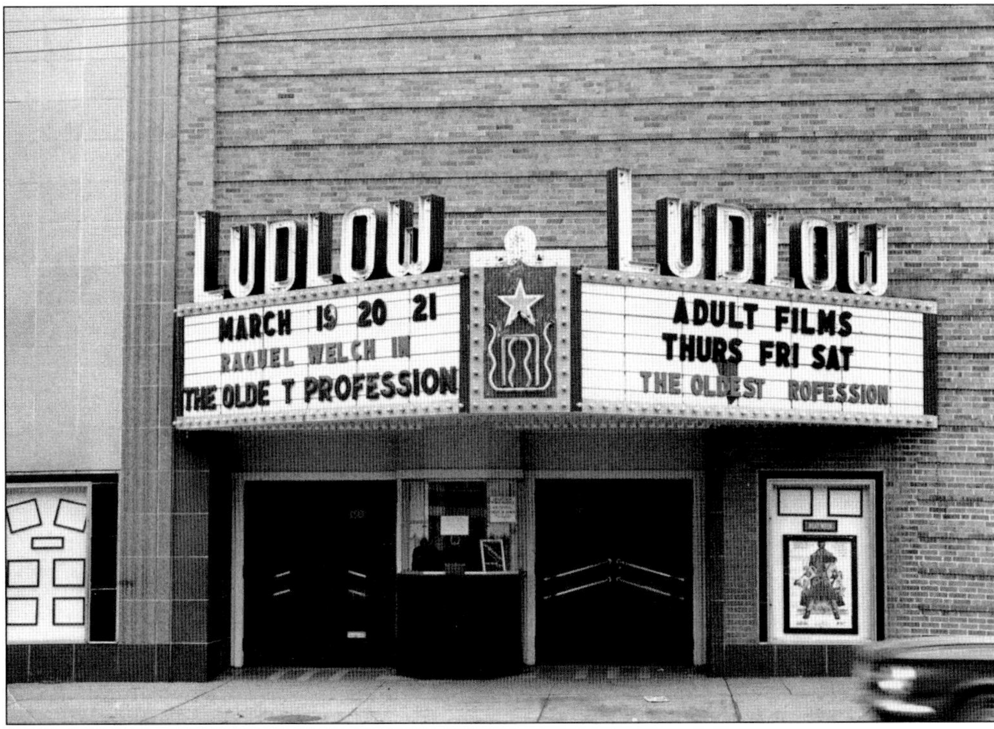

The Ludlow Theatre in Ludlow, Kentucky, is at the center of one of the strangest stories about the resurrection of an old theater. It opened as a movie house in 1946 but eventually went the way of other neighborhood cinemas. However, it came back as an entertainment center, of all things, housing a circus, the Circus Mojo, which began operations in the building in 2009. (Kenton County Public Library, Covington, Kentucky.)

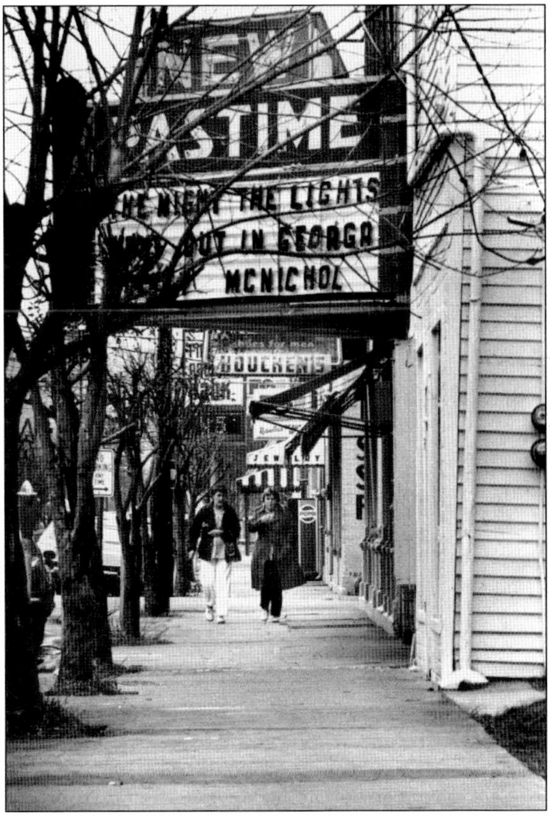

In this 1981 image, the marquee of the New Pastime theater in Falmouth, Kentucky, is advertising former child star Kristy McNichol in a film based on the popular song "The Night the Lights Went Out in Georgia." Neither the film nor the theater have survived the test of time. The building is now for sale. (Kenton County Public Library, Covington, Kentucky.)

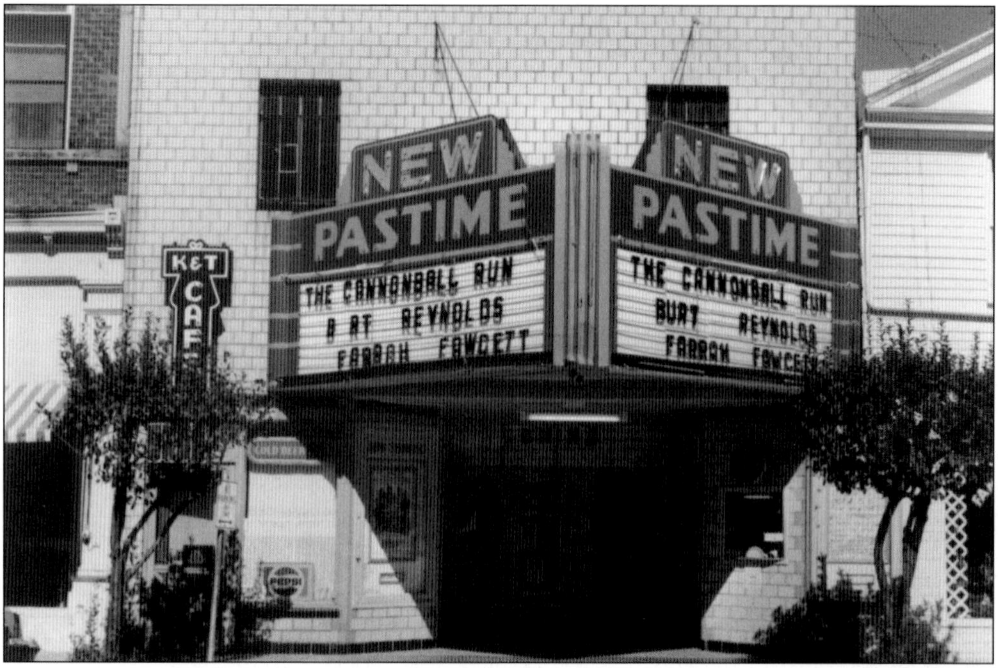

Located just a block from the Licking River, the New Pastime Theater in Falmouth, Kentucky, opened before the Second World War. It was originally known as simply the Pastime Theater. (Kenton County Public Library, Covington, Kentucky.)

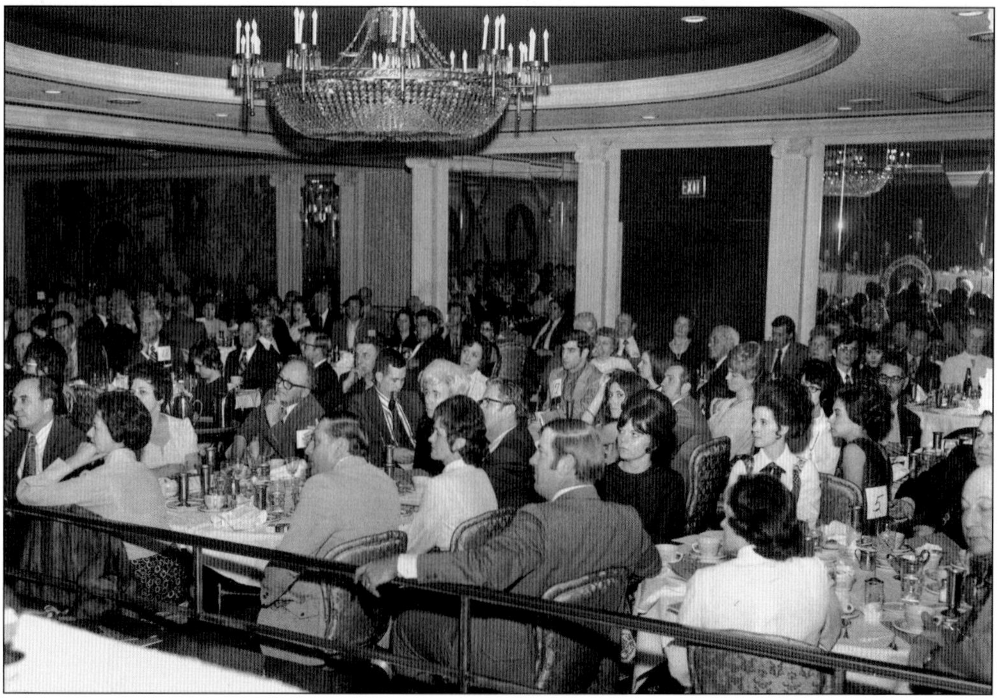

The Beverly Hills Supper Club in Southgate, Kentucky, attracted some of the finest acts, who would often fine-tune their material before going to Las Vegas. However, as elegant as the club was, it seemed to be under a curse. (Kenton County Public Library, Covington, Kentucky.)

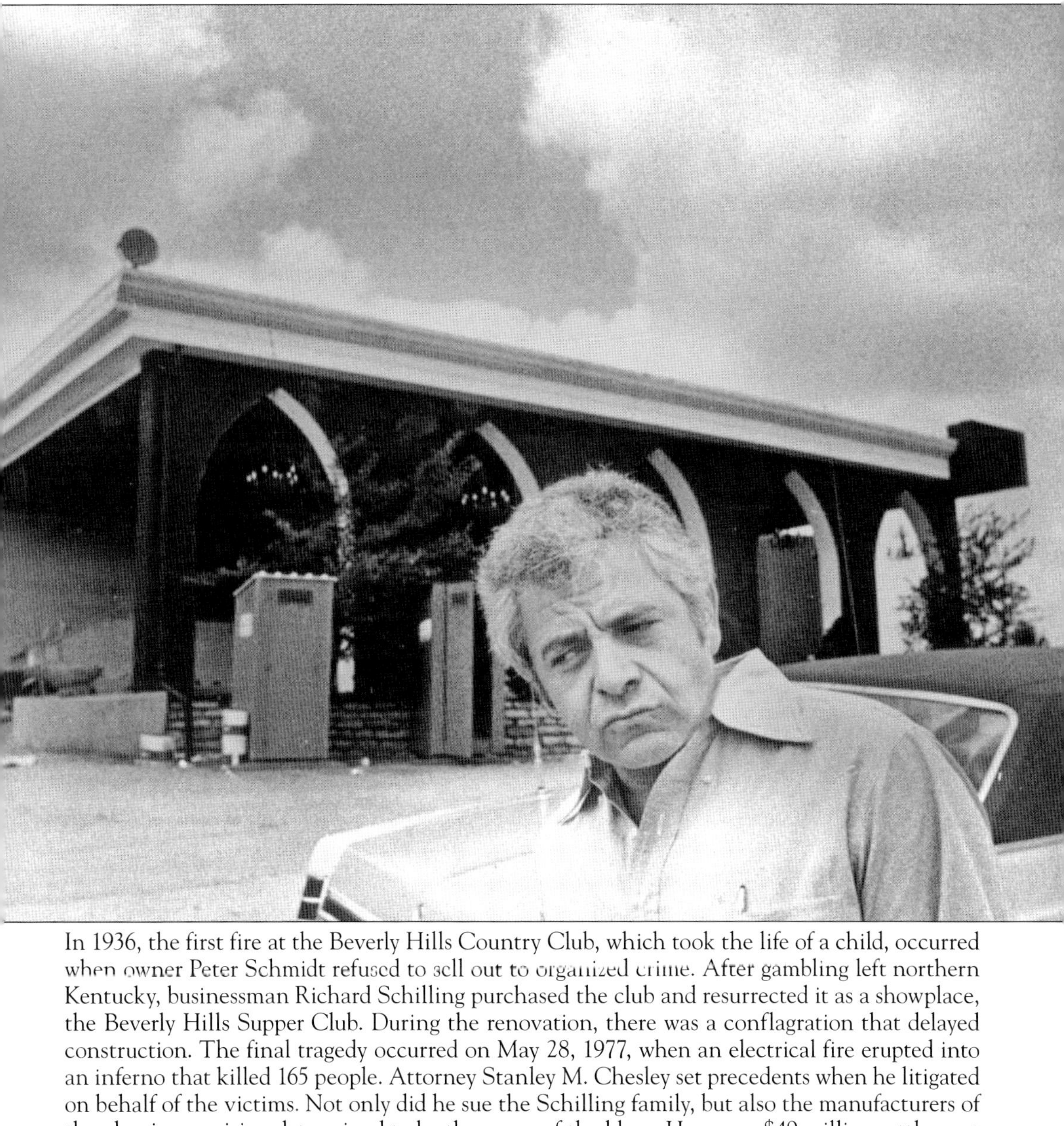

In 1936, the first fire at the Beverly Hills Country Club, which took the life of a child, occurred when owner Peter Schmidt refused to sell out to organized crime. After gambling left northern Kentucky, businessman Richard Schilling purchased the club and resurrected it as a showplace, the Beverly Hills Supper Club. During the renovation, there was a conflagration that delayed construction. The final tragedy occurred on May 28, 1977, when an electrical fire erupted into an inferno that killed 165 people. Attorney Stanley M. Chesley set precedents when he litigated on behalf of the victims. Not only did he sue the Schilling family, but also the manufacturers of the aluminum wiring determined to be the cause of the blaze. He won a $49 million settlement and helped to change building codes in an effort to prevent such tragedies from happening in the future. (Kenton County Public Library, Covington, Kentucky.)

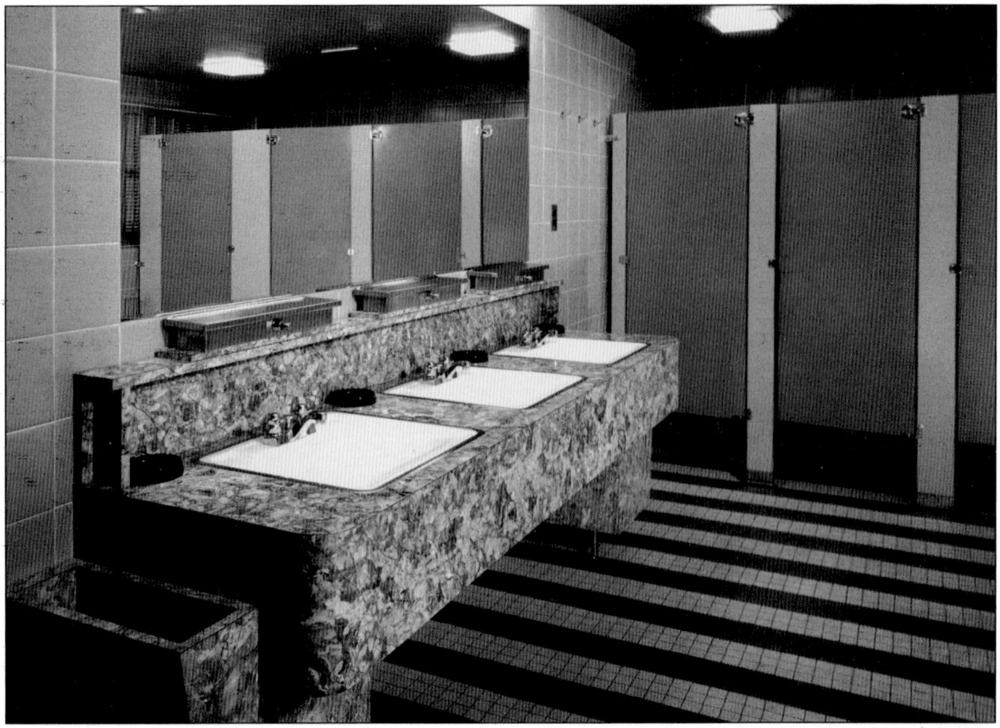

Gangs of organized crime wanted to take control of the original Beverly Hills Country Club, located in Southgate, Kentucky, from moonshiner Peter Schmidt because the nightclub was a prestige establishment, what the Mob called a "carpet joint." The rebuilt Beverly Hills Supper Club was no longer connected to organized crime, but as this photograph of the luxurious bathrooms attests, the supper club carried on the tradition of elegance and sophistication. (Kenton County Public Library, Covington, Kentucky.)

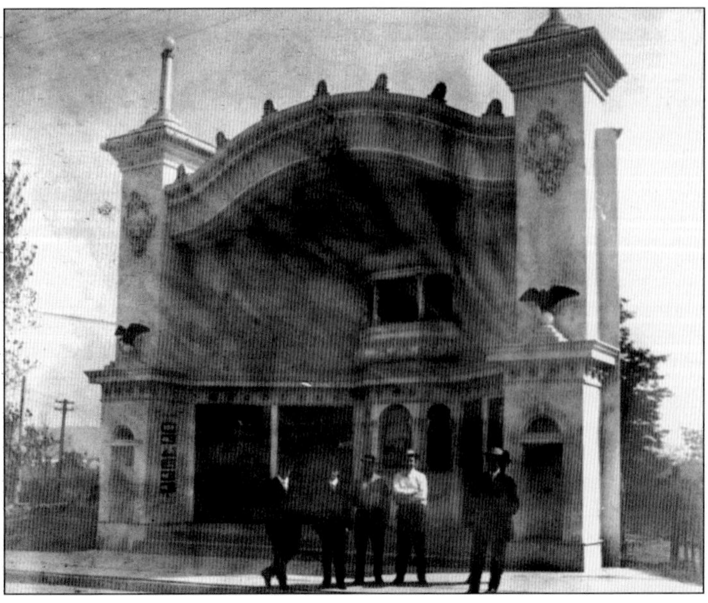

Although the quality of the photograph is poor, this is an extremely rare view of the Delbee Theater, which opened in Latonia in 1910, from the days when it showed hand-wound silent films. It was later known as the Derby Theater, which had a far more subdued facade. The Derby closed in the 1940s. (Kenton County Public Library, Covington, Kentucky.)

This 1983 photograph of Bellevue's Marianne Theater shows an Art Deco movie house in decline. (Kenton County Public Library, Covington, Kentucky.)

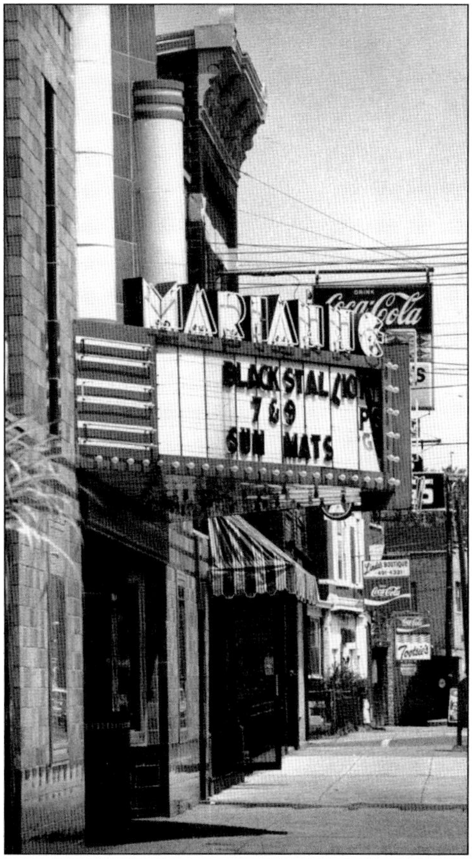

Today, this Art Deco building in Covington is home to Mike's Music, a store specializing in vintage instruments, but it once housed the Family Theater, opened by Nicholas Shafer in 1916. (Photograph by Doug Weise.)

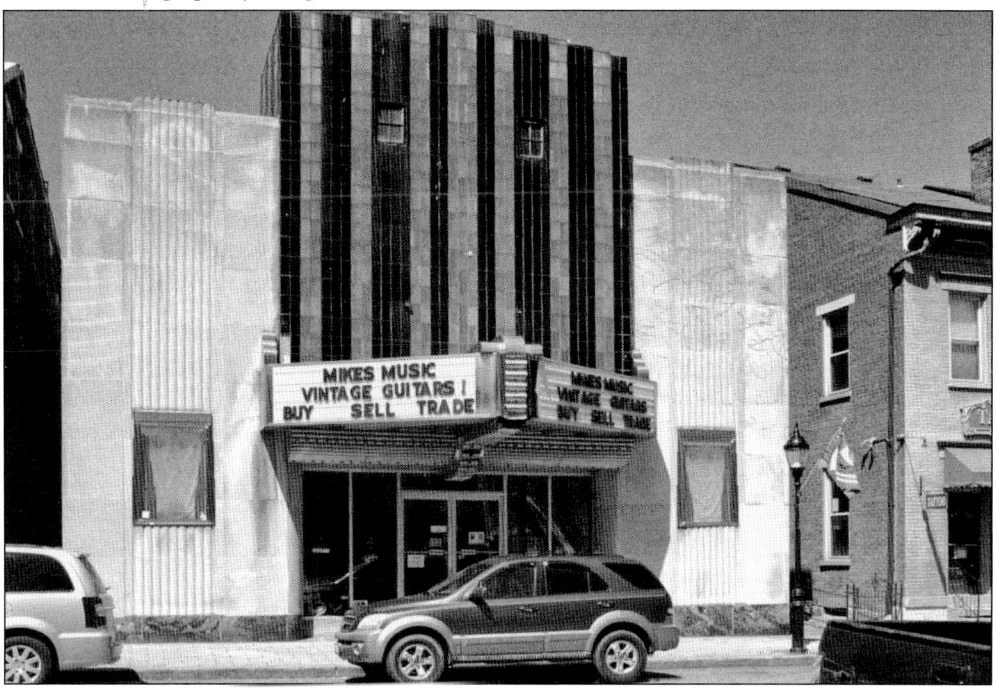

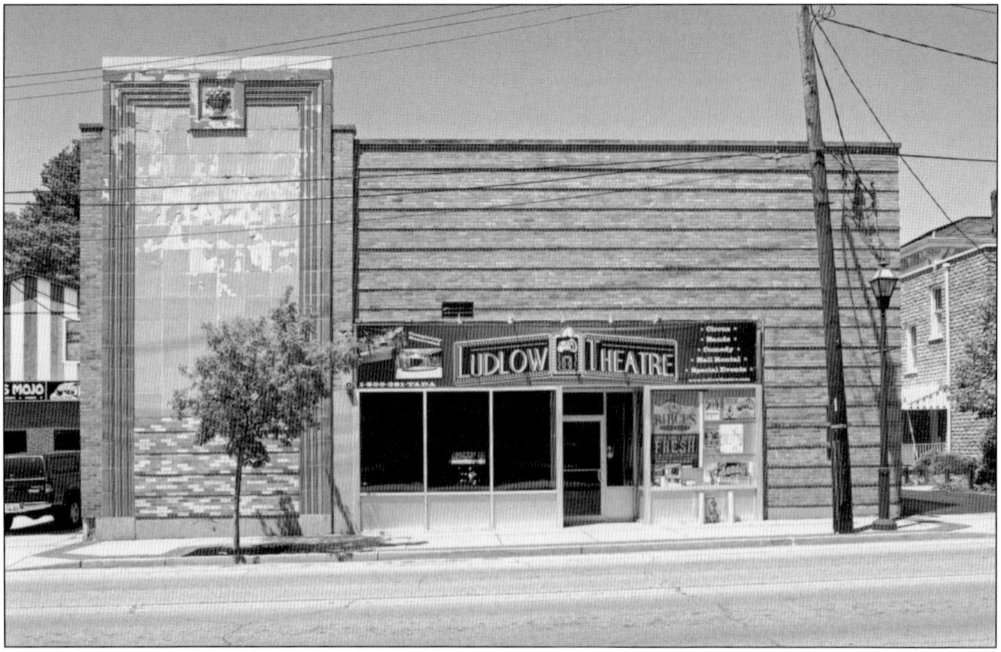

The Ludlow Theatre, located at 322 Elm Street in Ludlow, Kentucky, opened shortly after World War II. By the early 1980s, it had become a second-run dollar theater, which it remained until finally closing its doors forever. Thankfully, the beautiful Art Deco building has survived. (Photograph by Doug Weise.)

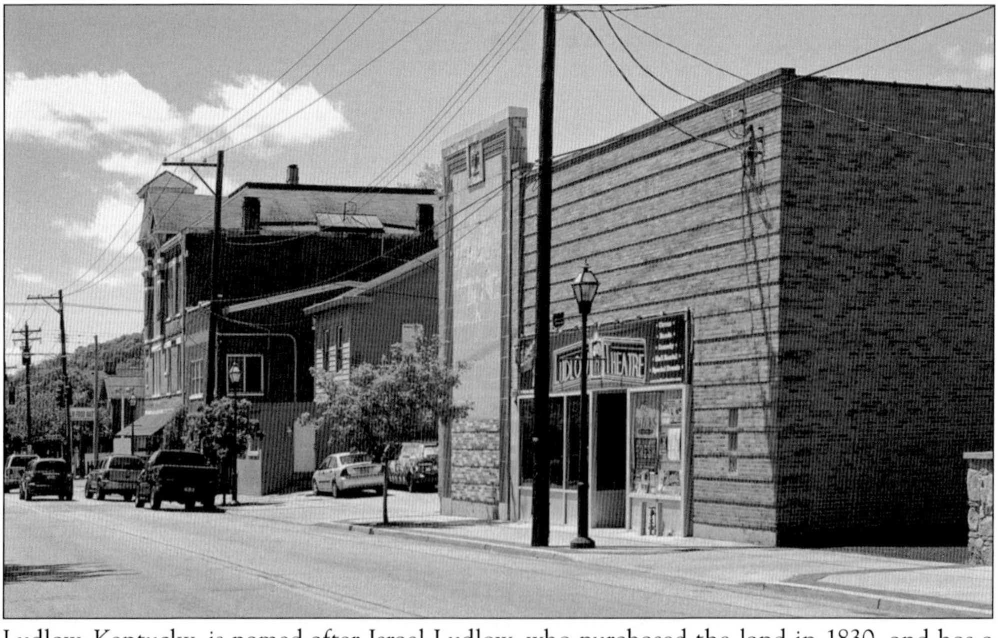

Ludlow, Kentucky, is named after Israel Ludlow, who purchased the land in 1830, and has a history of entertainment. Ludlow Lagoon, a massive man-made lake built in 1894, included five islands and an amphitheater for concerts; the park closed in 1918. The city later served as the setting for the film *Lost in Yonkers*. The old Ludlow Theater is slated to become a microbrewery and restaurant. (Photograph by Doug Weise.)

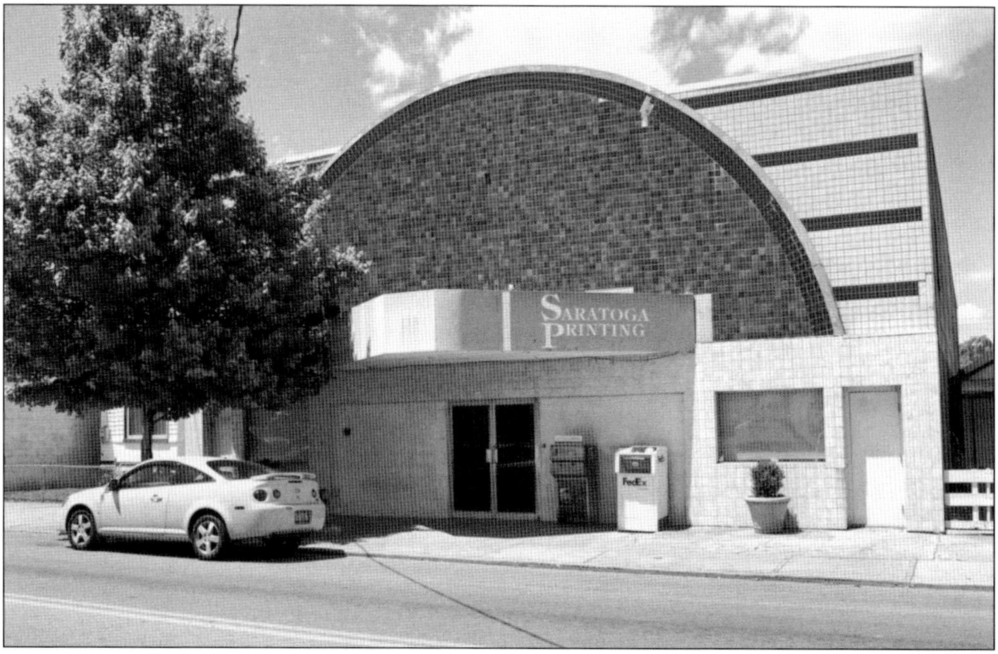

A look at the marvelous facade of this building reveals its former life as a movie house, the Dayvue Theater, located in Dayton, Kentucky. Woodrow and Jerome Bressler opened the Dayvue in 1941. It was situated quite close to the popular Marianne Theater in Bellevue. The theater closed in 1955 and now houses the Saratoga Printing Company. (Photograph by Doug Weise.)

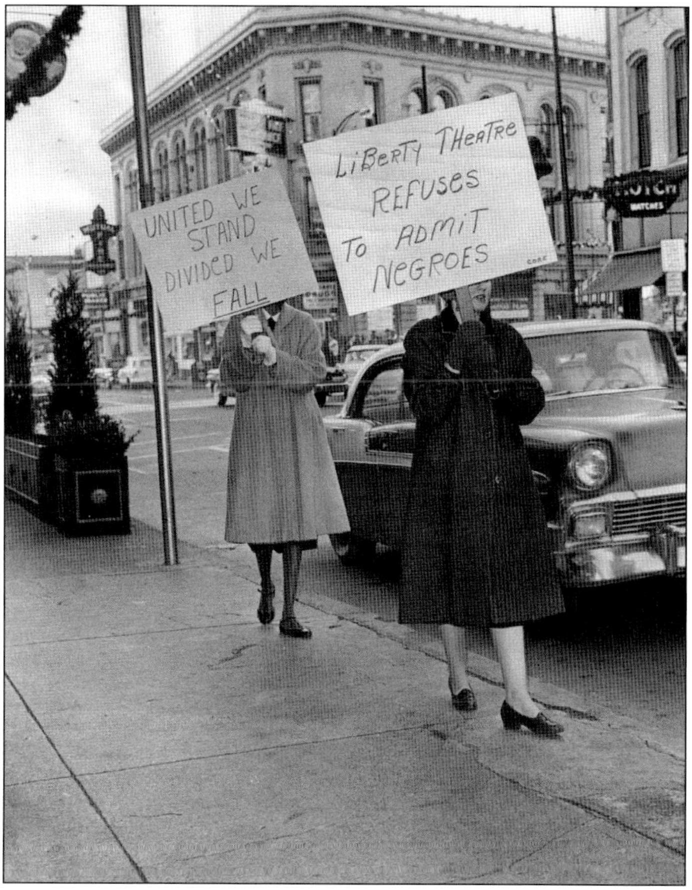

Protestors in the tristate area demonstrated against segregation at the Liberty Theatre in the early 1960s. Similar protests were staged at the Coney Island amusement park. (Kenton County Public Library, Covington, Kentucky.)

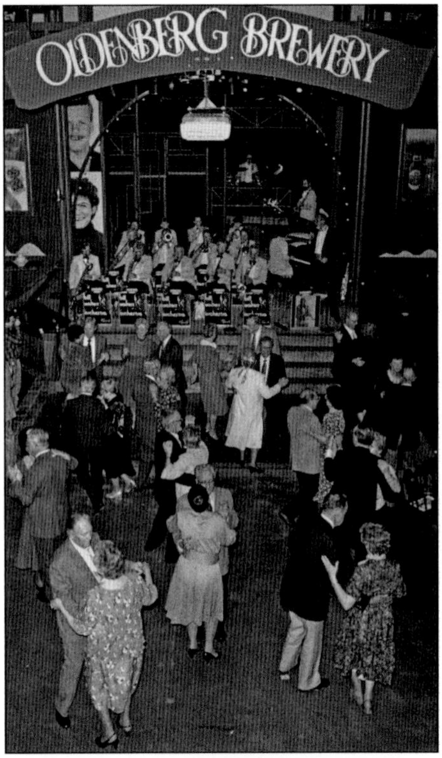

This photograph from the Oldenberg Brewery, located at Fort Mitchell's Drawbridge Inn, could be from Cincinnati's olden days of German biergartens. However, a close look at the pictures behind Bill Walter's Big Band reveals that this is a group of dancers reliving the glory days of Glenn Miller. (Kenton County Public Library, Covington, Kentucky.)

The Ludlow Theatre expresses its hometown pride with a salute to the Class A Champs on its marquee. This movie house opened shortly after World War II. Note the Art Deco facade to the left of the entrance, including the subdued decoration near the top. (Kenton County Public Library, Covington, Kentucky.)

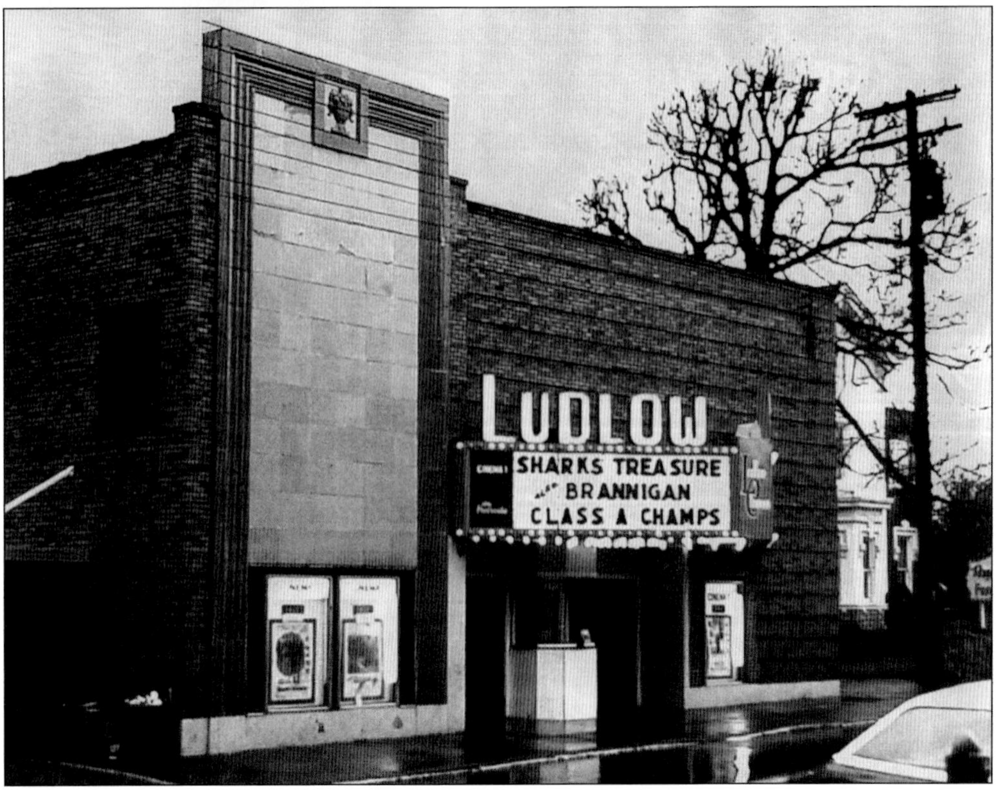

Five

Please Replace Speakers Before Exiting

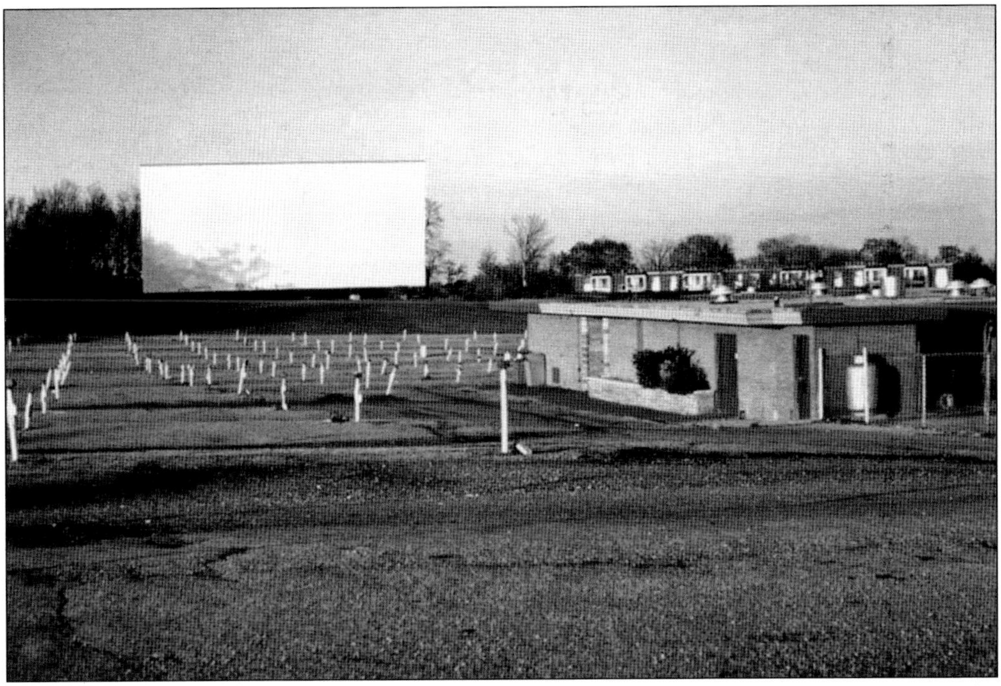

The Ferguson Hills Drive-In, located in the Western Hills area, opened in August 1958. As the years went by, and it became obvious that the final curtain was about to close, the owners attempted such schemes as showing horror movies and other bizarre films from sunset up until sunrise. The land is now home to a Walmart. (Phil Lind and the Ray Grothaus Collection.)

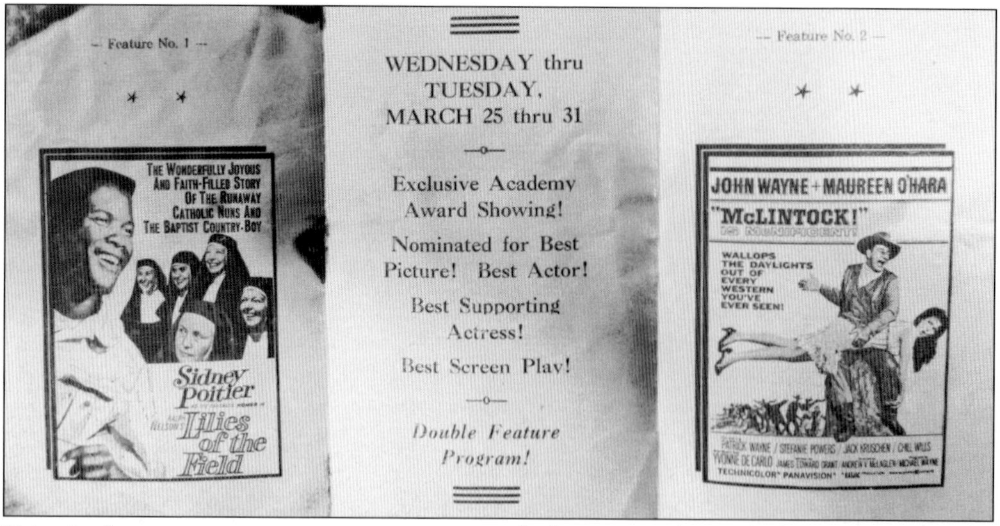

Drive-in theaters were in intense competition with the new medium of television. To keep the customers coming, they would enhance the experience by giving out informative pamphlets or gifts. This pamphlet from the Ferguson Hills Drive-In depicts a curious contrast: Sidney Poitier with a group of nuns on one side and a "McNificent" John Wayne administering corporal punishment on the other. (Tom Wernke.)

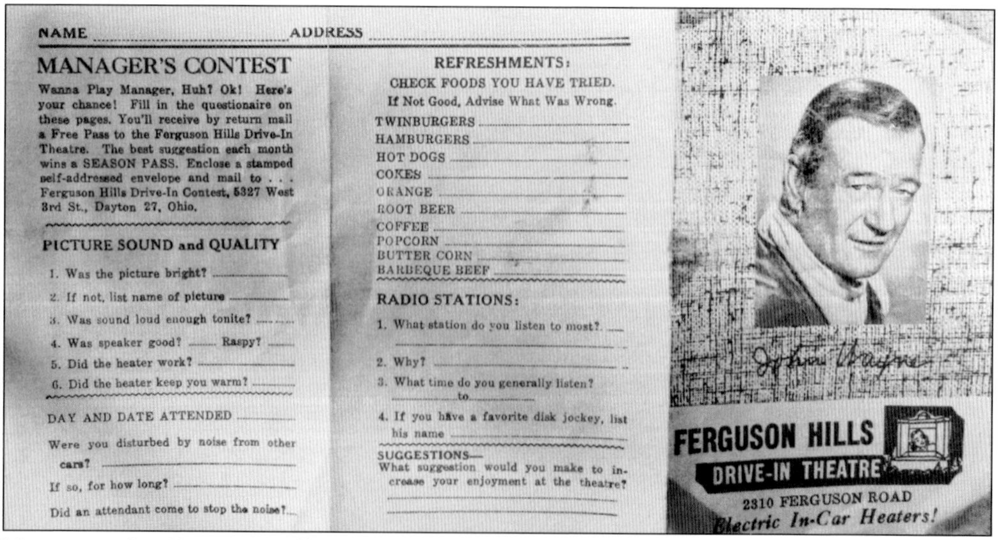
NAME .... ADDRESS ....

MANAGER'S CONTEST

Wanna Play Manager, Huh? Ok! Here's your chance! Fill in the questionaire on these pages. You'll receive by return mail a Free Pass to the Ferguson Hills Drive-In Theatre. The best suggestion each month wins a SEASON PASS. Enclose a stamped self-addressed envelope and mail to . . . Ferguson Hills Drive-In Contest, 5327 West 3rd St., Dayton 27, Ohio.

PICTURE SOUND and QUALITY

1. Was the picture bright? ....
2. If not, list name of picture ....
3. Was sound loud enough tonite? ....
4. Was speaker good? .... Raspy? ....
5. Did the heater work? ....
6. Did the heater keep you warm? ....

DAY AND DATE ATTENDED ....

Were you disturbed by noise from other cars? ....

If so, for how long? ....

Did an attendant come to stop the noise? ....

REFRESHMENTS:

CHECK FOODS YOU HAVE TRIED.
If Not Good, Advise What Was Wrong.

TWINBURGERS ....
HAMBURGERS ....
HOT DOGS ....
COKES ....
ORANGE ....
ROOT BEER ....
COFFEE ....
POPCORN ....
BUTTER CORN ....
BARBEQUE BEEF ....

RADIO STATIONS:

1. What station do you listen to most? ....
2. Why? ....
3. What time do you generally listen? .... to ....
4. If you have a favorite disk jockey, list his name ....

SUGGESTIONS—
What suggestion would you make to increase your enjoyment at the theatre?

John Wayne

FERGUSON HILLS
DRIVE-IN THEATRE
2310 FERGUSON ROAD
Electric In-Car Heaters!

Here is another Ferguson Hill Drive-In pamphlet with John Wayne—not spanking anyone this time. It also included a survey for their own marketing research. Notice the mention of "Electric In-Car Heaters" (which, for the record, never kept a car warm). These devices were an attempt to extend the season for going to the drive-in. (Tom Wernke.)

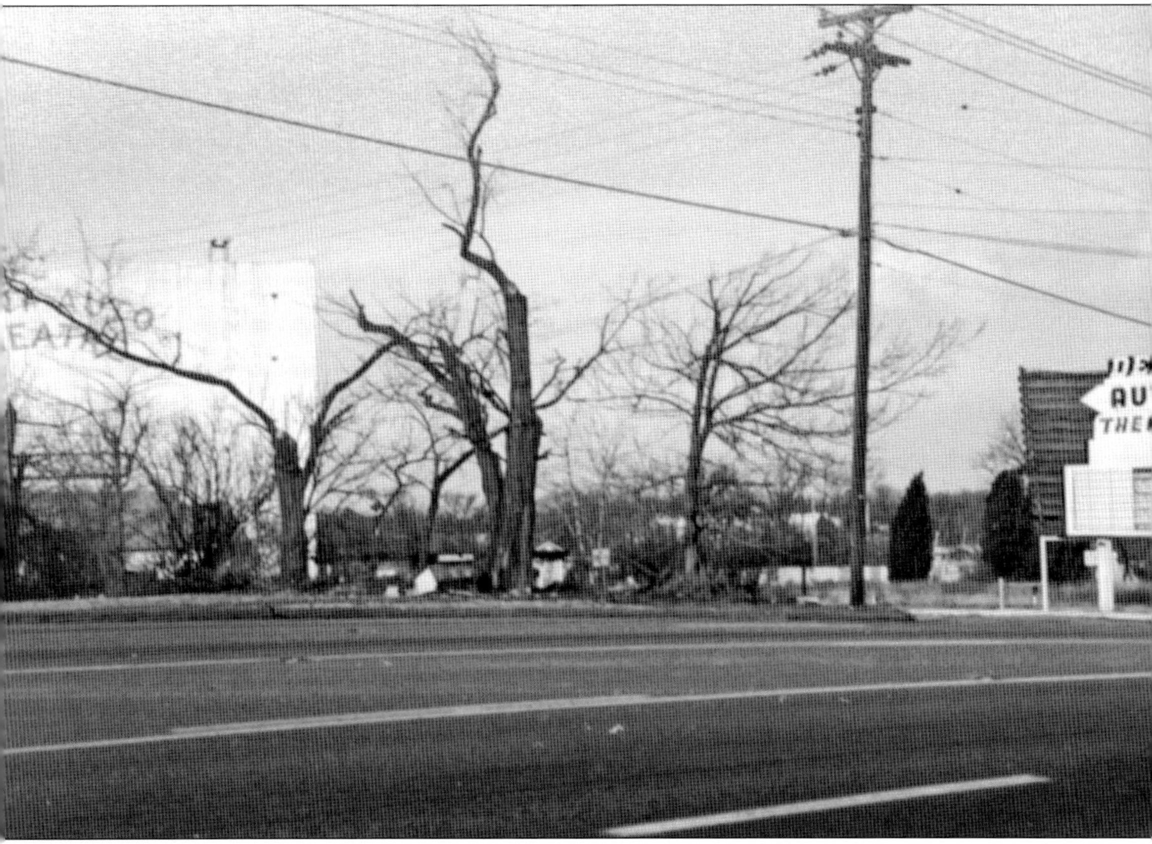

Sometimes words come together accidentally and give an entirely different, sometimes comical, meaning. In the mid-1800s, Rev. James Challenge owned a great deal of land west of the growing city of Cincinnati. The new rural community of mostly German farmers was first known as "Challengeville" to honor their founder. Later, the small village was renamed "Dent," leading to the most tongue-in-cheek name for a drive-in theater. Although the drive-in is gone, the area is today best known for a peculiar form of modern entertainment, the celebrated Halloween haunted house known as the Dent Schoolhouse. (Phil Lind.)

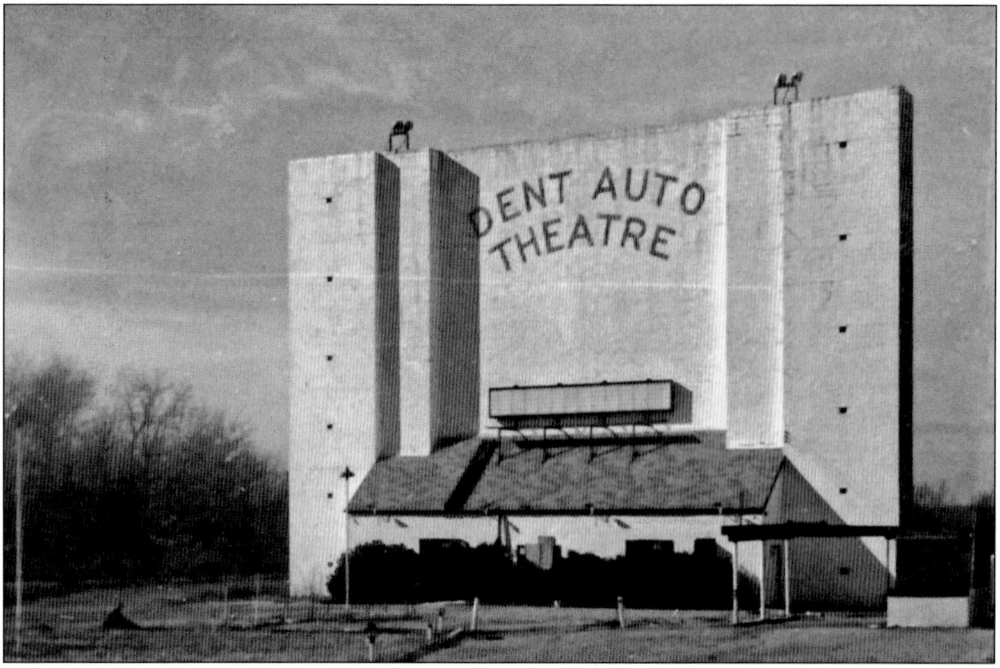

Although somewhat jokingly named, the Dent Auto Theatre was extremely popular on the west side of town. It opened in July 1949 with the film *Outpost in Morocco*, and throughout the 1950s and 1960s, it was extremely popular with young people. Today, the area is a park. (Tom Wernke.)

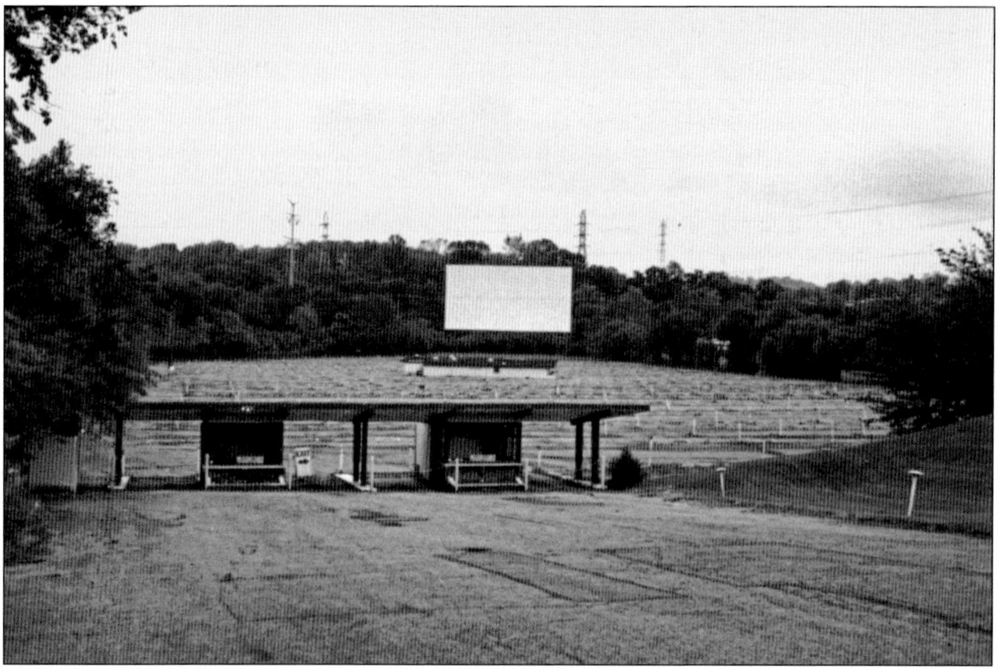

Here is a picture of tenacity. The Oakley Drive-In on Madison Road near Madisonville first opened its gates in 1952. Despite showing such first-run films as Tim Burton's classic *Batman*, time eventually caught up with the old tradition. Even the Caped Crusader could not rescue the drive-in, which closed in 2005. (Phil Lind and the Ray Grothaus Collection.)

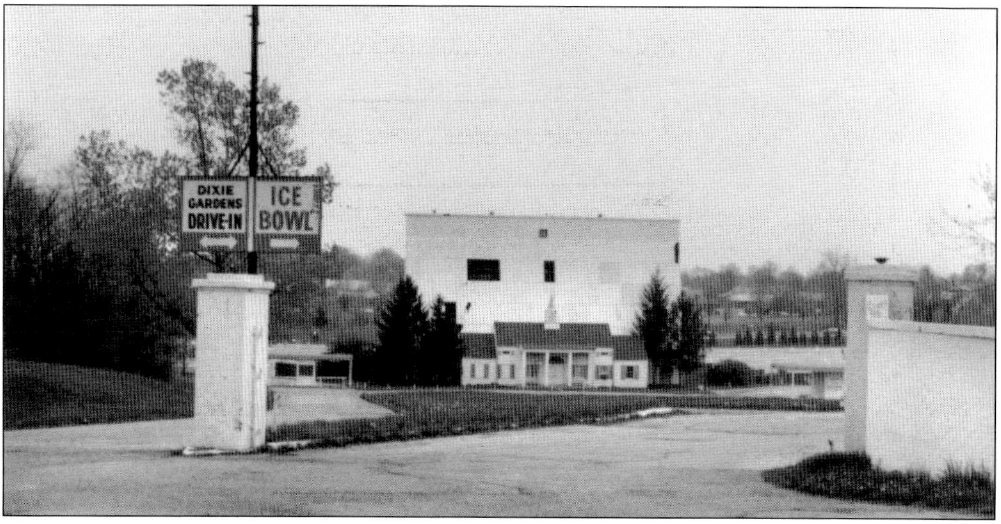

The Dixie Gardens Drive-In was next to the popular Dixie Gardens Ice Bowl skating rink, thus securing a steady flow of young customers. However, it was also visible from the nearby expressway, thus causing problems with nude scenes. The establishment opened in the late 1940s. By 1988, it had been demolished. (Kenton County Public Library, Covington, Kentucky.)

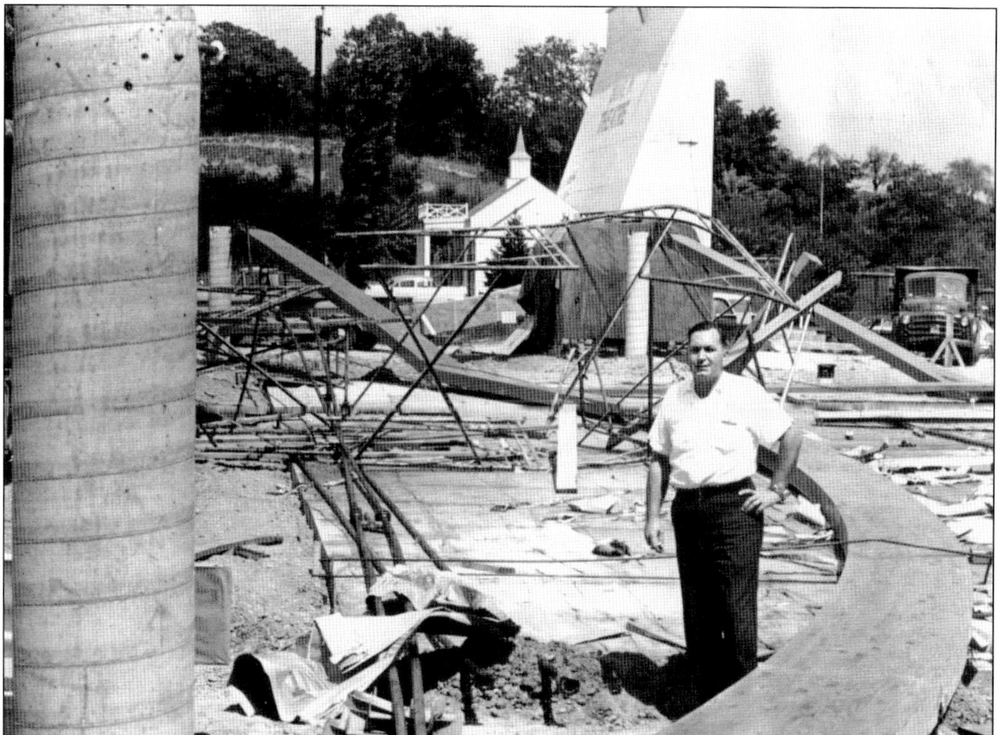

Jay Baglon surveys the damage after the roof collapsed at Dixie Gardens in Fort Wright in August 1964. Perhaps an attempt to prevent any further such mishaps, the theater opened a drive-in church in June 1969. However, even the Sunday-morning prayers could not stop it from closing in 1988. (Kenton County Public Library, Covington, Kentucky.)

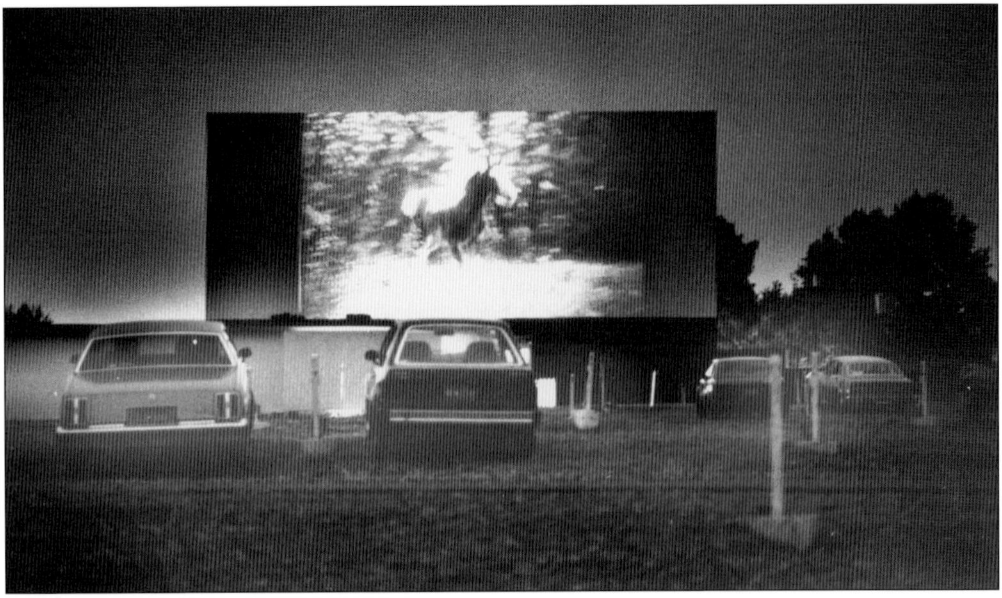

With only four cars present, this 1984 photograph of the Florence Drive-In shows why the institution was fading. Notice also that, for some reason, there are no heads visible in the center automobile. They must have been buying snacks. (Kenton County Public Library, Covington, Kentucky.)

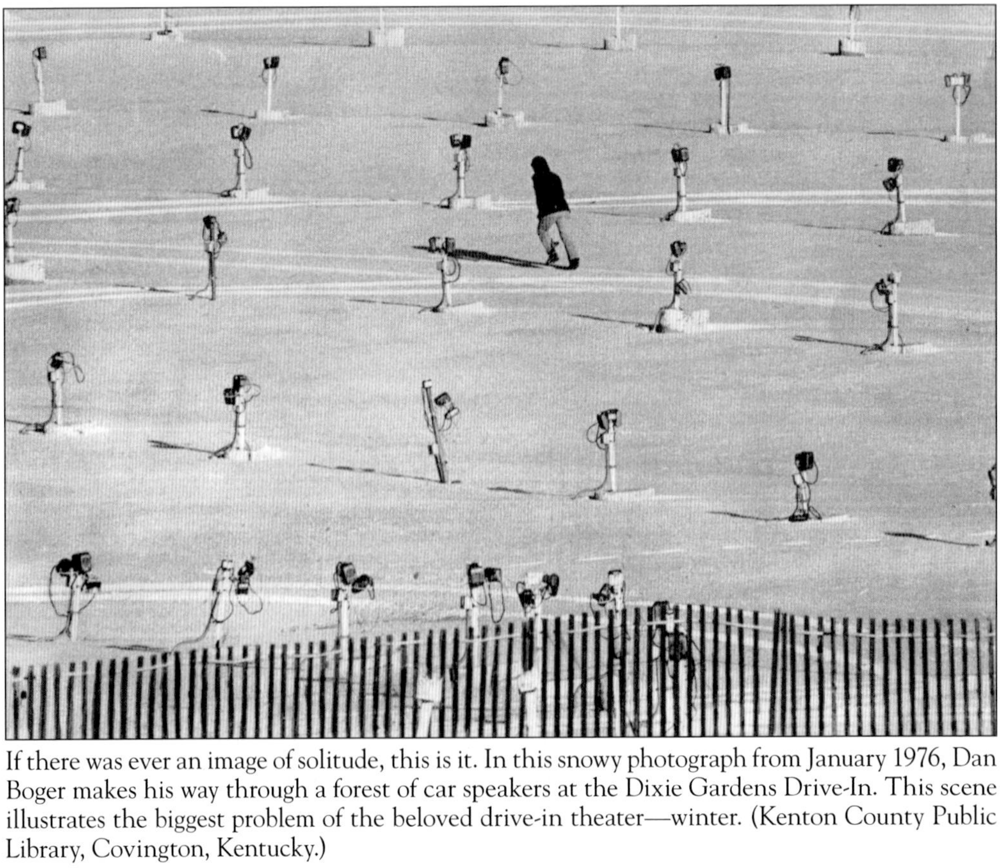

If there was ever an image of solitude, this is it. In this snowy photograph from January 1976, Dan Boger makes his way through a forest of car speakers at the Dixie Gardens Drive-In. This scene illustrates the biggest problem of the beloved drive-in theater—winter. (Kenton County Public Library, Covington, Kentucky.)

Six

The Genius of Waters Is Ready for Her Close-Up

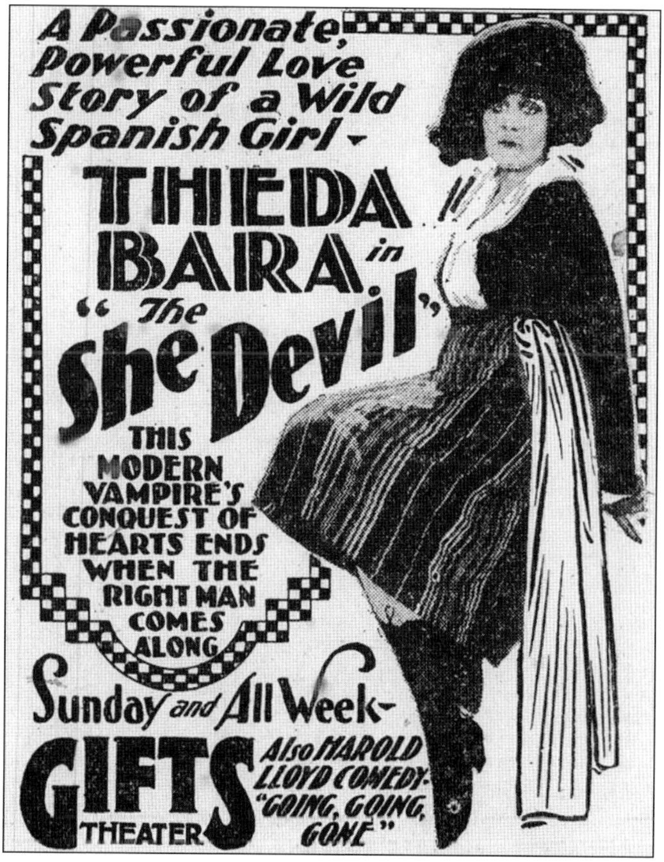

Eighty-nine years before *Twilight*, there was another type of cinema vamp. This 1919 advertisement spotlights Theda Bara, one of the first superstars of cinema to come from Cincinnati. The list of Hollywood stars from the Queen City includes acclaimed director Steven Spielberg, Columbia "torch lady" Evelyn Venable (Disney's Blue Fairy), and cowboy legend Roy Rogers. (Public Library of Cincinnati and Hamilton County.)

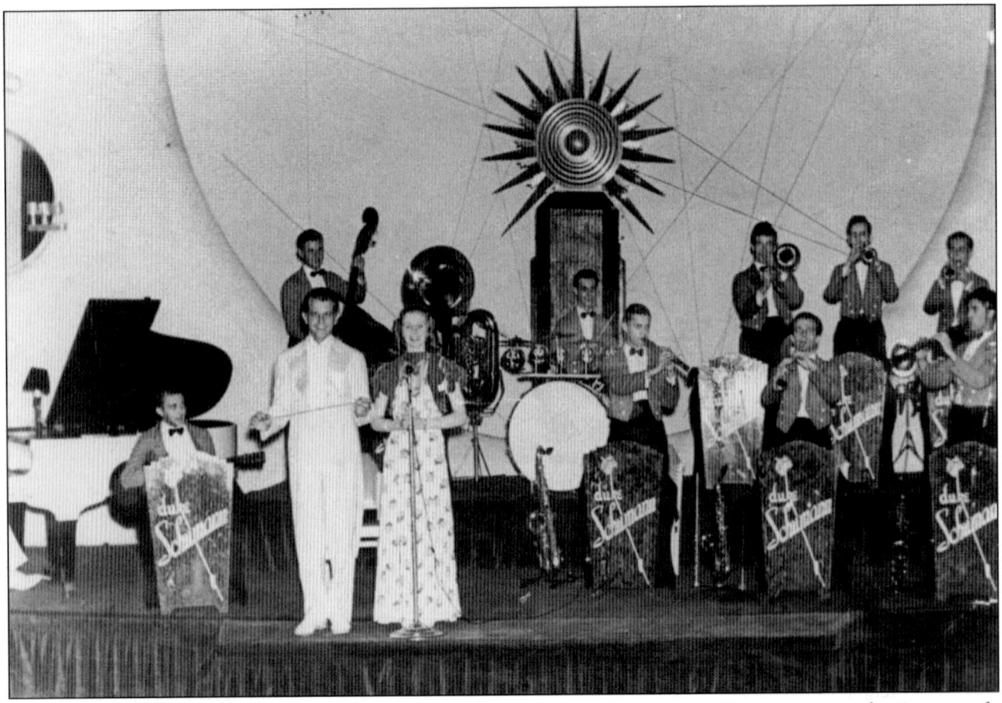

This lovely young lady was first known for her singing voice in various Cincinnati nightspots, such as the Netherland Plaza, shown here. Doris Kappelhoff was the daughter of German immigrants who rose to prominence in both singing with such greats as Benny Goodman and starring in numerous films. Of course, this was all under her stage name of Doris Day. (Hilton Netherland Plaza.)

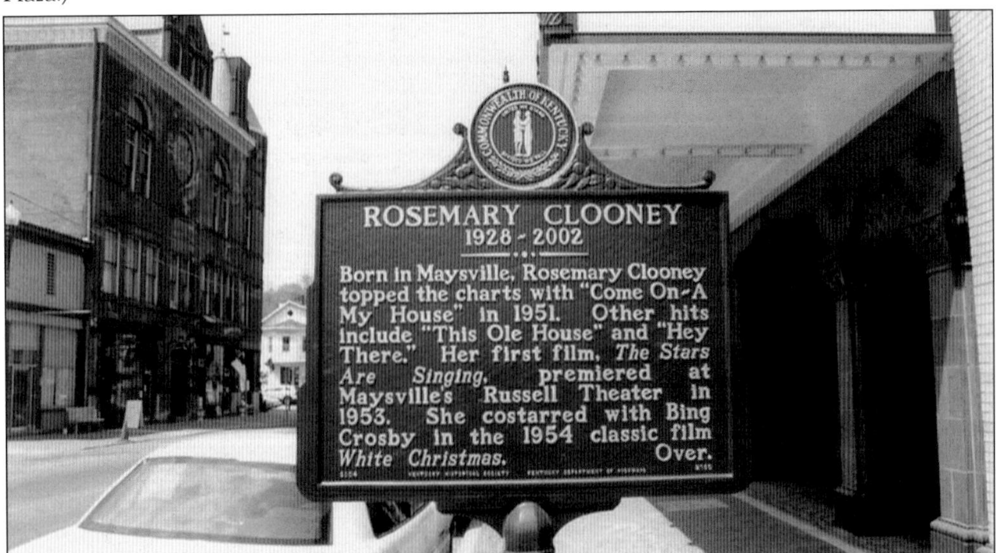

A hometown favorite was beloved actress Rosemary Clooney, memorialized by this plaque in her hometown of Maysville, Kentucky. After a stellar career, she passed away from lung cancer in 2002. Among the stars who attended her funeral was her nephew, actor George Clooney. (Kenton County Public Library, Covington, Kentucky.)

In 1989, Pompilio's co-owner Carmen Argento, along with Robin Kusten, unveiled commemorative artwork celebrating the popular Newport restaurant being featured in the blockbuster film *Rain Man*. The 1988 film starring Dustin Hoffman and Tom Cruise won Best Picture and four other Academy Awards. It showcased many locations in the tristate area. (Kenton County Public Library, Covington, Kentucky.)

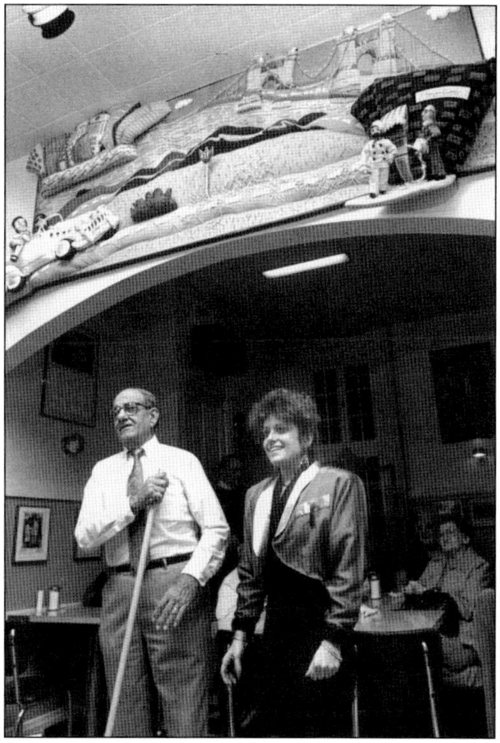

The tristate area has been the filming location for numerous motion pictures, as seen in this image from 1984. Northern Kentucky was a perfect place to film one of the many film adaptations of the popular American classic *Huckleberry Finn*. (Kenton County Public Library, Covington, Kentucky.)

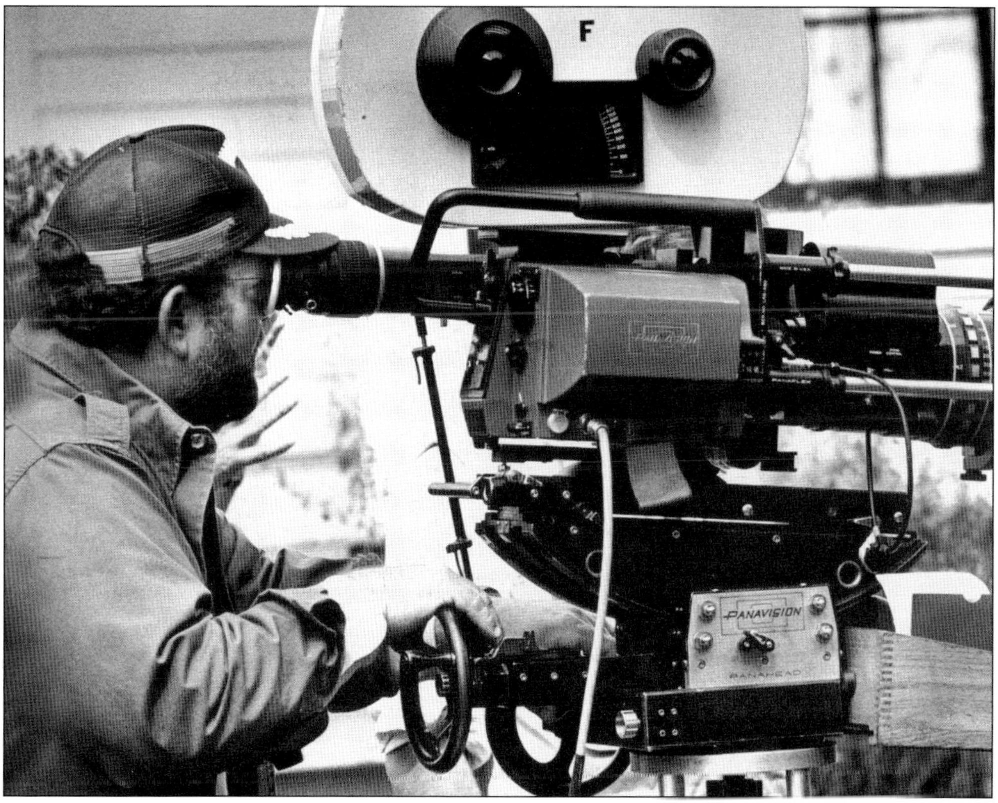

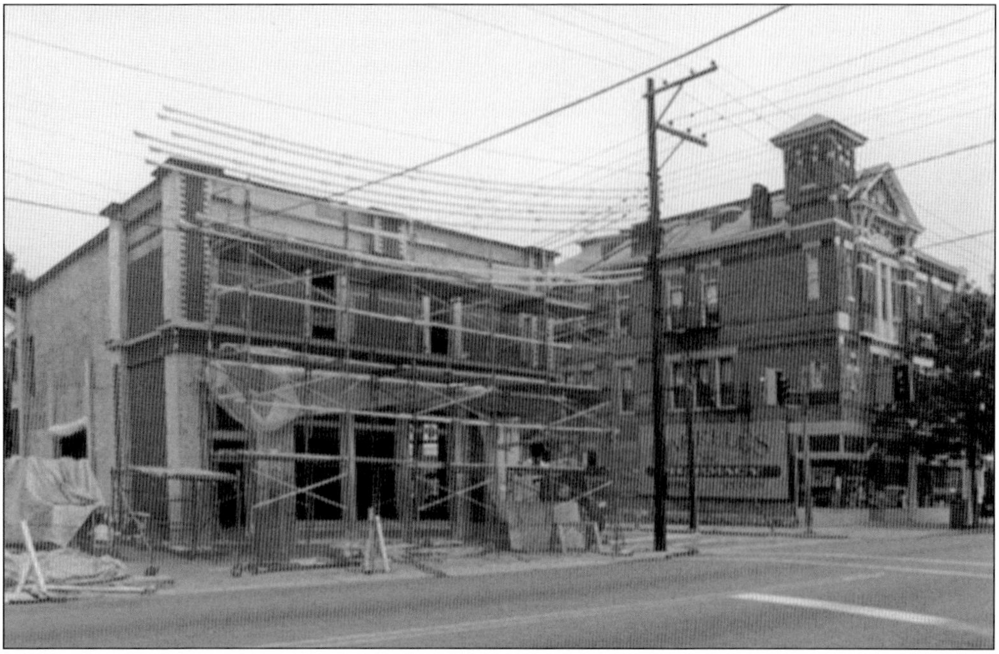

This 1992 photograph shows the amount of work that goes into making a feature film. This building is being prepared for Martha Coolidge's version of Neil Simon's *Lost in Yonkers*. They must certainly be lost, as this building was located in Augusta, Kentucky. (Kenton County Public Library, Covington, Kentucky.)

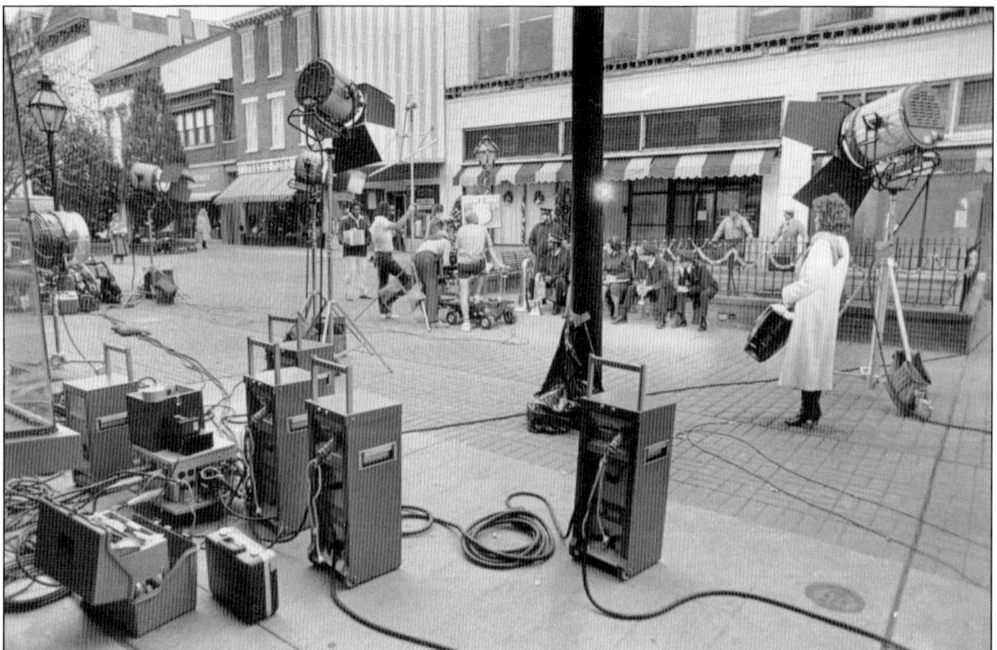

Once again, the tristate area is host to a film crew. While this may look like the set of a major motion picture, all this equipment is merely for the filming of a short commercial being made on the streets of Covington. (Kenton County Public Library, Covington, Kentucky.)

While this looks a great deal like the first theatrical experience in the Cincinnati area, these are actors filming *Centennial* in nearby Augusta, Kentucky. As is often the case in film, actors wearing makeup and costume find themselves just sitting about, waiting endlessly. (Kenton County Public Library, Covington, Kentucky.)

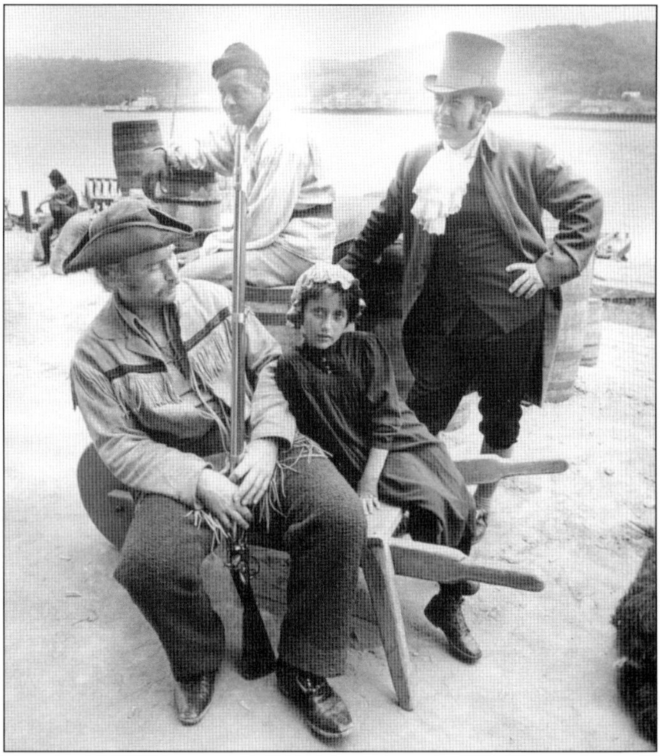

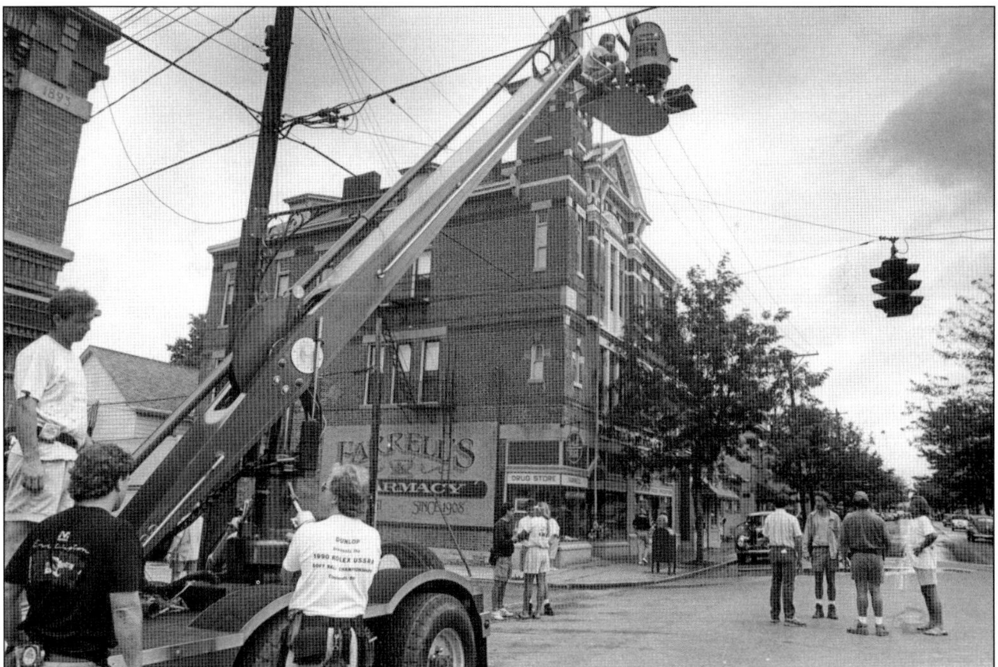

Here, production crews are seen on location for Martha Coolidge's 1993 film *Lost in Yonkers*. Notice the vintage automobiles parked along the street in the background. (Kenton County Public Library, Covington, Kentucky.)